Religions in the Making

Religions in the Making

Whitehead and the Wisdom Traditions of the World

Edited by
JOHN B. COBB JR.

CASCADE *Books* · Eugene, Oregon

RELIGIONS IN THE MAKING
Whitehead and the Wisdom Traditions of the World

Copyright © 2012 Wipf and Stock Publishers. All rights reserved. Except for brief quotations in critical publications or reviews, no part of this book may be reproduced in any manner without prior written permission from the publisher. Write: Permissions, Wipf and Stock Publishers, 199 W. 8th Ave., Suite 3, Eugene, OR 97401.

Cascade Books
An Imprint of Wipf and Stock Publishers
199 W. 8th Ave., Suite 3
Eugene, OR 97401

www.wipfandstock.com

ISBN 13: 978-1-61097-782-1

Cataloging-in-Publication data:

       Religions in the making : Whitehead and the wisdom traditions of the world / edited by John B. Cobb Jr.

       xx + 230 p. ; 23 cm. Includes bibliographical references

       ISBN 13: 978-1-61097-782-1

       1. Religions. 2. Whitehead, Alfred North, 1861-1947. 3. Ideology. I. Cobb, John B. II. Title.

BL80.2 R56 2012

Manufactured in the USA

Contents

Contributors

Rabbi Dr. Bradley Shavit Artson (www.bradartson.com) holds the Abner and Roslyn Goldstine Dean's Chair of the Ziegler School of Rabbinic Studies and is Vice President of American Jewish University in Los Angeles. A member of the Philosophy Department, he is particularly interested in theology, ethics, and the integration of science and religion. He supervises the Miller Introduction to Judaism Program and mentors Camp Ramah in California. He is the author of 10 books and over 250 articles.

Joseph A. Bracken, Professor Emeritus of Theology at Xavier University in Cincinnati, Ohio, has specialized over the years in linking the metaphysical scheme of Alfred North Whitehead with classical Roman Catholic views on the doctrine of the Trinity, the proper relations between religion and science, and the philosophical presuppositions of interreligious dialogue. His latest book is *Does God Roll Dice? Divine Providence for a World in the Making.*

John B. Cobb Jr. is emeritus professor of theology from the Claremont School of Theology and Claremont Graduate University. He is co-founder, with David Griffin, of the Center for Process Studies. His writings on religious diversity include *Beyond Dialogue, Christ in a Pluralistic Age, Transforming Christianity and the World,* and his contributions to *Deep Religious Pluralism,* edited by David Griffin. His reflection on the contribution of Whitehead's thought to Christian theology began with *A Christian Natural Theology.*

Roland Faber is Kilsby Family/John B. Cobb, Jr., Professor of Process Studies at Claremont Lincoln University and Claremont School of Theology, Professor of Religion and Philosophy at Claremont Graduate University, Executive Co-Director of the Center for Process Studies, and Executive Director of the Whitehead Research Project. Fields of research include

Process Philosophy and Process Theology; (De)Constructive Theology; Poststructuralism (Gilles Deleuze); Transreligious Discourse (epistemology of Religious Relativity and Unity) and interreligious applications (e.g., Christianity/Buddhism); Comparative Philosophy of Religion; Philosophy, Theology, Spirituality, and Cosmology of the Renaissance; Mysticism (Meister Eckhart, Nicolas of Cusa). Publications include *God as Poet of the World* and *Secrets of Becoming*.

Meijun Fan, PhD, is the co-director of the China Project, Center for Process Studies, Claremont; program director of the Institute for Postmodern Development of China; and editor-in-chief of *Cultural Communication*, a Chinese newspaper. She was professor of Chinese aesthetics at Beijing Normal University and a vice-chair of the philosophy department at BNU. Her areas of specialty include Chinese traditional aesthetics and aesthetical education. She has authored several books and numerous articles. The list includes *Aesthetic Development of Children, Beauty in Human Life, Contemporary Interpretation of Chinese Traditional Aesthetic, The Popular Aesthetics in Qing Dynasty*, etc. Her most recent publication is *Second Enlightenment* (with Zhihe Wang).

Christopher Ives is Professor of Religious Studies at Stonehill College. In his scholarship he focuses on modern Zen and ethics, and currently he is working on Zen approaches to nature and environmental issues. His publications include *Imperial-Way Zen: Ichikawa Hakugen's Critique and Lingering Questions for Buddhist Ethics; Zen Awakening and Society; The Emptying God* (co-edited with John B. Cobb Jr.); and *Divine Emptiness and Historical Fullness* (edited volume).

Catherine Keller is Professor of Constructive Theology in the Graduate Division of Religion and the Theological School of Drew University. She develops the theological spectrum of recent philosophical, feminist, and eco-political theories in interaction with histories of cosmology and mysticism. Books she has authored include *Apocalypse Now & Then; God & Power; Face of the Deep: A Theology of Becoming*; and *On the Mystery*. She has co-edited several volumes of the Drew Transdisciplinary Theological Colloquium, including *Postcolonial Theologies; Ecospirit; Apophatic Bodies*; and *Polydoxy*. She is currently writing *Cloud of the Impossible: Theological Entanglements*.

Jeffery D. Long is Associate Professor of Religion and Asian Studies and the current Chair of the Department of Religious Studies at Elizabethtown College and former chair of DANAM (the Dharma Association of North America). The author of two books—*A Vision for Hinduism: Beyond Hindu Nationalism* and *Jainism: An Introduction*—Long is an active member of the Ramakrishna Vedanta Society and the Hindu American Religious Institute.

Sandra B. Lubarsky chairs the Department of Sustainable Development at Appalachian State University in North Carolina. She holds a PhD in philosophy of religion from Claremont Graduate University and is author of *Tolerance and Transformation: Jewish Approaches to Religious Pluralism*; *Jewish Theology and Process Thought* (co-edited) and numerous articles on religious pluralism, Jewish theology, and the intersection of aesthetics and sustainability.

Mustafa Ruzgar was born in Turkey and completed his BA in Islamic Studies at Uludağ University in Bursa, Turkey. He earned his MA and PhD in Philosophy of Religion and Theology at Claremont Graduate University in 2001 and 2008, respectively. He is currently teaching at California State University, Northridge as an Assistant Professor of Religion. Dr. Ruzgar's research interests include Islamic thought, philosophy of religion, theology, process thought, religious pluralism, and interfaith dialogue.

Marjorie Hewitt Suchocki is Professor Emerita at Claremont School of Theology, where she was privileged to inherit the Ingraham Chair of Theology from her predecessor and mentor, John B. Cobb Jr. She has written many books and articles dealing with process theology, feminist theology, and film, including *God, Christ, Church: A Practical Guide to Process Theology*; *Divinity and Diversity: A Christian Affirmation of Religious Pluralism*; *The End of Evil: Process Eschatology in Historical Context*; and *The Fall to Violence: Original Sin in Relational Theology*. She currently directs the Whitehead International Film Festival.

Zhihe Wang, PhD, is the executive director of the China Project, Center for Process Studies, Claremont and the director of the Institute for Postmodern Development of China. His recent publications include: *A Study of Postmodern Philosophical Movement*; *Whitehead and China* (co-edited with George Derfer and Wenyu Xie); *The Roar of Awakening: A Whiteheadian Dialogue Between Western Psychotherapies and Eastern Worldviews* (co-edited with George Derfer and Michel Weber); and *Second Enlightenment* (with Meijun Fan).

Preface

—John B. Cobb Jr.

WHEN I STUDIED IN the Humanities Division of the University of Chicago as a veteran of World War II, I was hungry for exposure to the best thought of the time. But the more I absorbed, the more I found myself putting on glasses that presented me with a world in which I did not feel at home. It was completely alien to the world of a pious Methodist that centered on God and how one could serve God's creatures. The default position of most of what I read was a reductionist, determinist, materialist world in which any affirmation of norms or values was highly dubious. Since I had not put on these glasses voluntarily, I could not simply choose to take them off.

There was just one encounter that held me back from succumbing to what I would now call "modernity." Charles Hartshorne introduced me to the vision of Alfred North Whitehead. It was clearly different from the modern one. I had to decide whether that difference meant that it failed to take account of the vast array of information and critical thought that had gone into the construction of modernity. I did not want to choose it simply because it felt so much more comfortable. But it seemed to me that Hartshorne was familiar with the arguments for the modern vision and presented good reasons for taking another direction. As I encountered Whitehead's own thought directly, I was even more impressed. It seemed that he questioned more deeply and thought more originally than anyone else I had read. When I moved into the Divinity School, I continued to deal with Whitehead with growing appreciation.

At that time my application of Whitehead was limited to issues in philosophy and theology. Theology has been my central interest throughout my career. However, from the beginning I was deeply concerned not to adopt a philosophy incongruent with the present state of the sciences and relevant to the whole of reality. To adopt Whitehead's philosophy meant to put on a pair of glasses different from that of my youth, but also one strikingly at odds with that of modernity. I could not look at one range of issues with one pair of glasses and other issues with another. I knew the pain of having to give up a familiar and comfortable pair of glasses. I did not want to have to go through that again.

Nevertheless, in a few years, the new glasses were permanently in place. I could still talk about other ways of seeing the world, but my way had become the Whiteheadian one. To be a Whiteheadian is to know that one's way of seeing will always be correctable, that the best we can do is to have plausible and well-tested hypotheses. But these are not looked at objectively. They are the hypotheses that determine how one sees.

Those who wear the same glasses as most of their colleagues are often not aware that they are wearing glasses at all. But if one knows only a few other people who wear glasses similar to one's own, one is very much aware. One has to ask oneself again and again whether it is wise to go one's own way in spite of the social, scholarly, and intellectual pressures to go other ways. That meant for me to ask, again and again, whether what I saw in its difference from what most others saw was valid and valuable. Again and again I judged that it was, even if I could not persuade many others. I continue to judge that viewing the world through Whiteheadian glasses is clarifying and illuminating in many fields. There is far more evidence of this fruitfulness today than there was when I first struggled with the question of my own worldview.

From an early point I was particularly concerned about Whitehead's physics. This was a central interest of his, but it is a field in which knowledge has multiplied rapidly. I was quite confident that Whitehead's theories were congruent with the facts known when he wrote. But I feared that further developments might have shown them wrong. I was relieved that Ian Barbour used Whitehead in his *Issues in Science and Religion* (1966) without suggesting his conceptuality was outdated by later developments in physics. Of course, much more detailed work is needed, but I now think Whitehead's work is more relevant than when he wrote.

To put on Whiteheadian glasses is not to judge that Whitehead was correct in everything he said. To suppose such inerrancy would be thoroughly unWhiteheadian. He was a man of his time, in the sense that, on topics to which he did not give major attention, he often mirrored the prejudices and false assumptions characteristic of his culture. I find it hard to read what he says about North America as a largely empty continent when the Europeans came. In general, he had little appreciation for primal cultures. I disagree with his comments about the Old Testament and about Paul. He respected Buddhism, but he did not rightly understand it. I could go on.

But again and again I am even more impressed by his insights, even on topics that were at the margins of his philosophical and scientific inquiry. I would put on Whiteheadian glasses even if I did not find him, in the broad sense, a man of great wisdom; but I rejoice that, over a wide range of topics, his insights are still worth studying. I think the glasses he shaped in his philosophy enabled him to see many things clearly.

One area in which I have been involved for many years is that of the diversity of what are usually called "religions." There are still those who argue that because there are different teachings in different religions, no more than one can be correct. Some of those who think in this way are exclusivist Christians. Others are secularists who point out the extreme unlikelihood that any are correct. A third group uses this point to argue against taking religious utterances as having the prosaic character that would allow one to say they are either true or false.

The assumption underlying this kind of thinking is that when truth-claims differ, there is always a contradiction. Whitehead taught me that differences among truth claims may become "contrasts." That is, when the insights expressed are formulated with sufficient care the different statements may both be true, and holding them together may give rise to a more inclusive truth. His own philosophy embodies many such contrasts.

In recent decades a great deal of theological work has been done by Christians to rid Christian teaching of its deeply entrenched anti-Judaism. In some instances theologians have worked to achieve this primarily by setting aside those Christian teachings that Jews do not accept. But others, quite apart from any conscious use of Whitehead's idea of contrast, were able to show the distinctive emphases and convictions of Jews and Christians, while different, did not have to exclude one another. Christians could make central God's gracious incarnate presence in the world, paradigmatically actualized in Jesus, without contradicting Jewish thinking. This does not require that Jews join Christians in this emphasis. Jews could emphasize the centrality of Torah without insisting that Christians agree to obey the law, and Christians could appreciate the importance and value of this Jewish emphasis without sharing it. The world is made richer by having both forms of theism affirmed and lived out. Whiteheadians have contributed to this ongoing discussion of the complementarity of Judaism and Christianity without making any claims of leadership in this field.

The relation of Christianity and Judaism belongs to the inner-Western dialogue. Whitehead formed his vision over against the dominant modern theories, Cartesian, Humean, Kantian, and Einsteinian. In short, he was a Western thinker. I am a Westerner, and I would have been content to be helped as a Westerner to break out of the straightjackets that had been imposed on the Western mind. But I hoped for even more. Whitehead noted that his thought was in important ways closer to strands of Eastern thinking than to Western habits. Would Easterners find it convincing and useful? Could the thought of Western traditions such as Christianity and the thought of Eastern traditions such as Buddhism also be seen as complementary, making contrasts in Whitehead's sense?

I personally found what I learned from Whitehead extraordinarily helpful in my efforts to understand Buddhism. Even though Whitehead himself reflected the limited scholarly understanding of his time, his concepts were remarkably close to those of Nagarjuna, the most important thinker of Mahayana Buddhism. I felt that by using his concepts I could grasp the insights of this Buddhism even though I would never have been led to them simply by the study of Whitehead. I was deeply satisfied that, in general, my explanation of Buddhist thought in Whiteheadian categories gained approval from Buddhist thinkers.

It was my experience in inter-religious dialogue that most of the participants were convinced that all religious traditions relate their adherents to the same reality. These participants affirmed that the different traditions conceived and experienced this reality in different ways. At least in Buddhist/Christian dialogue, most of the Christians tended to hold the apophatic view of this ultimate, affirming that it is beyond all attributes or qualities, so that nothing can be said truly about it.

But as a Protestant oriented to biblical modes of thought I felt that dialogue should be not only between apophatic Christians and Buddhists, but should also involve those who worship the "Abba" addressed by Jesus. It occurred to me that Whitehead's thought allowed for both. What Whitehead called "ultimate" is creativity, and like the adherents of the apophatic tradition, he said that creativity as such has no attributes at all. In Buddhism the goal is to realize that one is an instance of this ultimate. One's deepest reality is an instance of "dependent origination," which is much better named as "nothing" or "emptiness" than as being. This all made sense in terms of what Whitehead called "creativity."

But Whitehead held that there is a primordial instantiation of creativity without which there would be no creativity. He called this "God." And Whitehead's God clearly belongs to the biblical family of thought. God is *an* actual entity, profoundly different from all others, everlasting and all-knowing, necessary to all the others as none of them are necessary to it, and interactive with creatures. It seemed to me important that in the Whiteheadian vision there are both creativity and God, that they are not the same, but that neither could be without the other. Based on this distinction, we can respect one another's views and practices as oriented to different features of reality, without supposing that one is superior to the other. People pray to God and worship God. People meditate is order to understand that what is most real in themselves is also the universal reality of emptiness.

I knew that in the Christian tradition in addition to the worship of God there had also been great interest in the reality that is known only apophatically. I discovered that in Buddhism there were also schools that oriented themselves to something much more like the God of the Bible. If the difference between creativity and God were fully recognized, as well as the inseparability and mutual dependence, it seemed to me that dialogue both within the several traditions and between them would be advanced. One might also find that some groups oriented themselves to creativity as primordially characterized by God.

My personal experience in dialogue was chiefly with Buddhists, but it seemed clear to me that the distinction between creativity and God was also illuminating of various schools of Hinduism and of Chinese religion. Accordingly, I wrote a good deal about the "two ultimates." Many differences that were obscured when it was assumed that all traditions are oriented to the same ultimate could be viewed as complementary, when one kept Whitehead's distinction between God and creativity in mind. But there were still other forms of religious life to which this distinction did not seem particularly relevant.

Despite what I have seen as the great advantage of distinguishing what Buddhists call Buddha-nature or *dharmakaya* from the biblical "God," and making similar distinctions in other traditions, most of the discussion has proceeded on the assumption that there can be only one ultimate focus of "religious" concern. I have come to the conclusion that the word "religion" is an obstacle to clear thinking. It can mean many things, but in general, use of this word tends to confuse the discussion in three respects. First, it draws a line between communities, traditions, or ways of life that constitute religions and others that do not. Second, it implies that what is "religious" in the former group as what is most important in them. Third it encourages the assumption that what is "religious" in all the "religions" is a relation to the same reality.

I propose that, instead of this approach, we describe what we consider "religious" activities, ideas, emotions, and attitudes. We note that some of them, such as a sense of the "holy," play an extensive role in human affairs, even those that consider themselves "secular," such as nationalism. In some communities and traditions these religious elements are emphasized. But they are not usually considered the most important aspect of the community's life. Indeed, by some definitions of "religious," some of the traditions usually thought of as "religions" will be strongly opposed to "religious" practices. The prophetic tradition in Israel was highly critical of such "religious" practices as sacrifices and communal observance of special occasions. Because "religion" is a term that developed in the West, it is sometimes associated with supernaturalism and theism. Zen Buddhists oppose both. Or "religions" may be thought of as efforts of people to attain salvation, according to which definition, Barth announced that authentic Christianity is not a religion at all.

It has seemed to me better to marginalize the issue of "religion." The terms that many traditions have used about themselves can often be rendered as "Way" in English. A Way is a way of life, a way of thought, a way of being in community, a way of relating to the natural world, a way of cultivating one's inner life. Christianity was first called "the Way." Although the Torah is usually translated as "law," it can equally well be thought of as describing the Way for the people of Israel. The term can be applied to Hindu and Buddhist traditions and to Chinese ones as well. I think that none object to this label or find it misleading. By most definitions of "religious" there are religious aspects of most ways. There are also secular aspects. Their relative importance varies, but there are no sharp lines separating the two types of community. If we understand that conversation between Buddhists and Christians does not relate two "religions" but rather two Ways, we may be more open to recognizing that these Ways differ in their judgment of what features of reality are most important to consider.

Since 1969 my deepest concern has been with the fate of the earth, the threat that human action now would make the planet almost uninhabitable in the future. I learned that neither the worshippers of God nor those who sought to recognize their identity with ultimate reality had resisted human damage to the earth. But there are also people whose feelings and practices relate them much more healthily to their natural environment. For them nothing is more ultimate than the world itself. Those who participate in such Ways today usually recognize that they are seeking to recover what "civilization" lost a long time ago. The focus on the earth is particularly characteristic of the primal Ways that have survived among Native Americans and in parts of Africa.

The Center for Process Studies has held conferences with Native Americans and Africans who affirm the traditional beliefs and customs of their peoples. The results have been encouraging. Despite Whitehead's own lack of appreciation of the primal vision, his understanding of the natural world and of the human place in it resonates well with this Way. Currently, some Congolese Catholics are organizing centers for Whiteheadian thought in order to provide an articulation of the Catholic message that is more congruent with indigenous African thought.

I found that Whitehead had explicitly located the world as a third everlasting and necessary feature of reality. Just as creativity and God depend on one another, so also the world requires both for its existence and neither can be apart from the world. Of course the planet earth and even this cosmos as a whole had a beginning and will pass away. But in Whitehead's view, there has always been, and will always be, some world. It is just as appropriate for some to order their lives around the celebration of the world as it is for others to order theirs around the realization of creativity or the worship of God. I proposed that we understand diverse religious traditions as oriented around one or another of these three "ultimates" or some combination of them.

I was convinced that Christians could learn to appreciate other Ways as complementary to ours. I thought that the others, too, with the help of Whitehead could develop better understanding of the diversity of traditions. David Griffin organized a conference made up of representatives of diverse traditions who were personally influenced by Whitehead to test the development by each tradition of an appreciative understanding of religious diversity. He published the result in a volume entitled *Deep Pluralism.*

Although the issue of religious diversity has become central in our time, it is by no means the only important topic from the perspective of any religious tradition. Christians have been making use of Whitehead's thought in relation to our theology for some time now. The *Handbook of*

Process Theology edited by Jay McDaniel and Donna Bowman, shows the many ways Christians have found Whitehead's thought useful for reframing and rethinking questions of theological importance.

I have thought and hoped that participants in other Ways would find Whitehead's conceptuality fruitful in dealing with their own questions and issues. But it is not for Christians to tell Muslims or Hindus with what questions or issues to wrestle and whether or how a particular conceptuality might help. We can only invite those from other traditions who are attracted to Whitehead to explore these matters. By speaking of Ways instead of "religions" it is easier to include a chapter on China, which speaks not so much about the specifics of Taoism or Confucianism but about the current search of the Chinese people for the Way that will work for them in this critical period of their history. This book is a response to the invitation to participants in a variety of ways to consider how Whitehead may help them.

Given my personal preference to avoid the term "religion," it is somewhat ironic that when we discussed a title for the book, we ended by playing off of Whitehead's title "Religion in the Making." Pluralizing "religion" makes clear that we are talking about what most people mean by "world religions." Their adherents will recognize that as communities of people with shared beliefs and practices, they are "in the making," even if they hold to a final revelation that cannot be changed. I accept the idea that a suggestive and catchy title that uses familiar language is often best, and what is really intended can be stated better in a subtitle.

I am very grateful to the authors of these chapters for their willingness to work with us on this text. Their participation certainly does not mean that all share all the beliefs and ideas that I have mentioned above as leading me to want this kind of book. I particularly appreciate the leadership of Rabbi Artson who wrote his paper as a model of what we hoped for from all, and who participated throughout in planning the volume. Philip Clayton has helped to shape the book at every turn. Finally, although I am credited as editor of this volume, the actual preparation of the manuscript for Cascade Books was the work of Steve Hulbert, a doctoral student in Claremont Graduate University. Without his patient and even laborious work, there would be no book. He plans to prepare the index as well. I am deeply indebted to him and celebrate his accomplishment.

The variety of topics and approaches suggests we can all learn from one another, not just on particular topics but also in asking new questions that Whitehead's conceptuality might help to answer. One can envision much further creative work in the future. But what is already offered here is a rich fare. It strengthens my commitment to the hypothesis: anyone who puts on Whiteheadian glasses will see the world in fresh and valuable ways.

1

A Jewish Perspective
Divine Power and Responsiveness

—Rabbi Bradley Shavit Artson

EDITOR'S INTRODUCTION

Mordecai Kaplan, the founder of Jewish Reconstruction, may be counted as a process thinker along the lines of John Dewey, but this nontheistic movement has not been attractive to many Jews. A number of Jews have identified themselves with Whiteheadian process thought, but thus far it has not been considered as a serious option in the Jewish community as a whole. Rabbi Artson thinks it is time that far more Jews became aware of its helpfulness and basic congeniality. Some Christians have in the past recognized that not all the obstacles to acceptance of process theology among Christians apply to Jews, and Artson's citations from the tradition indicate that this is correct. The orthodox philosophical theology shared by Jews and Christians has had less hold on Jewish thought. There seems to be a real possibility that if large numbers of Jewish thinkers considered the possible replacement of traditional Greek categories by process ones, many would agree that these meet the needs of Judaism better.

The basic issues discussed in this chapter are important for all members of the Abrahamic traditions. How can the understanding of God as good be reconciled with the evil in the world? And how can the theistic under-standing of the world be reconciled with modern science. Although some of the sources that Christians and Muslims cite would be different, much the same responses are relevant to all. Although specifically and emphatically Jewish, this chapter deals directly with how the process understanding of God and the world can help the Abrahamic traditions generally. Even those in nontheistic traditions will find the account of process theology here offered interesting and illuminating.

PROCESS THEOLOGY—A CONSTELLATION OF ideas sharing the common assertion that the world and God are in a flux of dynamic change, of related interaction and becoming—can be unsettling at first glance. We take for granted what it means to be conventionally religious, and those traditionalist assumptions make it difficult to open ourselves to an engaging and explanatory way to conceive and connect to an embracing faithfulness. Much of what I will offer as an alternative may sound shocking, perhaps even irreligious if this is your first encounter with process thinking. I want to provide an image that makes it possible, at least, to work through the shock and discomfort to some degree. You may wind up rejecting this dynamic/relational approach in the end, and that is your privilege too, but the opening image may help create the possibility of a new understanding.

I live in west Los Angeles in a home that was built in the 1950s. Our dining room has wood paneling along its four walls. When we first bought the house a decade ago, the room was painted a sickly green, presumably in the late 70s during the high watermark of the Brady Bunch and Partridge Family aesthetics. The actual wood grain and tone were covered, though I think that in that era people thought such a look was cutting edge. With that greenish coat of paint, the walls looked fake and cheap. When we finally got around to repainting the upstairs of the house, we asked our painter if he could just paint the phony paneling a simple white because the green was hideous. He pondered for a moment, then took his thumbnail and scratched on the panel. The paint peeled away, and he said, "You know, I think that under this green there is actual wood." His team spent three days sandblasting and then varnishing. At the end of the week our dining room was transformed! The wood is so rich and the patterns in the grain are magnificent. It is now my favorite room in the house. I had thought, erroneously, that it was the wood itself that was that sickly green, when in fact, that trashy look was just the coating that someone had painted over it.

Modern Western people often approach religion as I did the paneling: they assume that the only way to be religious is to accept the sickly green overlay of Greek philosophy. They take Aristotelian and Platonic presuppositions and filter religion through those ideas. Then, because they have insurmountable problems with those assertions, they assume that the quandary involves religion itself, or the Bible, the Talmud, observance, or God. What process thinking offers is the opportunity to sandblast the philosophical overlay of ancient Greece and medieval Europe off the rich, burnished grain of Bible, Rabbinics, and Kabbalah so that we can savor the actual patterns in the living wood of religion, the *Etz Hayim*,[1] and appreciate religion for what it was intended to be and truly is.

PROBLEMS WITH THE DOMINANT VIEW

Because we are habituated to the pale green overlay, we assume that drab impression is what religion necessarily entails: specifically, the kind of theology that most Christian theologians call "classical," by which they mean Augustine, Aquinas, the broad spectrum of medieval philosophy—which presupposes that God must be omnipotent, omniscient, and omnibenevolent.[2] Based on Aristotelian presumption, God has—and must have—all the power (that is what omnipotent means).[3] God has—and must have—all knowledge, knowing everything that is, was, and will be. God is omnibenevolent—pure good. The challenge for many contemporaries is that certain intolerable consequences result from these three axioms.

For God to be omnipotent implies that no power exists that is not God's, which means, first of all, that any occurrence is God's responsibility.

1. "Tree of Life," Genesis 3:24; Proverbs 3:18—a favorite Rabbinic metaphor for Torah in the broadest sense, the entirety of God and Jewry's ongoing revelation.

2. As a religious Jew, while I revere the great medieval theologians—Rav Saadya and Rambam preeminent among them—I reserve the term "classical" for Torah, Tanakh (the Hebrew Bible), and Rabbinics (Mishnah, Talmud, Midrash). I think that the medieval sages would have concurred with that prioritization. I acknowledge the influence and domination (but not the normative privilege or superiority) of the "classical" philosophical theology—Jewish, Christian, and Muslim—as "dominant."

3. For a superb presentation of Aristotelian premises and logic in the context of religious philosophy, there is no better presentation than Samuelson, *Revelation and the God of Israel*, 22–28.

Sometimes we like what happens, sometimes we do not; regardless, all that happens comes from God. So God gets the credit for anything good in life; for anything bad in life, God gets the blame. There is no escape from that inexorable logic, which engenders many people's vehement rejection of religion. A God who could have stopped doing "X" but did not is a God with whom most of us want nothing to do. Everyone, at some point in life, suffers terrible trauma. At the moments that monotheists most need God and a sense of God's love, they are coerced by their Greek-overlay theology into conceding that God must have a legitimate reason to cause (or at least to not prevent) the trauma from occurring. The fault, by default, must be their own. That relentless conclusion leads them to do what far too many Western people have done across the millennia, which is to abandon their moral compass and generally-reliable sense of right and wrong in order to blame themselves or their loved ones when bad things happen.[4] The inescapable consequence of this theological straightjacket is that not only does something horrible happen, but beyond their suffering, the victim also feels delinquent, abandoned, or punished.

But there is yet another way in which the concept of omnipotence creates an insurmountable challenge. Power is always relational. One has power only to the extent that one has more of it than someone else does. To the extent that one has *all* the power, one actually has no power what-soever, because power only works when there are two parties engaged in a power dynamic, one the object of the power of the first. Without that relationship, there is no possibility of demonstrating or utilizing power at all. Absolute power is self-erasing.[5] The philosophical presumption that God is omnipotent was reinforced by the fact that many translations of the Bible refer to God as the "Almighty," which derives from a mistranslation of El Shaddai.[6] The Torah has terms for great power and unsearchable strength,[7] but it has neither concept nor term for omnipotent. The prophets have no such term, nor does the Talmud. There is no Hebrew/

---

4. Job, by the way, provides brilliant evidence here that such a response is not the only Biblical ideal. His theologian friends work to get him to see the logic of accepting the blame in order to preserve God's omnipotence and omnibenevolence, yet Job refuses. God's response is to applaud Job's integrity and vision and to chastise Eliphaz and the other theologians: "I am incensed at you and your two friends, for you have not spoken the truth about Me as did My servant Job" (Job 42:7).

5. See Jonas, "The Concept of God after Auschwitz," 138–39; Mesle, *Process Theology*, 26–32; Cobb and Griffin, *Process Theology*, 52–54.

6. See Sarna, *Genesis*, 384–85.

7. Psalm 145:3; Job 9:10.

Aramaic term for being able to do anything whatsoever. In fact, that philosophical concept leads to clever theological tricks, for example: a person is more powerful than God because it is possible for a person to construct a weight so heavy that she cannot lift it. But if God is all-powerful, then God should be able to create a weight so powerful that God cannot lift it. But if God cannot lift it (or if God cannot make such a weight), then God is not all-powerful. That kind of conundrum of language highlights the fact that this particular concept of omnipotence is fatally flawed. The Bible and Rabbinics portray God as vastly, persistently powerful, yes, but not as all-powerful.

A similar conflict emerges with the claim that God is all-knowing. Omniscience assumes that God knows everything, including the future as well as the past. Nothing is hidden from an all-knowing God. But if God knows the future absolutely, then there is no room for divine or creaturely freedom. Human beings know the future probabilistically: I know it is likely if I write in an interesting way, you will be able to focus most of the time you are reading. That is probably true, and I have written and read enough that I can reasonably expect what has been true in the past will most likely continue to be true. But I do not know absolutely. Today something could have happened in your life to make it impossible to focus your attention, so that, try as you might to focus, your attention drifts. My "knowledge" of your being able to attend is probability knowledge—my perception is likely to be true. But this kind of statistical probability does not qualify as omniscience. If God knows *as a matter of certainty* that I am going to lecture at three o'clock, then where is my freedom to refrain? Is my choosing to speak an illusion? For God to be all-knowing makes real substantive human freedom impossible. And if God knows the future absolutely, then God also knows God's future choices absolutely. Such perfect foretelling strips God of any freedom as well, a contradiction lurking within the dominant theological scheme.

The philosophical conviction that God is eternal, unchanging, and impassible (impassible meaning *lacking feelings*, because to feel is to change) emerges from this welter of omnipotence, omniscience, and omnibenevolence. To change, after all, is to either improve (becoming perfect while previously having been imperfect), or to worsen (by having started as perfect and then becoming imperfect). In this line of reasoning, God cannot abandon perfection, and God was always perfect—hence God must be eternally unchanging. For God to be perfect and unchanging, God has to be beyond time, outside of space. Therefore, God cannot be changed by the choices we (all of creation) make, by the things we do. God was perfect before creation, perfect during creation, perfect after creation, and in that sense, separate from creation, above creation and time, independent of creation.

That static timeless perfection is not how Jewish traditions portray the Divine, even though that is how many Jewish philosophers tell us we should understand God. Despite the impressive lineage of philosophers (and rabbis) arguing for an immutable, impassible, omnipotent and omniscient God, the Torah and rabbinic midrash portray a God who gets angry, who loves, grieves, gets frustrated and surprised, and who repents! When the Holy Blessing One recalls God's children, who are plunged in suffering among the nations of the world, God lets fall two tears into the ocean and the sound is heard from one end of the world to the other—and that is the rumbling of the earth.[8]

As the philosopher Han Jonas reminds us: "Such an idea of divine becoming is surely at variance with the Greek, Platonic-Aristotelian tradition of philosophical theology that, since its incorporation into the Jewish and Christian theological tradition, has somehow usurped for itself an authority to which it is not at all entitled by authentic Jewish (and also Christian) standards."[9] The biblical/Rabbinic portrayal of an engaged, relating, interacting God is no surprise to process thinkers or to observant Jews, most of whom prioritize religious practice (including study) above theological reflection.

The conflict is basic: A God who possesses unlimited power and knows everything yet to come could have chosen to fashion a very different world. If an omnipotent and omniscient God knowingly created a world in which babies die in their cribs, a world in which people suffer from malaria and expire in mid-life, in which their children are orphaned, then God is responsible for that (and every) evil. If God could have prevented the Holocaust, and chose not to, it is well nigh impossible to consider that God, good. In the words of Rabbi Harold Kushner: "A God of power extorts obedience, but cannot command love. A God who could spare the life of a dying child, who could prevent the earthquake but chooses not to, may inspire our fear and our calculated obedience, but does not deserve our love."[10]

---

8. Talmud *Berakhot* 59a.

9. Jonas, "The Concept of God after Auschwitz," 137.

10. Kushner, "Would an All-Powerful God be Worthy of Worship?," 90.

Western theologians would rather deny their moral compass than change their theology. When confronted by such a moral outrage, theologians too often obfuscate behind the term "mystery." Or they assert that God's definition of good and evil is different than our own. If a million babies murdered is not evil by God's definition, then the term "evil" has no meaning. Such an atrocity is surely evil, regardless of the perpetrator.

Rather than cling to this outmoded (and unbiblical/unrabbinic) philosophical notion of God and power, process thinking offers a way to recover a more biblically and rabbinically dynamic articulation of God, world, and covenant, integrating that portrayal with contemporary scientific knowledge of the cosmos and of life into a speculative philosophy worthy of our engagement.

INSIGHTS OF PROCESS THINKING

Process thinking recognizes reality as relational. That is to say, our perception of the world as apparently independent substances that bang against each other and only interact externally is a coincidence of our size and our metabolism. It is an adaptation to our own species' evolutionary needs but it is not an objective description of the cosmos or of its residents. The cosmos actually is constantly interacting, constantly social, always in process, and always dynamic. That relating should sound familiar to any Jew because our word for that dynamic relating is "*brit*, covenant." Covenant is always interactive, always connecting, and always relational. Just like the cosmos: at a quantum level (the very smallest level) there are no solid substances bouncing into each other, there are only probabilities, packets of energy intertwined in their own uncertainty. At the largest scale, our spacetime bubble singularity (or, possibly, the infinitely larger "sea" of eternal inflation seething expansion) reality is eternally generating new pockets of spacetime. Only on one-size scale (the middle one, ours) can one speak with any coherence about stable, permanent substances. And even on our size scale it is quite clear that we are always on the way, always changing from who we were to who we will become, along with the rest of our dynamic biosphere, planet, and cosmos.[11]

---

11. This dynamism and relatedness is magnificently recounted in three books: Primack and Abrams, *The View from the Center of the Universe*; Swimme and Berry, *The Universe Story*; Morowitz, *The Emergence of Everything*.

We and the rest of creation are not static substances. We—and everything that is—are events.[12] To grasp our nature scientifically, we must simultaneously embrace different levels of being, despite our propensity, when we think of ourselves to focus on our conscious level. But our multilayered reality complicates any simple self-identity. If we think about humans also as collections of atoms, those atoms do not know when they are part of a particular person and when they are part of the air around us, or when they are part of nearby objects. They float in and out of what we think of as "us" all the time. We are completely permeable; in fact, we do not exist on an atomic level. And that level is no less real than the level of our conscious thought. On a molecular and even a biological level, we also exchange with our environment: inhaling air, ingesting food, absorbing heat or cold, sweating, defecating, shedding hair and skin. On atomic, molecular, biochemical, cellular, biosystemic, bodily, even conscious levels, we are not stable substances at all. We are constantly engaging in a give-and-take with the rest of creation, all simultaneously. We are immediately connected to all that came before us, up until this very instant.[13] Each immediately contains in ourselves everything that has led to each of us.

Freedom is an inherent quality of the world because the cosmos and its denizens are relational, dynamic processes. The world is always becoming, always facing possibilities, and always making choices. There certainly are constraints to those choices. Past decisions create the context in which we now exist. We each know that in our own lives, choices that we made years ago shape the kinds of choices we have available now. One can choose to stay married to a spouse or not. But having chosen years ago to marry that spouse, our choices are different than if we had not made that particular choice. We always make our choices from the particular context that is the sum total of our previous choices; the sum total of the world's previous choices.

The world, then, is self-created and self-creating. The cosmos is a partner with God in the becoming. We are partners with the cosmos and with God in our own becoming. We have agency; all creation has standing. The past is offered to us,[14] and God meets us in this moment, as in this

12. Whitehead called this "occasions of experience." See *Process and Reality*, 16; Griffin, *Reenchantment without Supernaturalism*, 108–9.

13. Whitehead's word for that is, "prehension"—that we immediately prehend all of existence. See Cobb and Griffin, *Process Theology*, 19–20.

14. Whitehead called that 'the primordial aspect of God" that part of God that is eternally fixed; the part of God that is unchanging because it has already been decided. See McDaniel and Bowman, eds., *Handbook of Process Theology*, 7–8.

The future is radically open!

Rabbi Bradley Shavit Artson—*A Jewish Perspective*

moment we come to be anew. In every moment we are coming into being again and again. Think again about the level of electrons and protons,
and neutrons you are flashing into being, flashing out of being instantly,
instantly; over and over again. And, at each moment you are met in the
sum total of the choices you made, with the choices you now face. And
you get to decide where you are going to go with that opportunity. That
moment of becoming—the present—is called "concrescence," in which
everything comes into being. And after you make the choice, the selected
option becomes part of God's consequent nature.[15] God holds out a choice
to you that you are free to take, free to reject, and then God meets you in
the next choice, with the next possibility. That means that the future is
radically open.

- Why was this world created through the letter 'ה, hey'? Because the
  world is an *exedra* (closed on three sides, open on one): you may
  proceed if you wish.[16]

- Free will is granted to all. If one desires to turn to the Path of good
  and be righteous, the choice is given. Should one desire to turn to the
  path of evil and be wicked, the choice is given.[17]

God does not, cannot know the future, because the future has not
yet been decided. In choosing to create, God made a world that has the
capacity to make choices, too. And therefore, ibn Ezra describes God as
the One "who can probe all thoughts and see all deeds."[18] God can only
know what is possible to know, past actions and current intentions. The
future has not been chosen.

"Lover, indeed, of the people,"[19] "God" is how we address the creative responsive love that pervades the world. Here I want to mention a
particularly useful tool. Conventional theology thinks of God in mono-
polar terms: if God is simple, God cannot be complex. If God is eternal,
God cannot be dynamic. If God is perfect, God cannot be in relationship:
one polar extreme or the other. A Jewish philosopher at the turn of the
twentieth century, Morris Raphael Cohen, first articulated the principle of
dipolarity. Dipolarity is the notion that something can be one trait in one
context and another trait in another context. For example, I am son and
father at the same time. That is not logically incompatible, unless I claim

15. Ibid., 6.

16. Yehudah bar Ilai, *Menahot* 29b.

17. Rambam, *Mishneh Torah*, Hilkhot Teshuvah 5:1.

18. Rabbi Abraham ibn Ezra, Leviticus 22:31.

19. Deuteronomy 14:1.

9

to be both poles to the same individual. But I am son to my father, and father to my son, and I can, in fact, be both. In fact, the fullest possible understanding of me in my complexity and multipolarity is only possible if we utilize all possible aspects of my being, what Cohen called dipolarity. Process thinkers apply that notion of dipolarity to God and to God's creation.[20] Interestingly, we find this insight in several Jewish sources, as well:

- Am I only a God near at hand—says the Holy One—
  And not a God far away?
  If a person enters a hiding place,
  Do I not see him?—says the Holy One.
  For I fill both heaven and earth—declares the Holy One.[21]

- In God's greatness and the bulk of God's might, God created the whole world in pairs, each reflection resembling the other, and each corresponding to the other. For God made them in his wisdom, to make known that every thing has its partner and its reflection, and were it not for the one, the other would not be.[22]

Dipolarity is kind of a Yin-Yang in which we comprehend both polarities to understand the fullness of what is in front of us: "Everything that exists in the world is either of a certain essence or its opposite."[23] This dipolarity extends even to God, who is infinite in some respects, and finite in some respects. God is infinite in how God is in potential prior to creation. Having created, God enters into relationship with us, and in entering into relationship there are aspects of God that are finite.

The word 'Elohim,' the designation for God in that same first verse of Genesis, refers to a contraction. Since God is endless the creation of the world had to involve a contraction of the light, so that God might enter the lower worlds. God remains infinite, and the worlds cannot contain God, but since God desired their creation God so self-contracted, as it were, that they could bear to contain God. It is in this aspect that God is called Elohim.[24]

God is separate from creation in some respects, and in some respects, part of the creation. The prophet Isaiah proclaims, "Holy, holy,

20. Most originally, Charles Hartshorne. See Hartshorne and Reese, *Philosophers Speak of God*, 1–15.

21. Jeremiah 23:23–24.

22. *Midrash Temura*, chapter 1.

23. Rabbi Judah Loew of Prague, *Hiddushei Aggadot*, 2:89.

24. Rabbi Menachem Nachum of Chernobyl, *Me'or Eynayim*, "Hayei Sarah."

holy—the Holy One of Hosts, God's presence fills all the world."[25] God is not separate. God cannot fill something God is separate from. One can only fill it by being in it, by being co-extensive with it. In *Pesikta de-Rav Kahana* we find, "There is no place lacking the Divine presence."[26] God is not separate from spacetime, God permeates it; God fills it, as the Talmud notes, "God's presence is in all places."[27] That means that God is eternal in some respects (God's reliability, God's being the steady source of creating, absolutely eternal) and dynamic in some respects. God's static eternality is ontology, the study of being. God's dynamism is hyathology, the study of becoming.[28] The details of God's creating—once we move away from the abstract to the concrete—that is always incomplete, in process, on the way: "Whatever was created by God during the six days of creation needs further improvement."[29]

Apparently, this ability to exceed previous perfection—to be vulnerable to creation and open to change—includes the divine as well. For example, in the very beginning of the book of Genesis, after God fashions humanity, we are told "the Holy One regretted that He had made man on earth, and God's heart was saddened."[30] What does it mean for God to regret and feel sorrow? A timeless, changeless God cannot regret. Regret means being different than you were a moment ago. So the Torah itself asserts God's dynamism in the context of relationship. Over and over again the Torah emphasizes a God who expresses emotion, a God who is always meeting people in relationship, and changing because of that relationship. God for process thinking is the ground of novelty. God is the fact that a universe established through fixed, changeless laws, still generates novelty all the time; new unprecedented things that did not previously exist. And, in process thinking, God shares the experiences of all creatures, and is experienced by all creatures:

> The essence of divinity is found in every single thing—nothing
> but it exists. Since it causes every thing to be, no thing can live

25. Isaiah 6:3.

26. *Piska* 1:2.

27. Talmud *Bava Batra* 25a.

28. "Hyathology" is a neologism based on God's self-identification as "Ehyeh-Asher-Ehyeh, I will become what/who I will become" to Moses in Exodus 3:14. Coined by Professor Tetsutaro Ariga of Kyoto University it was used by Charles Hartshorne to articulate process thinking's prioritization of becoming. See Hartshorne, "Some Causes of My Intellectual Growth," 43.

29. *Bereshit Rabbah* 11:6.

30. Genesis 6:6.

by anything else. It enlivens them; its existence exists in each existent. Do not attribute duality to God. Let God be solely God. If you suppose that Ein Sof (Without Limit) emanates until a certain point, and that from that point on is outside of it, you have dualized. God forbid! Realize, rather, that Ein Sof exists in each existent. Do not say, 'This is a stone and not God.' God forbid! Rather, all existence is God, and the stone is a thing pervaded by divinity.[31]

Nothing that happens escapes God's perception and experience, and we are always in touch with the Divine. In *Bereshit Rabbah*, we learn: "From the first day of creation, the Holy Blessing One longed to enter into partnership with the terrestrial world, to dwell with God's creatures within the terrestrial world."[32]

God is our partner, dwelling in the world; a statement that no dominant theologian could make, but with which the rabbis are content. "God is the place of the world, but the world is not God's place."[33] God permeates the world. God dwells within the world.

NOT BY MIGHT, NOR BY POWER, BUT BY MY BREATH[34]

One key shift then, for process thinking, is that God does not exercise coercive power; God exercises persuasive power. Western people conceive of belief in God, and many concur—both believers and atheists—as affirming a bully in the sky who compels behavior from unwilling, passive agents, or who restrains behavior and precludes outcomes that sinning creatures would otherwise pursue. Process thinking dissents, reminding us that God does not work through coercion; God works through persuasion and invitation, through persistently inviting us to make the best possible choice, and then leaving us free to make the wrong choice. But then the minute we have made our choice, God persistently lures us toward the making of the best possible subsequent choice.

God does not break the rules to force a desired outcome, working instead with and through us, with and through natural law. Here is that timely assurance from Midrash *Tanhuma*:

---

31. Rabbi Moshe Cordovero, *Shiur Qomah* to *Zohar* 3:14b (Idra Rabba).
32. *Bereshit Rabbah* 1:10.
33. *Bereshit Rabbah* 68:9.
34. Zechariah 4:6.

All the might, the praise, the greatness, and the power belong to the Sovereign of Sovereigns. Yet God loves law. It is the custom of the world that a powerful tyrant does not desire to do things lawfully. Rather, he bypasses law and order by coercing, stealing, transgressing the will of the Creator, favoring his friends and relatives while treating his antagonists unjustly. But the Holy Blessing One, the King of Kings, loves law, and does nothing unless it is with law. This is the meaning of 'Mighty is the King who loves law.'[35]

The ancient rabbis decontextualize this verse and construe it to teach that when one talks about God's might, one celebrates God's willingness to live within natural law. God does not "break" the laws of physics, the laws of chemistry, the laws of biology, the laws of morality. In that wondrous way, God's power is not simply an amplification of human power, it is qualitatively superior and unique.[36] God works within the constraints of law. The way God works on us, in us, through us is called the 'lure,' what Whitehead calls, the 'initial aim'[37] and Jonas calls "the mutely insistent appeal of his unfulfilled goal."[38] That is to say, at this very moment (and at every moment) God meets each of us, and all of creation, offering us the best possible next step. We have the opportunity (and the freedom) to decide whether to take that best possible next step, or not. That next step, best of all possible, the initial aim, becomes for us, our subjective aim; what we choose to do.

We know what the initial aim is; we know it intuitively because we prehend it. We do not have to be told we are each connected to all, and to the creative-responsive love that is God. So we intuit the lure from the inside. Sometimes we choose not to make the right choice, or do the right thing because of the other powers that impinge upon us: our physicality, drives, selfishness, desires, or laziness. A wide diversity of excuses accounts for our subjective aim perverting God's initial aim, which leaves God in covenant, hence vulnerable: "When Israel performs the will of the Holy One, they add strength to the heavenly power. When, however, Israel does not perform the will of the Holy One, they weaken (if it is possible to say so) the great power of the One who is above."[39]

35. *Tanhuma*, Mishpatim, 1.

36. See Keller, "After Omnipotence," in *On the Mystery*, 69–90.

37. McDaniel and Bowman, eds., *Handbook of Process Theology*, 7; Griffin, *Reenchantment without Supernaturalism*, 146–47, 150–51.

38. Jonas, "The Concept of God after Auschwitz," 141.

39. *Pesikta*, Buber, xxvi, 166b.

Here again we meet a dynamic, relating God who suffers, a God who becomes vulnerable in having created us. This is not an all-powerful, impassible, eternal God, but a God so connected through relationship that the best way to describe this temporal, passionate covenant partner is in the language of love. The prophet Hosea understands this, when he speaks on God's behalf to Israel.

> I will espouse you forever:
> I will espouse you with righteousness and justice,
> And with goodness and mercy,
> And I will espouse you with faithfulness.
> Then you shall know the Holy One.[40]

The rabbis recognize this passage as the very heart of the relationship binding the Jew and God, inserting it into the morning liturgy to be recited as the Jew wraps the bands of Tefillin on the arm in preparation for the morning prayers. To be in covenant with God is akin to marriage: "See, God's love for you is like the love of a man and a woman."[41]

To love someone is to become vulnerable to his or her choices. It is to suffer another's pain, and to exalt in the lover's triumph. It is to want to be steadily a partner and helper, and to sometimes be hurt by his or her rejection or bad choices. In such a way, God suffers and rejoices in the world, and with the world: "In all their troubles God was troubled."[42] In Psalm 91, we are told, "I will be with him in his suffering."[43] In Mishnah *Sanhedrin*, Rabbi Meir says, "When a person is sorely troubled, what does the Shekhinah (God's indwelling Presence) say? She says, my head is ill; my arm is ill; I am not at ease."[44] Our suffering pains God. God is diminished by our not rising to the best choice. The God of Israel is not merely an unchanging, external perfection (although there is an aspect of God which is unchanging and eternal); we encounter the divine in the dynamism of *brit*, relationship. During the rituals of Hoshanot,[45] observant Jews march around the sanctuary and one of the hymns is, "As you saved together, God and people, so save us." There is a dynamic interconnection between

40. Hosea 2:21–22.

41 Talmud *Yoma* 54a.

42. Isaiah 63:9.

43. Psalm 91:15.

44. Mishnah *Sanhedrin* 6:5.

45. Toward the end of the Festival of Sukkot, on Hoshanah Rabbah, the day of the Great Hoshanah, Jews march around the sanctuary with their palm fronds, chanting.

God, humanity, and all creation. That interconnection changes how we understand life's big questions.

IT IS BEYOND MY KNOWLEDGE:[46] APPREHENDING WITHOUT CERTAINTY

One of the changes that process thinking encourages is to take pluralism seriously, to approach knowledge in a spirit of humility, relationality, and dynamism. Dominant style theologies of creation present a single telling of creation, or afterlife, imposing a certainty and an objectivity that verifiable knowledge does not mandate. At least from the medieval period into the present, scholars have remained aware that there is no way to step outside of the cosmos to verify or falsify many of our theoretical explanations, no way to prove a definitive single encompassing account for the beginning. As Saadia Gaon notes in tenth-century Baghdad:

> The problem dealt with . . . is one on which we have no data from actual observation or from sense perception, but conclusions which can be derived only from postulates of pure reason. We mean the problem of the origin of the world. It cannot be grasped by the senses, and one can only endeavor to comprehend it by thought.[47]

While it is certainly true that contemporary scientists have "seen" a great deal more than the pre-modern natural philosophers (background cosmic radiation, galaxies and nebulae extending to the visible cosmic horizon, etc.), it also remains true that we cannot explore and test various spacetime bubbles; we cannot step outside of our own cosmos to compare and contrast with others.

Furthermore, we are limited to an intuitive sense that pertains to our range of size and our durations of time.[48] For size ranges vastly larger than our own (planets, galaxies, spacetime) or vastly smaller (molecules, atoms,

---

46. Psalm 139:6.

47. Saadia Gaon, *Book of Beliefs and Opinions*, 38.

48. See Primack and Abrams, *The View from the Center of the Universe*, 156–66. As they point out, from the limit of our cosmic horizon, at 10^{28}cm as a maximum to the Planck length at the smallest (10^{-25}cm), there is about 60 orders of magnitude. Our intuition works near the center, from 10^{-5}cm to 10^{5}cm. At sizes much larger or smaller than these sizes, our assumptions, intuition, and logic no longer hold. The same limits pertain to time frames vastly more quick or more slow than the middle range of our own.

atomic particles, and quanta), human intuition and logic isn't reliable, not having evolved to cope with such enormity or smallness. Nor do our common sense perceptions function intuitively with the briefest quantum time intervals or with the expansive duration of cosmic events. In such durations and sizes, the only effective system of human relation and expression (constrained by our scientific knowledge) is the Three M's: Math, Myth, and Metaphor, Meditation, and Music. Each provides a syntax and narrative to link our consciousness and existence to those realms of reality vastly larger or smaller than our own size range, or vastly shorter or longer than the time frames we are evolved to recognize and intuit.

When contemplating the possible origins of this universe, consequently, we are thrown back to a similar position as the medievals—mustering all available evidence and then generating plausible tellings based on our own presuppositions and use of human reasoning.

CREATION RENEWED EVERYDAY

Instead of thinking of creation as *ex nihilo*, as if there was nothing existent previously and then, in an instant, everything suddenly existed, process thinking takes a more developmental view. I think it fair to say that most process thinkers, beginning with Whitehead, have understood God as the organizing force of an eternally existing reality. Such a view surprises those who restrict their view of creation to the first and third sentences in the book of Genesis, ignoring the second sentence and creation images from elsewhere in the Bible, Midrash, and Kabbalah. The dominant view filters the Genesis telling through a pre-existent ideology of an omnipotent, eternal, impassive Deity, forcing readers to constrain the text within the procrustean confines of an effortless, spontaneous moment that created everything that exists today. Such an approach conflicts with fundamental scientific evidence, such as: the age of the planet, the cosmic materials out of which life is constructed, that living things have developed from previous living things, and the several mass extinctions that have punctuated life on earth prior to the appearance of today's species, to mention only a few. Equally significantly, such a theological imposition (more green paint!) depends on ignoring the second verse of Genesis: "the earth being unformed and void, with darkness over the surface of the deep and a wind from God sweeping over the water."[49] So much for taking the Bible literally!

49. Genesis 1:2. All biblical translations taken from Stein, *JPS Hebrew-English*

A contextual reading of the opening chapters of Genesis yields the recognition that the unformed and void darkness (*tohu va-vohu*) existed when God began creating. That bubbling, irrepressible depth remains the source of self-creativity, potentialities, and resistance to all imposed power.[50] God's creating is not necessarily one of instantiating *ex nihilo* from without, but rather a process of mobilizing continuous self-creativity from within:

> An epiphany enables you to sense creation not as something completed, but as constantly becoming, evolving, ascending. This transports you from a place where there is nothing new to a place where there is nothing old, where everything renews itself, where heaven and earth rejoice as at the moment of creation.[51]

Because, of course, every moment *is* the moment of creation! This richer view of continuous creation, it turns out, is also reflected in Jewish sources, beginning with the beginning itself. The book of Genesis begins with the word, *B'reisheet*, which the New Jewish Publication Society version correctly translates as "When God began to create heaven and earth—,"[52] with God's spirit fluttering over preexistent *tohu va-vohu*. Chaos is already there, God fluttering over its surface, and then God begins to speak it into increasing order and diversity. By the end of the first chapter of Genesis, God has spoken creation into a symphony of diverse becoming.

At each stage of the blossoming process of creating, God turns to creation itself and issues an invitation, a lure, let there be 'whatever,' and let it flourish according to its own laws, *le-minehu*.[53] God invites creation to be a co-partner in the process of creating. It is not that God, once and for all, speaks everything that currently lives into existence from the outside. God coaxes, summons, and invites the sun and stars and planetary objects into becoming, then the earth to distinguish oceans and dry land, then to generate plants, and which cascade into increasing diversity of grasses, shrubs, trees and vegetation; God invites the earth to spring up as animal life, and then asks each species to continue its own internal growth by its own inner logic—*le-minehu*, after its own kind.[54] It is worth noting that

Tanakh: The Traditional Hebrew Text and the New JPS Translation, 2005.

50. See Keller, *Face of the Deep.*

51. Rav Abraham Isaac Kook, *Orot Ha-Kodesh.*

52. Genesis 1:1.

53. Genesis 1:12, 21, 24.

54. See, for instance, Genesis 1:24. Discussion is found in Gnuse, *The Old Testament and Process Theology,* 103–7.

God sees creation as a process with developmental stages each with their own integrity and each worthy of celebration. At the end of each day, "God saw that it was good."[55] At the creation of humanity and the beginning of the Sabbath, God "found it very good."[56] As Robert Gnuse notes, "The statement that God found the creative act of each specific day to be good is highly important, for it means that at each stage of the creative endeavor God stopped and took account of what was unfolding. Perhaps the text even speaks of divine pleasure exhibited at the end of each individual creative act. If we focus on this language in Genesis 1, we may see the cosmic creation as a dynamic, evolutionary process."[57]

We are told in *Massekhet Haggigah* that God "renews every day the work of creation." That is not a single intervention with a clear temporal beginning and a sharp conclusion after which it's complete; the Talmud is suggesting that God is constantly creating, indeed is inseparable from the process of creating. The *Zohar* takes that even further. It quotes from the book of Proverbs, "By understanding God continually established the heavens."[58] The *Zohar* asks, what does the phrase "continually established" mean?

> God goes on arranging the Sefirot every day, and never stops. They were not arranged at one particular time, but God arranges them daily because of the great love and the pleasure that the Holy Blessing One feels for them and for their preciousness in God's sight.[59]

Creation, then, is the process of God luring emergent being into order, abundance, diversity, and goodness. Creation is God's inviting creation into the process of becoming. That means there can be no break with natural law at any point in the process. God works with and through material reality. The universe is not merely passive stuff that God molds into shape; it is a self-creating universe.

> God created the world in a state of beginning. The universe is always in an uncompleted state, in the form of its beginning. It is not like a vessel at which the master works to finish it; it requires continuous labor and renewal by creative forces. Should these

55. Genesis 1:4, 10, 12, 18, 21, 25.
56. Genesis 1:31.
57. Gnuse, *The Old Testament and Process Theology*, 102.
58. Proverbs 3:19.
59. *Zohar* 1:207a.

cease for only a second, the universe would return to primeval chaos.[60]

God permeates that *tohu va-vohu* stuff and expresses through it the ability to live:

> The activating force of the Creator must continuously be present within the created object, to give it life and continued existence . . . And even as regards this physical earth and its inorganic components, their life-force and continued existence is the 'word of God.' . . . There is a kind of soul and spiritual life-force even in inorganic matter such as stones and dust and water.[61]

There are two contemporary, scientific ways to contextualize the process of continuing creation we have described, each accepted at present by large segments of the scientific community. Both provide plausible accounts of the data we have at present, and both leave certain large assumptions unproven and unprovable in theory. The two plausible options correspond in broad outline to the two medieval cosmic options—an eternal creation and a creation of space and time as part of the creative act:

- *Eternal inflation* asserts that our spacetime bubble is located in a cosmic "sea" of infinite, eternal inflation. This "sea" is sometimes referred to as the superuniverse, or the multiverse, or the meta-universe.[62] Within the eternal inflation, only quantum rules govern, although on rare occasions due to long-shot quantum odds, exceptional space-time bubbles emerge into being within which expansion does not pertain. Within each bubble there is a coherent spacetime, and we live in one such bubble. So what we think of as the Big Bang and all of existence, in this understanding, is really one space-time bubble in an infinite sea of eternal inflation that erupts into other new space-time bubbles. In this eternal realm, neither space nor time have meaning—time because it has no direction, and space because it is the same in every direction and in every place. Of course, this eternal inflation, existing beyond spacetime is unverifiable and immeasurable in principle. It lies beyond human cognition or description, in a realm of myth, math, and metaphor (where, it turns out, all human conceptualization and meaning-making occurs).

---

60. Reb Simcha Bunam of Przysucha, *Siach Sarfei Kodesh*, 2: 17.

61. Rabbi Shneur Zalman of Liadi, *Tanya*, chapter 25.

62. Primack and Abrams, *The View from The Center of the Universe*, 190.

- *Big Bang theory* starts with the instant in which space-time exploded into existence, that primal singularity some fourteen billion years ago which created the vast cosmos in which we live and move and have our being. The Big Bang itself is held to be inexplicable, the laws of physics fail as we move back in time toward the singular moment itself. Within that singularity, we can only marvel at the remarkable fine-tuning of the major forces of the cosmos, a slight variation of any of which would have made life impossible.[63]

These two understandings of creation—of an infinite, eternal infla-tionary multiverse or of a singular Big Bang—may be disturbing to people who have read the Bible exclusively through dominant theological lenses, but let me assure you, Jewish traditional voices have resources to accom-modate both. So let me offer a passage in *Kohelet Rabbah*, which quotes from the book of *Kohelet*, "As God has made everything beautiful in its time."[64]

Rabbi Tanhuma said, "In its due time was when the universe was created." It was not proper to be created before then; it was created at the right moment. Assuming there is one universe, it got created at the right moment. If you prefer to think of the cosmos as co-extensive with our space-time bubble (and there are plenty of scientists who do), Rabbi Tan-huma (and many other sages) shares your view. There is no way for us to stand outside of our space-time bubble to test whether there are other space-time bubbles, let alone an infinite and eternal expansion. It is logic (and existential preferences) that drive the people who posit multi-verses; not experience. They may be right, but we will never know with certainty.

But that same Midrash goes on to say, "Rabbi Abbahu said: 'From this we learn that the Holy Blessing One kept on constructing worlds and destroying them, until God constructed the present one and said, this one pleases me, the others did not.'"[65] In the second part of the same Midrash is the idea of an infinite number of universes of which ours is only one. Apparently ours is not the first generation to speculate on the possibility of previous, perhaps infinite, universes. Apparently, these rabbinic sages were comfortable understanding God the Creator, not as having created once, but as the God who is always creating.

At these two choices—an eternal inflation with repeated space-times or a singular space-time that encompasses all—individual scientists have

---

63. See Rees, *Just Six Numbers*; Tyson and Goldsmith, *Origins*, 98–107.

64. Kohelet 3:11.

65. *Kohelet Rabbah* 3:13.

strong preferences, but science as a whole does not definitively weigh in. We are left with two conceivable possibilities, each scientifically plausible and each religiously compatible with the understanding of creation as an ongoing process that the Bible and Rabbinic sources present. We are (still? once more?) in the position that Maimonides explicated in his magisterial *Guide of the Perplexed*: "It was to our mind established as true that, regarding the question whether the heavens are generated or eternal, neither of the two contrary opinions could be demonstrated."[66]

God may be the One who created everything out of nothing, or the One who created something out of eternity and infinity. Process saves us from having to weigh in beyond what we can know. We can indulge a little dipolarity here—rather than asserting a false certainty beyond what knowledge can assert, rather than creating a false dichotomy between the two plausibilities, we can embrace both understandings as useful metaphors to orient and motivate ourselves within the cosmos. In either telling, God continually lures this dynamic creation, working in/with/through all that exists to generate greater order, expressiveness, diversity and abundance.

WHAT OF THE NIGHT?[67] EVIL & SUFFERING

If God is not the coercive despot who created all as it is, if God is found in the steady relational love that invites creation into diverse becoming, then evil is that aspect of reality not yet touched by God's lure or that part of creation that ignores God's lure.

Another way to address suffering and evil is to acknowledge that much of what we term evil or suffering is a matter of perspective. Maimonides, speaking out of the naturalism that Neo-Aristotelian thought makes possible, articulates it best. He points out how often what we term evil is simply our perspective on a particular event:

> The ignoramus and those like him among the multitude consider that which exists only with reference to the human individual. Every ignoramus imagines that all that exists exists with a view to his individual sake; it is as if there were nothing that exists except him. And if something happens to him that is contrary

---

66. Maimonides, *Guide of the Perplexed*, II:22, 320.
67. Isaiah 21:11.

to what he wishes, he makes the trenchant judgment that all that exists is an evil.[68]

Much of what we understand to be evil is the very source of dynamism and life. The fact that our planet is churning, so that the rocks do not settle in order of heaviness, but the heavy ones keep getting kicked up to the surface, that is why there is life on the surface. Were it not for the tectonic activity of the core, there would be no life on the surface of this planet. Events that are disasters for some are sources where novelty and development emerge. So the process of evolution is driven precisely by a tension between limits on the one hand and possibilities on the other. Maybe that is why Isaiah says God is the one who "makes peace and creates evil."[69] God has to be *borei ra*, the Creator of evil, because out of what is experienced as evil comes life itself. You cannot have one without the other.

The cosmos itself does not follow God's script, as though predetermined. Every level of the cosmos follows its own inner *hokhmah*, its own inner dynamic, and therefore is in the process of becoming, as are we. As Maimonides goes on to explain, most human suffering is not a divine punishment or test, but is the result of three broad realities of life.

- The first reality is that it is the nature of material reality to come into being, to grow and flourish for a time, and then to fall apart prior to going out of existence:

  > The first type of evil is that which befalls people because of the nature of coming-to-be and passing-away. I mean to say because of our being endowed with matter. Because of this, infirmities and paralytic afflictions befall some individuals either in consequence of their original natural disposition, or they supervene because of changes occurring in the elements, such as corruption of the air or a fire from heaven and a landslide.[70]

This realm of suffering is the logical manifestation of dynamism and change. The only alternative, a world of static eternity, is one that few of us would choose—even if it means embracing an alternative that also brings suffering and death. It is also possible to understand large swaths of suffering and evil as the result of our freedom, the freedom of the entire cosmos. And sometimes we individuals, or

68. Maimonides, *Guide of the Perplexed*, III:12, 442.

69. Isaiah 45:7. NJPS translates as "I make weal and create woe."

70. Maimonides, *Guide of the Perplexed*, III:443.

humanity at large, make bad choices, and sometimes the rest of the cosmos makes disastrous choices. This freedom accounts for the final two channels we perceive as evil and experience as suffering:

2. The evils of the second kind are those that people inflict upon one another, such as tyrannical domination of some of them over others.[71] This second category of suffering is the result of human freedom and our ability to impose bad choices on innocent others. This requires no additional supernatural intervention, but is the immediate consequence of our freedom and our relatedness.

3. The third and final category of evil and suffering is related to the second: our freedom to make poor choices also means that we inflict harm on ourselves when we don't muster the strength and vision to implement the divine lure.

> The evils of the third kind are those that are inflicted upon any individual among us by his own action . . . All people lament over evils of this kind; and it is only seldom that you find one who is not guilty of having brought them upon himself . . . This kind is consequent upon all vices, I mean concupiscence for eating, drinking, and copulation, and doing these things with excess in regard to quantity or irregularity or when the quality of the foodstuffs is bad. For this is the cause of all corporeal and psychical diseases and ailments.[72]

The dynamic, ephemeral nature of becoming, the competing lures that tempt us and distract us from God's lure, our ability to impose ourselves on others and our ability to mislead ourselves—these remain sources of suffering and evil. Process thinking allows us to recognize their sources as proximate, within nature, and not as the judgment or punishment of the Divine. In turn, this realization allows us to continue to perceive God as our ally and strength in times of tribulation, to be able to reorient ourselves to focus receptively on implementing the divine lure before us, to choose as free creatures to affirm those relations (and make those choices) which bring us strength, joy, and health.

In the dominant theology, an omnipotent, omniscient God becomes the source of our suffering, either actively by commission or passively by refraining from intervention. In either case, it is easy to feel abandoned, betrayed, or persecuted by such a coercive power. In such a theology, evil

71. Ibid., 444.
72. Ibid., 445.

is a conceptual conundrum, to be resolved through better reasoning. Process thinking opens our eyes to a Biblical/Rabbinic/Kabbalistic view of God as relational and loving. "I am with you, declares the Holy One,"[73] working in/with/ through us to bring order to the chaos in our lives and societies, giving us the strength and insight to know how to struggle for health, connection, and justice.

Understanding God as the pervasive creativity and novelty that permeates all-becoming invites us to stop *thinking* about the status of evil, and to focus on how we fight for justice and compassion: "*You shall love the Holy One your God*—This implies that one should make God beloved by one's deeds."[74] Evil and suffering are not intriguing theological puzzles; they are existential goads calling us to repair the world. This shift, from ratiocination to action has ancient precedent. The rabbis perceive God as choosing righteous behavior rather than correct belief: "Would that they had rather forsaken Me but maintained my Torah, for the great light emanating from the Torah would have led them back to Me."[75]

If we are part of creation, if we also have the ability to align ourselves to the divine lure, then evil is a summons for us to implement justice, which is resolute love. What choices must we make now to obviate evil tomorrow? That question beckons as a revelation: what is it that God asks of us?

A STILL, SMALL VOICE: REVELATION[76]

Process enhances our ability to participate in revelation. Our museums retain Medieval illustrations of Moses receiving the Torah, the artists portray an arm descending from the sky holding a book, while Moses stands on the top of the mountain, reaching up—straining to grab the book that is handed to him! And that illustration is, I think, an accurate pictorial presentation of the dominant view of revelation as shaped by Greek philosophy—eternal God, static immaculate Torah, passive (although worthy) recipient. But if you can entertain a notion of God and cosmos as becoming, of the universe as relationship in process, then it is easy to recognize revelation as also ongoing, relational, dynamic and continuous. That should not be a surprise to Jews who are familiar with

73. Haggai 1:13.

74. Talmud *Yoma* 86a.

75. Talmud *Nedarim* 81a.

76. 1 Kings 19:12.

the Bible, Rabbinics, and Kabbalah because we find that openness in our own tradition, as well. Jewish tradition speaks of Matan Torah, the giving of Torah and Kabbalat Torah, the receiving of Torah, both active aspects of a dynamic relationship. Far from being relegated to the distant past, to a single day and a particular mountain, Sinai and the revelation name a quality of relation that is always and everywhere available: "*On this day they came to the wilderness of Sinai* (Exodus 19:1). Every day that you study Torah, say 'it is as if I received it this very day from Sinai."[77] Not only does this continuous revelation apply to the study of Torah (the book), but any fruitful teaching by any sage enjoys the status of Torah: "Everything that a diligent student will teach in the distant future has already been proclaimed on Mt. Sinai."[78]

This open-ended Torah harvests a <u>living, growing process, a pulsing relationship of love</u>. No mere abstraction or desiccated set of rules, Torah takes concrete form in the specific people through whom it emerges into the light of day. God's presence is manifest in their specific language, idiom, and culture. Moving backward through time, we can track this insight back across the ages:

- "The word of God can be uttered only by human mouths."[79]

- "Likewise with all the prophets and those possessed of the Holy Spirit: the supernal voice and speech vested itself in their actual voice and speech."[80]

- "The Shekhinah speaks from the throat of Moses."[81]

- "It is clear that [while God's precepts are given]through words uttered in Torah, they are also given through words uttered by elders and sages."[82]

As the Torah becomes real through the active participation of its human co-creators, the apparent conflict between the Documentary Hypothesis—the method through which God and the sages of Israel produced the Torah we now possess—and the veneration of Torah as the manifestation of the Divine in words finds resolution. Since the Torah represents the

---

77. *Tanhuma*, Yitro 7.

78. Yerushalmi *Peah* 2:17a. See also *Sifrei Devarim* 11:13; and Yerushalmi *Megillah* 1:7.

79. Jonas, *Memoirs*, 30.

80. Rabbi Shneur Zalman of Liadi, *Tanya*, Ch. 25.

81. *Zohar* 3:234a.

82. Pesikta Rabbati *Piska* 3.

response of the Jews to a heightened experience of God—an openness to the Divine lure—it is patently impossible and fruitless to argue about whether the Torah is divine or human. In good dipolar fashion, it is inseparably both. (God "speaks" with/in/through us.)

Recognizing Torah as a Divine/human partnership means that the authority of the Torah is no longer misperceived as coercive. Like God, Torah's authority is persuasive, an invitation to wisdom rather than intimidation through fear. Jewish tradition labels that fear of consequences the inferior *yirah*. But the superior yirah is marvel or wonder. It reflects reverent awe at the staggering grandeur of cosmos, consciousness, and life! Such yirah responds willingly to persuasive, not coercive, power. This inviting lure is found in the book of Deuteronomy, when we are instructed to keep the *mitzvot* and observe them, "for this is your wisdom and your understanding in the sight of nations, who when they hear of these statutes will say, 'surely this great nation is a wise and understanding people.'"[83] As we recognize the shift in the authority of Torah from corrosive coercion imposed to bubble-up wisdom offered, the Torah becomes compelling because it is wise, because it is beautiful, because it augments life. Obedience is no longer the desperate attempt to avoid punishment, but the free embrace of life-sustaining wisdom. In fact, the rabbis make the same point in a wonderful, ancient midrash: recall how the Jews are gathered at the foot of Mt. Sinai. The Torah says they are *tachtit ha-har*—under the mountain (Exodus 19:17). The rabbis understand that curious phrase to mean that God "covered them with the mountain as a vat. God said to them, If you accept the Torah, fine. But if not, your burial will be here."[84] But you cannot obligate someone into agreement through coercion, even if you are God! So if Sinai is a coercive imposition, the Jews are technically free of the obligations of the covenant. Astonishingly, the answer the Gemara records is that *we are not obligated by Sinai!* We are obligated to the Torah because of an event during the lives of Mordecai and Esther. When they wrote and disseminated the teachings of the tradition, the book of Esther records of the Jews, *kimu ve-kiblu*, "they established and they accepted it. As the Talmud notes, "They established that which they already had accepted."[85] It is only because they freely accepted the Torah, because they responded to the divine lure, freely offered and freely accepted, that the covenant linking God and the Jewish people was affirmed. God's initial

83. Deuteronomy 4:6.

84. Talmud *Shabbat* 88a.

85. Ibid.

aim—take this way of living that the nations will recognize as wise flowed into the subjective aim of the Jews' response, "we will observe and we will hear."[86] That relationship precludes coercion. Covenant thrives in invitation, a mutual yearning.

Such covenantal love also, of course, elevates the place of ethics, and it means that morality becomes the capstone of religious Jewish life. But this has been true from the beginning. Think of the Torah as a mountain; Genesis and Deuteronomy, the base; Exodus and Numbers, the second stand; and Leviticus at the peak. And the middle chapter of Leviticus is the Holiness Code. The Holiness Code details how to participate in holy community. The peak of Sinai, it turns out, is ethics, as the prophets themselves reiterate. In Jewish religious understanding, ritual matters because it generates ethical seriousness; it creates a pedagogy of goodness and an agenda of grateful inclusion.[87] Our beliefs enter life through our deeds: "What short text is there upon which all the essential principles of the Torah depend? 'In all your ways, acknowledge God (Prov 3:6).'"[88]

CHOSENNESS: SERVANT, LOVER, FIRSTBORN

In the dominant theology with its either/or dichotomies, either the Jews are chosen, hence superior, or all peoples are equal and none are chosen. If God is the active choosing partner then Israel must be the passive recipient of God's choice. But dipolarity allows us to transcend these binary dichotomies. Israel is an active partner in the process of chosenness: "We do not know whether the Holy Blessing One chose Jacob or whether Jacob chose the Holy Blessing One."[89] Another midrash reiterates the reciprocity: "As soon as the Holy Blessing One saw Israel's resolution, saw that they wished to accept the Torah with love and affection, with fear and reverence, with awe and trembling, God said I am the Holy One your God."[90]

Jews choose/are chosen to live Torah in the world, both to build communities of justice and inclusion and to model that such a life is possible to embody. But other peoples choose/are chosen, too, in other ways. The Torah reminds us, "It was not because you were more in number than any other people that the Holy One showered love upon you and chose

86. Exodus 24:7.
87. See Berman, *Created Equal*.
88. Talmud *Berakhot* 63a.
89. Sifre Devarim *Piska* 312.
90. Pesikta Rabbati *Piska* 21.

you, for you were the fewest of all peoples."[91] To this cautionary note, the rabbis add:

> Not because you are greater than other nations did I choose you, not because you obey My commandments more than the nations, for they follow My commandments even though they were not bidden to do it, and also magnify My name more than you, as it says, 'From the rising of the sun even to its setting, my name is great among the nations.'[92]

Jews choose/are chosen for Torah and mitzvot, although most emphatically not because of intrinsic superiority. Other peoples are chosen/choose their own paths to holiness and righteousness. This understanding comes not just from modern rabbis and theologians; it emerges from the Torah and Rabbinics, as well. The prophet Isaiah exults, "In that day, Israel shall be a third partner with Egypt and Assyria as a blessing on earth; for the Holy One of Hosts will bless them, saying, "Blessed be My people Egypt, My handiwork Assyria, and My very own Israel."[93] He also inquires, "Is it too light a thing that you should be my servant, to raise up the tribes of Jacob and to restore the preserved of Israel? I will give you as a light to the nations that my salvation shall reach to the ends of the earth."[94] We are God's servants both to return Israel to a covenantal life, but also to be a light to the nations of the world. The prophet Amos reminds us that others have been chosen too: "Are you not like the Ethiopians to me, O people of Israel? Says the Holy One. Did I not bring up Israel from the land of Egypt, and the Philistines from Caphtor and the Syrians from Kir?"[95] All peoples are God's people; all children are children of God. The rabbis, as well, comment that we chose/were chosen, not because we are greater, not because we are more observant, not because we glorify God's name more, we choose/are chosen because God is discerned in process, and that process is not abstract logic, it is a particular relationship, involving a people, a place, a history, and a way.

91. Deuteronomy 7:7.
92. Malachi 1:11.
93. Isaiah 19:24.
94. Isaiah 49:6.
95. Amos 9:7.

SALVATION & AFTERLIFE

As it was in the beginning, so it shall be in the end. Our stories of beginnings took advantage of dipolarity to embrace two plausible scientific/mythic tellings: Big Bang *and* Eternal Inflation, each redolent with biblical, Midrashic, and Kabbalistic imagery and insight. Each of these tellings takes us beyond the limits of empirical knowing (although they are each constrained by current scientific knowledge to reflect a minimal standard of plausibility). Now, turning to questions of death and afterlife, we seek yet again to peek behind the curtain, where certainty and knowledge cannot arbitrate. Process thinking joins Jewish traditions in offering two plausible paradigms. Rather than the false swagger of pretended certainty, we can embrace the openness of aggadic hope and multiplicity, knowing that truth flashes just under the surface of such tellings.

A process perspective on death and afterlife affirms the same speculative metaphysics as all process insight: We generally think of ourselves as substances, but we are really organized patterns of energy. Everything is in flux, everything is dynamic, everything is volts of electricity; which is to say, a great light that was made at the beginning and hidden away. As we serially flash in and out of existence, on every level, we are free to determine our next choice, constrained only by our previous choices and the instantaneous impact of the rest of choosing creation. God does not know the future. God knows objectively and retains forever all that has already occurred. Integrating and responding to our choices and actions is one of the ways God changes. After we are offered the initial aim—God's best possible option—we then select our subjective aim, choosing what we prefer. That choice, and series of events, then becomes eternally part of God. God's integration of those events that have been achieved is eternal.

Process thinking allows us to formulate a plausible understanding of life in the coming world (*Olam Ha-Ba*). *Olam Ha-Ba* is the biblical/Rabbinic term for our continuing as objectively real aspects of God's thought. We are not substances now in life, and we will not be substances after life ends. We are patterns of energy now, and there is no necessity to believe that we will not continue as patterns of energy in God's eternity.

At this point, however, the specifics of the nature of that continuing existence diverge, in process thinking as is true in Jewish thought as well. Judaism insists on belief in eternal life. The Talmud insists that one who won't proclaim the prayer for the resurrection of the dead is immediately removed as prayer leader,[96] and Maimonides lists affirmation of the afterlife as one of the core required beliefs of traditional Judaism.[97] Beyond affirming faith in some form of continuing existence, however, Jewish law is remarkably open. As Rabbi Louis Jacobs writes:

> Religious agnosticism in some aspects of this whole area is not only legitimate but altogether desirable. As Maimonides (1135–1204) says, we simply can have no idea of what pure spiritual bliss in the Hereafter is like. Agnosticism on the basic issue of whether there is a Hereafter would seem narrowness of vision believing what we do of God. But once the basic affirmation is made, it is almost as narrow to project our poor, early imaginings on the landscape of Heaven.[98]

This religious realism permeates Jewish theology—affirming what we can, specifying only when possible. In this instance, Judaism traditionally affirms an afterlife, but refrains from specifying a single vision of that future. Value-Concept terms—such as *Gan Eden* (Garden of Eden), *Pardes* (paradise), *Gehenna* (hell), *Olam Ha-Ba* (the Coming World), *Tehiyat Ha-Metim* (resurrection), *Gilgul Ha-Neshamot* (reincarnation), *Keitz Ha-Yamim* (End of Days), and *Yeshiva Shel Ma'alah* (Supernal Academy)—circulate in various Jewish conceptions of afterlife, but are never defined with precision or authoritatively. Using the building blocks of these value-concepts, many different tellings of life after death abound within religious Jewish traditions. Those options remain viable for a Jewish process thinker.

Once our lives are finished and done, we continue—as we have lived—on multiple levels. All of the stuff of which we are composed continues in the world. The atoms that constitute us don't stop with our death. The proteins that are us get recycled in the ongoing cycles of life. Everything that we are gets reused and continues.

- One possibility is that death marks the end of our individual consciousness. Our energy patterns continue unabated, but there is no governing organization, no self-reflective awareness that continues beyond death. In such a possibility, we merge back into the oneness from which we emerged. We sleep as discrete individuals and awaken as the totality of the cosmos.

---

96. Talmud *Berakhot* 26b, 29a.

97. Maimonides, *Commentary to the Mishnah Sanhedrin*, introduction to chapter 10.

98. Jacobs, *A Jewish Theology*, 321.

• A second possibility builds on the first, adding the plausible hope that consciousness and identity continue unimpaired. As God is process, and as God is the one who is supremely connected to everything, supremely related, and forgetting nothing, we remain eternally alive in God's memory, in God's thought, which, it turns out, is what we have been all along.

SELECT BIBLIOGRAPHY

Process Thinking

Cobb, John B. Jr. *The Process Perspective: Frequently Asked Questions about Process Theology*, edited by Jeanyne B. Slettom. St. Louis: Chalice, 2003.
Cobb, John B., Jr., and David Ray Griffin. *Process Theology: An Introductory Exposition*. Louisville: Westminster John Knox, 1976.
Cousins, Ewert H., editor. *Process Theology: Basic Writings*. New York: Newman, 1971.
Ford, Lewis S. *Transforming Process Theism*. SUNY Series in Philosophy. Albany: SUNY Press, 2000.
Griffin, David Ray. *Reenchantment without Supernaturalism: A Process Philosophy of Religion*. Cornell Studies in the Philosophy of Religion. Ithaca, NY: Cornell University Press, 2001.
Hartshorne, Charles. "Some Causes of My Intellectual Growth." In *The Philosophy of Charles Hartshorne*, edited by Lewis Edwin Hahn, 3–45. LaSalle, IL: Open Court, 1991.
Keller, Catherine. *On the Mystery: Discerning God in Process*. Minneapolis: Fortress, 2008.
McDaniel, Jay, and Donna Bowman, editors. *Handbook of Process Theology*. St. Louis: Chalice, 2006.
Mesle, C. Robert. *Process Theology: A Basic Introduction*. St. Louis: Chalice, 1993.
Whitehead, Alfred North. *Process and Reality: An Essay in Cosmology*. Corrected Edition. Edited by David Ray Griffin and Donald W. Sherburne. New York: Free Press, 1978.

Jewish Process Thinking

Jonas, Hans. "The Concept of God after Auschwitz: A Jewish Voice." In *Mortality and Morality*, edited by Lawrence Vogel, 131–43. Northwestern University Studies in Phenomenology and Existential Philosophy. Evanston: Northwestern University Press. (Originally published in *Journal of Religion* 67 [1987] 1–13).
———. *Memoirs*. Waltham, MA: Brandeis University Press, 2008.
———. *Mortality and Morality: A Search for the Good after Auschwitz*. Northwestern University Studies in Phenomenology and Existential Philosophy. Evanston: Northwestern University Press 1996.

Kaufman, William E. *The Evolving God in Jewish Process Theology.* Jewish Studies 17. Lewiston, NY: Mellon, 1997.

Kushner, Harold. "Would an All-Powerful God be Worthy of Worship?" In *Jewish Theology and Process Thought*, edited by Sandra B. Lubarsky and David Ray Griffin, 89–91. SUNY Series in Constructive Postmodern Thought. Albany: SUNY Press, 1996.

Lubarsky, Sandra B. and David Ray Griffin, editors. *Jewish Theology and Process Thought.* SUNY Series in Constructive Postmodern Thought. Albany: SUNY Press, 1996.

Steinberg, Milton. *The Anatomy of Faith.* Edited by Arthur Cohen. New York: Harcourt, Brace, 1960.

Process Thinking & The Bible

Beardslee, William A. *A House for Hope: A Study in Process and Biblical Thought.* Philadelphia: Westminster, 1972.

Beardslee, William A., and David J. Lull, editors. *Old Testament Interpretation from A Process Perspective, Semeia* 24 (1982) 1–116.

Ford, Lewis S. *The Lure of God: A Biblical Background for Process Theism.* Philadelphia: Fortress, 1978.

Fretheim, Terence E. *God and World in the Old Testament: A Relational Theology of Creation.* Nashville: Abingdon, 2005.

———. *The Suffering of God: An Old Testament Perspective.* Overtures to Biblical Theology. Philadelphia: Fortress, 1984.

Gnuse, Robert K. *The Old Testament and Process Theology.* St. Louis: Chalice, 2000.

Keller, Catherine. *Face of the Deep: A Theology of Becoming.* London: Routledge, 2003.

Other

Berman, Joshua A. *Created Equal: How the Bible Broke with Ancient Political Thought.* Oxford: Oxford University Press, 2008.

Gaon, Saadia. *The Book of Beliefs and Opinions.* New Haven: Yale University Press, 1948.

Jacobs, Louis. *A Jewish Theology.* New York: Behrman House, 1973.

Hartshorne, Charles and William L. Reese, editors. *Philosophers Speak of God.* Amherst, NY: Humanity Books, 2000.

Maimonides, Moses. *Commentary to the Mishnah Tractate Sanhedrin.* New York: Sepher Hermon, 1981.

———. *The Guide of the Perplexed.* Translated by Shlomo Pines. Chicago: University of Chicago Press, 1963.

Morowitz, Harold, *The Emergence of Everything: How the World Became Complex.* New York: Oxford University Press, 2004.

Primack, Joel R., and Nancy Ellen Abrams. *The View from The Center of the Universe: Discovering Our Extraordinary Place in the Cosmos.* New York: Riverhead, 2006.

Rees, Martin. *Just Six Numbers: The Deep Forces that Shape the Universe.* New York: Basic Books, 2000.

Samuelson, Norbert M. *Revelation and the God of Israel.* Cambridge: Cambridge University Press, 2002.

Sarna, Nahum M. *Genesis*. JPS Torah Commentary. Philadelphia: Jewish Publication Society, 1989.

Stein, David E. S., editor. *Hebrew-English Tanakh: The Traditional Hebrew Text and the New JPS Translation*. Philadelphia: Jewish Publication Society, 2005.

Swimme, Brian, and Thomas Berry. *The Universe Story: From the Primordial Flaring Forth to the Ecozoic Era—A Celebration of the Unfolding of the Cosmos*. New York: HarperOne, 1994.

Tyson, Neil deGrasse, and Donald Goldsmith. *Origins: Fourteen Billion Years of Cosmic Evolution*. New York: Norton, 2004.

2

A Catholic Perspective
Church and Sacrament[1]

—Joseph A. Bracken

EDITOR'S INTRODUCTION

In the years following the Second Vatican Council, there seemed to be a possibility that the Catholic Church would be profoundly influenced by process theology. The process theology in question was specifically that of Teilhard de Chardin, but many followers of Teilhard saw a close relation to Whitehead. The first book with "Process Theology" as its title was edited by a Catholic Teilhardian but included more essays by Whiteheadians than by Teilhardians. Unfortunately, from the process perspective, the Catholic theological community moved away from this possibility, returning to its previous emphasis on Thomas Aquinas. Many Catholic theologians who had been discussing process themes shifted to other topics.

A few continued to identify with the process community. Joseph Bracken in particular has continued to publish in this field. He has also led in reflection about why the church has been so resistant to this change in its metaphysics. This chapter deals directly with that question and with how

1. A modified version of this essay appears in my *Does God Play Dice? Divine Providence for a World in the Making.*

Catholic process thinkers can overcome the problem. Bracken appreciatively summarizes a book of Bernard Lee, which was the most thorough presentation of a process-oriented Catholicism written at the peak of Catholic openness to this kind of thinking. Appropriate for Catholicism, the focus is on the church and its sacraments. Bracken then shows that, despite the attractiveness of Lee's formulations, on the fundamental question of the one and the many, he followed Whitehead too far in the direction of the primacy of the many. Bracken proposes interpreting or developing Whitehead's philosophy in a way that achieves a better balance, one that would enable the church to adopt his philosophy.

❖

METAPHYSICS IN CATHOLIC THEOLOGY

METAPHYSICS HAS TRADITIONALLY BEEN an important feature of Roman Catholic systematic theology. As Joseph Cardinal Ratzinger (now Pope Benedict XVI) noted in his book, *The Nature and Mission of Theology*, "Faith does not destroy philosophy; it champions it. Only when it takes up the cause of philosophy does it remain true to itself."[2] By philosophy, to be sure, Ratzinger had principally in mind Aristotelian-Thomistic metaphysics. Initially, this particular synthesis of philosophy and theology was looked upon with suspicion by more conservatively oriented theologians and at least some church authorities in the thirteenth century because it ran the risk of subordinating divine revelation as given in Sacred Scripture to the independent judgment of philosophical reflection.[3] But over time the synthesis of reason and revelation presented by Thomas Aquinas in the *Summa Theologiae* and other works has become the benchmark for Roman Catholic philosophy and theology.

In the twentieth century Transcendental Thomism emerged as a way to come to terms with Immanuel Kant's "Copernican Revolution" in Western philosophy without sacrificing the objectivity of human knowledge of the world of nature and the transcendent reality of God. Influenced by Kant, Transcendental Thomists like Bernard Lonergan and Karl Rahner made individual human subjectivity the starting-point for their metaphysical reflections. However, whereas Kant believed the existence of God, the

2. Joseph Cardinal Ratzinger, *Nature and Mission of Theology*, 29.
3. See here Copleston, *History of Philosophy*, Vol.II, Part 2, 152–55.

non-empirical self, and the world as an ordered totality cannot be empirically proven but must be treated as postulates of practical reason necessary for the pursuit of the moral life, Transcendental Thomists found a way to affirm the objective reality of human knowledge of the natural world and the existence of God as the object of the unrestricted desire to know, or as the "infinite horizon" of the human desire for self-transcendence.[4]

Some more conservatively oriented Thomists were suspicious of this heavily anthropological approach to metaphysics, grounded in individual human subjectivity rather than in cosmology or the objective world order presupposed by Aquinas in reliance on the philosophy of Aristotle. But the same basic categories came into play within both metaphysical schemes: act and potency, matter and form, substance and accident. Furthermore, there was an even deeper affinity between the two approaches in that both dealt with the age-old problem of the One and the Many in the same way. Both classical Thomistic metaphysics and Transcendental Thomism continued to affirm the priority of the non-empirical One over the empirical Many as initially proposed by Plato.

THE ONE AND THE MANY

Plato sought a middle ground between two earlier Greek philosophers: Heraclitus with his focus on constant becoming and Parmenides with his attention to unchanging being. Plato found that middle ground in the affirmation of an unchanging non-empirical One (the idea of the good) which gives order and intelligibility to the ever-changing empirical Many. This same paradigm for the relation between the One and the Many found an echo in Aristotle's and Aquinas's affirmation of the ontological priority of form over matter and the transcendence of God to the material world. Likewise, even within the more dynamic approach to reality characteristic of Transcendental Thomism with its starting-point in individual human subjectivity, the same basic relation between the One and the Many prevailed. The self is more than the sum of its contingent experiences; it is a spiritual entity with a connatural desire for union with God as the ultimate, non-empirical One.

This classical Platonic approach to the problem of the One and the Many has entered deeply into the institutional life of the Roman Catholic Church. The ontological priority of the One over the Many is reflected in the priority of the Pope as the Vicar of Christ over his brother bishops,

4. See, Lonergan, *Insight*, 3rd ed.; and Rahner, *Foundations*.

the priority of the bishop over the priests in his diocese, and the priority of the pastor over the parishioners in the local parish. Likewise, this same thought-pattern is reflected in the conscious or unconscious attitude of many Roman Catholics to ecumenical dialogue with members of the other Christian denominations and to interreligious dialogue with representatives of the other major world religions. As they see it, the Roman Catholic Church should be the basic point of reference or the One in dealing with other Christian denominations and the non-Christian world religions since these other religious bodies are collectively the derivative reality of the Many. Thus Roman Catholics can certainly learn from their dialogue-partners, but in the end the truth to be gained in and through the dialogue will find its full expression only in current Roman Catholic belief and practice.

At the same time, in recent decades a new mind-set seems to have taken hold, at least among liberally oriented Roman Catholics within the institutional church. The Second Vatican Council caught many Catholics by surprise. In many of the documents of Vatican II there was a totally unexpected focus on reform and renewal of church life. Furthermore, the enthusiastic reception of those same reform-minded documents among liberally oriented Roman Catholics was implicit testimony to a felt need for change in traditional belief and practice. From a philosophical perspective, what seemed to have happened both at Vatican II and in the years immediately following it within certain quarters of the Roman Catholic Church was an awakening to the inevitable limitations of the classical paradigm for the relation between the One and the Many. More attention should be paid to the reality of the empirical Many (the people of God) and to the ultimate dependence of the One (the institutional church with its established beliefs and practices) on the Many for its own legitimacy.

Within this post-Vatican II ferment among liberally oriented Roman Catholics, Bernard Lee, SM, found in the thought of Whitehead and some early Whiteheadian process theologians, notably John Cobb, support for the primacy of the Many over the One. He published *The Becoming of the Church*, a book on church and sacraments. His book made clear how Whitehead's philosophy can have a significant impact on Roman Catholic belief and practice. The account offered in the next part of the paper closely follows his.

Afterwards, I will offer some comments on why in my judgment this book has not had more influence on the thinking of Roman Catholics (both professional theologians and educated laity) in the United States. It may be that Lee's dramatic shift in focus from the One to the Many (i.e., from official belief and practice within the church to felt beliefs and actual practices of people in the pews) was too big a change for even liberally oriented Roman Catholics to assimilate. What might be needed for broader acceptance of the tenets of process theology among those same Roman Catholics could well be a middle-ground position whereby traditional belief and practice could be reconciled with a new focus on change, activity from the bottom-up, within the church. If this middle-ground is still to make use of Whiteheadian thought, it requires some modest rethinking of Whitehead's metaphysics, in particular, his understanding of the category of "society." Most interpreters of Whitehead emphasize that causal efficacy is located only in individuals and give little attention to the role of societies as such in shaping those individuals. It is possible to develop Whitehead's thought so as to provide a more balanced view of the relation of One and Many, thus to legitimate a more acceptable revision of the relationship between the One and the Many in contemporary Catholic belief and practice. Accordingly, the remainder of this essay is divided into two sections, one summarizing the ideas of Bernard Lee and the other proposing modifications that bring process thought into better connection with the Catholic Church.

LEE'S WHITEHEADIAN ALTERNATIVE TO THOMISTIC CATHOLICISM

Roman Catholic Church leaders are concerned with the growing phenomenon of secularization within Western civil society and by extension within the church as well.[5] This secularization is a positive rather than a negative phenomenon, and its appearance in Western life was virtually inevitable, given other factors at work both in society at large and in the church. The first such factor was the growth of modern science and the technology which accompanied it.[6] The second factor was historical and biblical criticism, subjecting the text of Sacred Scripture to rational analysis.[7] The third and last factor was the popularity of existentialist philosophy with its emphasis on human freedom, the ability to become whatever one wished to be, free of restraints in terms of God's will or natural law.[8] The

5. Bernard Lee, SM, *Becoming of the Church*, 10.
6. Ibid., 12–20.
7. Ibid., 20–22.
8. Ibid., 22–28.

last factor, to be sure, had its historical antecedents in the Pelagian heresy at the time of Augustine, in Aquinas's effort to reconcile nature and grace, and among Roman Catholics in the modernist heresy at the beginning of the twentieth century.[9] In any case, to meet the challenge thus presented to the church by secularization, theologians must look for new symbols and new modes of thought, chief among them the process philosophy of Whitehead, better to express the ancient faith.[10]

Whitehead's language is unfamiliar because he is consciously moving from a thing—or substance-oriented to an event-oriented view of the world. As a result, "the final real things of which the world is made up" are 'actual entities,'" momentary self-constituting subjects of experience.[11] Also called "actual occasions" by Whitehead, these self-constituting subjects of experience are the momentary events, which in dynamic interrelation make up the world of people and things from moment to moment. Every actual entity is unique in the way it mirrors the world around it in and through its self-constitution here and now. Yet there is also identity between itself and its predecessors and successors in the same "society" or assemblage of actual entities if the pattern of self-constitution remains basically the same from moment to moment.[12] This pattern or "common element of form" is a structure of intelligibility or "eternal object" by which a later subject of experience can "prehend" (on a feeling-level grasp) what a previous subject of experience has made itself to be.[13]

God enters into this process-oriented world in two ways: through the divine primordial nature and the divine consequent nature. In virtue of the divine primordial nature, God sets up the conceptual ranking of eternal objects for "prehension" by finite subjects of experience in their concrescence. Choices by finite subjects of experience, after all, involve "de-cisions," a "cutting-away" of some possibilities for self-constitution in order to actualize still another possibility.[14] But each such possibility to be actualized carries with it consequences both for the individual subject of experience and for the society/societies to which it belongs. The divine primordial nature is an unchanging vision of all these eternal objects together with their logical consequences, a vision to which the finite

---

9. Ibid., 28–42.

10. Ibid., 42–52.

11. Ibid., 57, 62. See also Whitehead, *Process and Reality*, 18.

12. Lee, *Becoming of the Church*, 64.

13. Ibid., 65–69.

14. Ibid., 69–70.

subject of experience has access through what Whitehead calls a "hybrid prehension," a physical prehension of God, not in terms of God's own self but in terms of God's conceptual vision of possibilities for that subject of experience.[15] So, through this hybrid prehension of God, an actual entity or finite subject of experience is able to establish a "subjective aim" for its own self-constitution which, at least in some measure, conforms to what God has in mind for it in terms of a divine "initial aim" for it.[16]

But for God to provide from moment to moment reliable initial aims for concrescing actual entities, God has to know what is going on everywhere in the world at any given moment. Furthermore, God has to organize all these contingent events into a coherent whole or universe from moment to moment. Otherwise, the cosmic process, based as it is on the contingent decisions of so many actual entities at every moment, could rapidly descend into chaos. This is what Whitehead calls the "divine consequent nature."[17] It is the way in which God turns apparently contradictory events into harmonious contrasts and thereby "saves the world as it passes into the immediacy of his own life."[18] To sum up Whitehead's approach to the God-world relationship, one can say that it matters to God what happens to us. But, by the same token, it should also matter to us that God is so deeply involved in our ongoing existence and activity.

Catholic interest in process thought has in fact been stimulated more by another processive thinker than by Whitehead. This was Pierre Teilhard de Chardin, the Jesuit priest/paleontologist. The world view or metaphysical vision of the two men, however, is strikingly similar. Both agree "that the world is both radically particulate and essentially related."[19] Likewise, both seek to overcome the dichotomy between matter and spirit in scientific research and in religious practice. Teilhard, accordingly, postulates that all energy is basically psychic but is at work in nature under two different forms: tangential energy, which links together entities of the same size and complexity so as to constitute the "without" or external appearance of things, and radial energy, which draws an individual entity towards ever greater complexity and centricity and thus constitutes its "within."[20] Whitehead comes basically to the

15. Ibid., 72–73, 89.

16. Ibid., 95.

17. Ibid., 98.

18. Whitehead, *Process and Reality*, 346.

19. Ibid., 127–28.

20. Ibid., 129–30.

same conclusion with his notion of an actual entity. An actual entity is internally an immaterial subject of experience and externally a material reality, aspects of whose objective pattern of self-constitution can be physically "prehended" by subsequent actual entities.[21]

Moreover, the action of God in the world is quite similar for both men. "Teilhard also sees the action of God as a kind of lure. With something of a dipolar sense of God, he speaks of evolution as 'stirred by the Prime Mover ahead.'"[22] For both Whitehead and Teilhard, accordingly, God and creativity, the urge for novelty and progress, are closely linked. Likewise, the basic understanding of the supernatural in Teilhard's work is horizontally rather than vertically conceived. That is, the supernatural represents not what is above and beyond the cosmic process but what lies ahead in the cosmic process.[23] But here the differences in the thought of the two men are important. For Teilhard the evolutionary process moves toward a final consummation. For Whitehead, on the contrary, there will be an end to the present "cosmic epoch" but no end to the cosmic process as a whole. For, process is reality.[24]

Whereas Whitehead was a philosopher who made only scattered comments about Jesus, Teilhard was a Catholic priest who, in his philosophical/theological writings reconciled his scientific belief in cosmic evolution with the traditional teaching of the Roman Catholic Church about the divinity of Jesus and, above all, his Second Coming at the end of the world. Teilhard, thinking more as a theologian than as a philosopher, feels free to use the New Testament to support his belief in the cosmic Christ as the Omega or end-point of cosmic evolution. His vision is that the cosmic Christ brings the process of cosmic evolution toward a close that initiates the "new creation" (full union with the divine persons in eternity) when the energy-levels of this world are depleted.[25]

Clearly, there is no one "process Christology." However, Whitehead's understanding of the way God participates in the constitution of occasions can be used to develop Christological ideas. John Cobb showed in *The Structure of Christian Existence*,[26] that God's role in constituting

21. Ibid., 25–26.

22. Lee, *Becoming of the Church*, 135. Reference is to Teilhard's major work, *The Phenomenon of Man*, 271.

23. Lee, *Becoming of the Church*, 139–40, 151.

24. Ibid., 56, 172, 204.

25. Teilhard de Chardin, *Phenomenon of Man*, 273–89.

26. Lee, *Becoming of the Church*, 109–19. See also Cobb, *Structure of Christian Existence*.

human existence can differ in the way it affects and is incorporated by people. The divine initial aim and the subjective aim of the concrescing actual entity can explain how Jesus was different from other human beings, even from the Hebrew Prophets, in his personal life and message. Just as God has a specific initial aim for every finite actual entity in its process of concrescence, so God had a special initial aim for Jesus at every moment of his life.[27] What made Jesus different from other human beings in their reception of a divine initial aim at each moment of their lives is that Jesus realized better than others that it was an inspiration directly from God and responded to what God wanted of him at that moment. As a result, Jesus's sense of self-identity at every moment of his life was constituted by his conformity to the Father's will for him at that same moment. Thus, he could speak to his contemporaries with the authority of God in a way that no one else, not even the Hebrew Prophets, could claim.[28]

Of special importance to Catholics is the understanding of the church and the sacraments. Whitehead's metaphysics offers a new understanding of the workings of the church and the efficacy of the sacraments. "Whitehead gives us a metaphysics of the individual-in-community, which should be one word, so intimate and inextricable are individual and community; reality is essentially social. Yet if we *had* to weight one a little more than the other, it would be in behalf of the individual. Actual entities are all that there is."[29] Whitehead's generic description of "society" as an assemblage of actual entities, momentary self-constituting subjects of experience, linked by a "common element of form" can be applied to the church as a "structured society" or society composed of sub-societies of actual entities.[30]

Lee begins by asking himself what the "common element of form" should be for Christians as members of the church and concludes that it is "the Jesus-event."[31] Later he will specify what he means by the Jesus-event. But for now he is simply interested in the "dynamics" of church life, how the Jesus-event is what links Christians to one another as members of the church. Following Whitehead, he concludes: "The defining characteristic of a society emerges in an individual through certain conditions imposed upon him by his prehensions of those who are already members of the

27. Lee, *Becoming of the Church*, 116.

28. Ibid., 118–19.

29. Ibid., 164.

30. Ibid., 174–81.

31. Ibid., 175–76.

society."[32] New members come to understand and assimilate the Jesus-event by noting how it functions within the lives of fellow members of the church. But a further step is needed. Once the new member of the church appropriates the Jesus-event as constitutive of his/her own existence, then she or he thereby reinforces that common element of form for other church members, both new and old. Both the individual and the group in this way "emBody" the Jesus-event, make it present to one another within the church and to the world at large.[33]

According to Cobb: "Christian existence is spiritual existence that expresses itself in love."[34] Not just any kind of love is herewith implied, of course, but only "a love which frees us from needing to be loved by anyone else to know that we are loved, and frees us to love more largely than ever."[35] Jesus, in other words, both in his life and in his message affirmed the unconditional love of God for human beings, based upon his own experience of God the Father's unconditional love for him even under the trying circumstances of his passion and death on the cross.[36] Thus understood, the Jesus-event transforms Christian life to make it the sacrament of God's love: in the first place for church members in their dealings with one another but in the second place for church members in their dealings with the non-Christian world where skepticism and even hostility toward this kind of self-giving love is all too often experienced.[37]

Finally, Lee applies to the church as a Whiteheadian structured society the same goals of group survival and intensity of experience for component parts or members that would be applicable to biological organisms within the cosmic process.[38] That is, in order to survive within an ever-changing environment, physical organisms have to be relatively unspecialized, have a simple structure or pattern of existence. But, to further evolve and grow, an organism must have component parts or members which in their dynamic interrelation exhibit intensity of experience. "As a society the Church meets the same challenge, to maintain itself in existence and to occasion an intense life in the membership."[39] But how is this to be done?

32. Ibid., 176. See also Whitehead, *Process and Reality*, 34.
33. Lee, *Becoming of the Church*, 177–79.
34. Ibid., 183. See also Cobb, *Structure of Christian Existence*, 125.
35. Lee, *Becoming of the Church*, 183.
36. Ibid., 185.
37. Ibid., 186.
38. Whitehead, *Process and Reality*, 100–101.
39. Lee, *Becoming of the Church*, 197.

Whitehead's concept of "conceptual reversion" can help. This is the way in which contemporary members of a "society" reshape the "common element of form" governing their dynamic interrelation in order to adjust to novelty within the environment.[40] Applied to the structured society which is the church, this means that the church "must make provision for contact between the Jesus-event and immediate situations so that new appropriations of the Jesus-event can be made in terms of the new challenges which history proffers."[41] This is the privileged role of the sacraments in church life. "Each Sacramental experience is a possible initiative 'to receive the novel elements of the environment into explicit feelings with such subjective forms [emotional tone] as conciliate them with the complex experiences proper to members of the structured society.'"[42] In this way, sacraments are for Lee events, not things. Likewise, the church is not a stable institution with a fixed body of beliefs and practices, but an ongoing process constituted again and again by sacramental events.[43]

To explain sacraments as sacred events, not sacred things, Lee first appeals to the exodus event in the Hebrew Bible and the annual celebration of Passover every spring by the Jewish people. "The event was not completed once and for all. It continues to take hold of each man's life."[44] The annual Passover celebration makes that identity-shaping event present to Jews ever after. In similar fashion, the sacraments allow Christians to prehend the Jesus-event as something both past and present, something "felt *there* and made to be *here*."[45] That "something" in Whiteheadian terms is an eternal object, a structure or form which was objectively present in the life and message of Jesus and which subjectively affects a Christian in his or her self-constitution here and now. The church as an institution has to supervise this symbolic reference of the Jesus-event from the past into the present.[46] Otherwise, there is clear danger that some Christians will unconsciously misread the Jesus-event as something past and make it present to themselves here and now in the wrong way with negative consequences for themselves and others. "The combination of the New Testament, tradition, and the life of the community seems to guarantee

40. Whitehead, *Process and Reality*, 102.
41. Lee, *Becoming of the Church*, 200.
42. Ibid. See also Whitehead, *Process and Reality*, 102.
43. Lee, *Becoming of the Church*, 200–207.
44. Ibid., 211.
45. Ibid., 212.
46. Ibid., 213, 220.

the Sacramental signs as offering forms of definiteness through which the Jesus-event can truly be made present."[47]

"Because each of the Sacraments is *societally* creative, there needs to be a ritual sameness through which elements of the Church's identity might be touched wherever and whenever there is a Sacramental experience. That is a survival dynamic."[48] "In each Sacramental experience there is need also for intensity dynamics as well as survival dynamics. The intensity dynamics are concerned with the immediacies of appropriating the Jesus-event. The intensity dynamics are of extraordinary importance as presence-making agents."[49] A sacramental ritual, however well performed, only makes a difference to an individual Christian if it brings home the meaning and value of the Jesus-event to him or her here and now. In this sense, the preoccupation of the Roman Catholic Church with the "matter" and the "form" of the sacrament was largely misplaced. The sacrament is not a thing composed of matter and form, but an event designed to make a difference in the lives of Christians sharing in the event.[50]

"Many prehensions go into a concrescence [of an actual entity]. Each prehension has a subjective form, that is, its own emotional tone. Each emotion is a response to some quality or another (forms of definiteness, eternal objects)."[51] This is a technical basis for saying that the sacramental rituals have somewhat different effects on different people. The ritual, after all, only partially objectifies the Jesus-event for any given Christian. Both as a historical and as a contemporary reality, the Jesus-event exceeds the capacity of the ritual to express and of the participant to comprehend. But, if the ritual is properly performed, some specific dimensions (forms of definiteness) of the Jesus-event will be conveyed with sufficient emotional power so as to catch the attention of the participants and bring home to them the importance of the Jesus-event for their self-constitution or self-identity here and now. This seems to correspond to a time-honored distinction in classical sacramental theology between *ex opere operato* and *ex opere operantis*. The objective long-term efficacy of the sacrament is heavily dependent upon the readiness of the individual Christian to act upon the grace of the sacrament.

47. Ibid.
48. Ibid., 217.
49. Ibid.
50. Ibid., 227.
51. Ibid., 217.

The indispensable role of the Christian community in conveying and sustaining the importance of the Jesus-event for the individual believer is especially clear in baptism, confirmation, and eucharist. With respect to Baptism, for example, the person to be baptized or the person newly baptized needs to prehend the Jesus-event at work in other members of the Christian community (in the first place, family members) in order to begin seeing himself/herself as likewise molded by the Jesus-event. "His fundamental understandings are given him by the community in which he finds life. His own sense of identity is shaped by those around him."[52] This is akin to the first stage in the self-constitution of an actual entity, concrescence, where it is heavily conditioned by other actual entities in its environment. With respect to confirmation, the person baptized is "confirmed" by the bishop or other church authorities as "one to whom others ought to be able to look to see a workable 'pattern of assemblage' according to which a Christian life has been put together."[53] This, in turn, corresponds to the second stage in the self-constitution of an actual entity, that of superject, where the actual entity's pattern of self-constitution is available for prehension by subsequent actual entities for their self-constitution.

It is primarily in the Eucharist as a sacred event that the community plays a key role. Lee calls attention to the fact that in Paul's account of the first Eucharist in 1 Corinthians 11:23–26 the consecration of the bread and the wine into the body and blood of the Lord do not take place at the same time during the Paschal Meal (Last Supper): "The cup is taken only after the meal . . . The breaking of the bread is earlier in the meal."[54] In Luke's account there are two cups shared, one during the meal and one at the end; only the second cup is offered as Christ's blood to be shed in testimony to the new covenant.[55] In their re-enactment of the Eucharist, however, the early Christians followed the account of the institution of the Eucharist in Matthew and Mark where the bread and wine are consecrated and shared in quick succession during the meal. However, the institution narrative in Paul and Luke allow us to claim that the consecration of the bread and the wine are different symbolic actions (events) with related but still different meanings.[56]

"The Sacramental symbols, as reported in Paul's letter (and for the most part, also in Luke's account) are not *things* of bread and wine, though

52. Ibid., 236.
53. Ibid., 242.
54. Ibid., 246–47.
55. Ibid., 247.
56. Ibid.

they are part, but the *action* of breaking bread and partaking, and of blessing the cup of a new covenant in Jesus' blood and partaking in it."[57] So the classical doctrine of transubstantiation, whereby bread and wine are transformed into the body and blood of the Lord, has a misplaced emphasis. The emphasis should be not on a miraculous change of one substance into another but on two powerful community-building actions or events, breaking consecrated bread and sharing consecrated wine in a special context which reminds those who participate that they now belong to the new covenant, the new relationship of humanity with God established by Jesus through his life and message, but above all through his passion and death on the cross.

That special context, of course, was the Passover, the annual ritual re-enactment of the exodus from Egypt which, in Jewish belief, forever establishes their covenant with God through Moses. In both cases, bread is broken and shared and blood is symbolically shed as key symbols of the enduring covenant of God with his chosen people. "In a way, the content of Jesus' New Covenant is not greatly different. The locus of it is in the spirit of love and not in prescriptions of a written law . . . Jesus does, however, un-nationalize the Covenant. It is meant for all men. It is universalized. Hebrew history erupts into world history in the Jesus-event."[58] In both cases, of course, the covenant is a community-building event, the community of God with human beings, the community of human beings with one another in their con-celebration of a ritual meal.

A process-oriented approach to Church and Sacraments should make a major difference in the lives of ordinary Christians. Becoming a Christian is not a one-time event but a life-long process of assimilating features of the Jesus-event into one's own ongoing self-constitution or self-identity: "the name Christian belongs to an identity which is larger than individual actions, which is as large as patterns of life, a pattern which inundates our process, communicating its identity to the whole assemblage of life's events."[59] This is not to say that all Christians will assimilate the Jesus-event in the same way. Because different Christians will incorporate different dimensions of the Jesus-event into their lives, there is still another reason for life in Christian community. Through their prehending one another's different personal assimilation of the Jesus-event, individual

57. Ibid., 248.
58. Ibid., 252.
59. Ibid., 257.

Christians will over time gain a certain balance in the way they conduct themselves before the world as Christians.[60]

When Christians positively prehend one another's way of being Christian, in effect, "unpack their lives" in one another's presence,[61] they influence one another's process of becoming Christian and thereby generate a higher unity, a common subjective aim for their life together as members of a Christian community.[62] The same dynamic, of course, applies to our relationship with God. What matters to me matters to God, and what matters to God should also matter to me: "this extension of our caring to all that we know matters to God is precisely the stuff of union with God, of shared life."[63] The purpose of prayer, then, is to help us better realize what matters to God here and now within the world of creation and to enable us to direct our energies into effecting what God wants for us and all God's creatures at this moment.[64] "Jesus becomes central to our interpretation of human life for he is the primordial symbol of God. Because of Jesus' participation in God, the Christian has access to God in his participation in the Jesus-event."[65]

ADAPTING WHITEHEAD AND LEE TO CATHOLIC NEEDS

Unquestionably, Lee's use of Whiteheadian metaphysics to interpret what it means to be a Christian in the modern world has much to recommend it. His approach to church life at the parish level offers a new way to conceive the workings of the church in the modern world which is reflected within some of the documents of Vatican II.[66] His event—or process-oriented approach to Christian life makes membership in the church much more dynamic for the individual believer. One feels much more connected with the Jesus-event both as a historical event and as an ongoing reality shaping one's own life and the life of others within the Christian community. One sees much better how Christians need one another to understand and interpret the deeper significance of the Jesus-event for their lives together in community. Christian community is thus not only a matter of going to

60. Ibid., 258–60.

61. Ibid., 261.

62. Ibid., 268.

63. Ibid., 269.

64. Ibid., 271.

65. Ibid., 273.

66. Ibid., 190–92.

church on Sundays and putting an envelope in the collection basket to pay one's share of necessary expenses. It is much more a matter of Christians becoming together the body of Christ in this place and at this time in cosmic history.

Lee thus provides us an understanding of community that can contribute significantly to our understanding of the church. In advance, however, he sets forth a cardinal principle for the workings of White-headian societies: "Whitehead gives us a metaphysics of the individual-in-community, which should be one word, so intimate and inextricable are individual and community; reality is essentially social. Yet if we *had* to weight one a little more than the other, it would be in behalf of the individual. Actual entities are all that there is."[67]

Lee is basically correct in this interpretation of Whitehead. As already noted, Whitehead clearly states in *Process and Reality* that actual entities are "the final real things of which the world is made up."[68] The "common element of form" or social order prevailing between actual entities in a society is derivative from their dynamic interrelation from moment to moment.

Such a hypothesis might well be a "hard sell" for Roman Catholics accustomed to life within a church with strong central authority. In any case, does his account of church and sacrament not over-simplify the way in which the Roman Catholic Church and other Christian denominations actually function? Are not other factors involved in church life as a Roman Catholic, Baptist, Methodist, Lutheran, Presbyterian, etc., over and above the ongoing appropriation of the Jesus-event by the individual? If so, is this not a type of top-down causation at work in church life in addition to the bottom-up causation in terms of individual appropriation of the Jesus-event? Lee himself grapples with this issue in his analysis of how the sacraments work.

Lee's approach with its focus on the "how" as opposed to the "what" of the Jesus-event seems to prescind from the concrete details of life within one or another Christian denomination. The process of internalizing the Jesus-event and becoming church together with other like-minded Christians would seem to apply indiscriminately to Roman Catholics, Baptists, Methodists, Presbyterians, etc. In one respect, this may be an advantage. But, in another respect, it seems to ignore the top-down causation of a given ecclesial environment, placing emphasis only upon the bottom-up

67. Ibid., 164.

68. Whitehead, *Process and Reality*, 18.

causation of the individual and his or her faith-community in interpreting and acting out the Jesus-event here and now.

But, if so, can one remedy that "defect" without taking leave of Whiteheadian metaphysics as one's governing conceptuality for rethinking church and sacraments in contemporary life? For, as already noted, Whitehead laid heavy emphasis on actual entities as "the final real things of which the world is made up"[69] and at least seemed to regard societies of actual entities as realities strictly derivative from the interplay of their constituent actual entities at any given moment. Can one modify Whitehead's scheme in such a way as to give more enduring meaning and value to Whiteheadian societies and thereby allow for more effective top-down causation on individual Christians and their faith-communities in efforts to internalize the Jesus-event and become church here and now?

For many years now, I have argued on strictly philosophical grounds that Whitehead's category of society is notably under-developed. Since my thinking on this matter is well documented in previous publications,[70] I will simply state here my hypothesis and try to show its pertinence to Lee's overall approach to church and sacraments. I propose that Whiteheadian societies should be understood as enduring structured fields of activity for their constituent actual entities at any given moment. So, instead of thinking of societies as (in Lee's words) "assemblages" of actual entities with a "common element of form" or "defining characteristic," I claim that actual entities as momentary self-constituting subjects of experience always arise within an already given context or antecedently structured common field of activity. Furthermore, at the end of their individual processes of concrescence, these same actual entities contribute the pattern of their own self-constitution to the overall structure of the field for the next set of actual entities. The field, in other words, provides the necessary continuity of pattern or form for successive generations of actual entities. At the same time, the structure of the field itself will slowly but surely evolve as new sets of actual entities arise within the field and appropriate that governing structure in somewhat new and different ways.

Roman Catholics trained in classical metaphysics will immediately see here a certain affinity to the Aristotelian-Thomistic category of "substance." But there is a clear difference between a "structured field of activity" and a "substance." For, while both concepts account for continuity

69. Ibid.

70. See Bracken, *Society and Spirit*, 39–56; *The Divine Matrix*, 60–61; *The One in the Many*, 98–100, 147–49; *Subjectivity, Objectivity and Intersubjectivity*, 130–36.

of form or structure in the midst of ongoing change, only the notion of a field of activity allows for gradual evolution of form with the passage of time. An Aristotelian-Thomistic substance, in other words, is a fixed intelligibility corresponding (for Aquinas at least) to an idea in the mind of God. Thus, individual substances come into and go out of existence, but the form or basic intelligibility of the substance never varies from one individual substance to another. A field of activity, on the contrary, is an evolutionary reality. Its governing structure is relatively independent of any single set of actual entities here and now, but over time that structure will evolve to correspond with the somewhat different way that successive sets of actual entities "prehend" one another and thereby set up new relations to one another and to the broader world around them. In brief, then, the category "substance" presupposes heavy, top-down causality, the priority of form over matter. The category "structured field of activity," on the contrary, presupposes the conjoint working of both top-down and bottom-up causality. The constituent actual entities contribute to the ongoing structure of the field of activity in which they arise, but the field in turn evolves in its basic structure as the pattern of interrelation among the constituent actual entities subtly changes with the passage of time.

So much for pure theory. How does this revised understanding of Whiteheadian societies affect a process-oriented approach to church and sacraments? Here I suggest that we should think of Christianity as a Whiteheadian structured society with the different Christian denominations as its constituent sub-societies. Each of these subsocieties is a structured field of activity for its church members (Roman Catholics, Episcopalians, Methodists, etc.). Yet each of them also contributes to the "common element of form" or "defining characteristic" of the structured society which is Christianity as opposed to the other world religions. In my view, all of the world religions likewise contribute to an even bigger structured society, which in biblical terms may be called the Kingdom of God, or in more neutral terms the community of all world religions. But this last point is not pertinent to our present discussion. What I am striving for here is a way from a Whiteheadian perspective to justify what I earlier called top-down causality within each of the various Christian denominations. Each of these subfields of ecclesial activity within the overall field of activity proper to Christianity as a whole has an abiding internal structure consistent with its institutional history, but which makes it different from the other Christian denominations with their own structured fields of activity for their members. Within this conceptual scheme, the sacraments still function as events, not as things, in line with Lee's proposal. But their reality as sacred events is somewhat different within each Christian denomination, each subfield of ecclesial activity. That is, both the number of sacraments (seven for Roman Catholics, only two or three for many others) and their accompanying rituals differ from one denomination to another so that the Jesus-event is not experienced quite the same way by Christians belonging to different denominations. This is perfectly consistent with a field-oriented approach to Whiteheadian societies whereby each society has its own ontological identity and yet can co-participate with other societies in perpetuating the meaning and value of the broader structured society. Applied to the Jesus-event, this means that the various Christian denominations need one another to give full expression to their ongoing corporate reality as the body of Christ.[71]

Finally, within such a field-oriented approach to Whiteheadian societies, one can rethink and re-present to one's faith community traditional Christian beliefs that are also key features of life together for many, even if not all, of their members. As I have explained at length in previous publications, a field-oriented approach to Whiteheadian societies allows one to defend, within a process-oriented context, the doctrine of the Trinity as an ongoing community of divine persons. Similarly, one can claim that creation as a whole came into being and continues to evolve in size and complexity within the field of activity proper to the divine community. From this, one can derive a new understanding of the notion of *creatio ex nihilo* as an expression of divine self-giving love rather than of unilateral divine power as it is sometimes represented by Whiteheadians.[72] Finally, within this field-oriented approach to the God-world relationship as a society of subsocieties or cosmic community, one can expand upon Whitehead's own rather sparse remarks about the possibility of subjective as well as objective immortality within what he called the divine consequent nature.

Whitehead, after all, was a philosopher who was interested in theological issues only as a corollary to the formulation of a process-oriented philosophical cosmology. Hence, his conceptual scheme should be available for professional theologians to rethink and re-present to their faith communities certain basic beliefs within their denominations in a more readily intelligible way. Whitehead's metaphysical scheme can be employed then not only to foster intensity of religious experience for individual

71. See Bracken, *Christianity and Process Thought*, 53–64.
72. See Griffin, *Two Great Truths*, 5–11.

Christians (as Lee proposes) but also to allow for legitimate diversity in belief and practice within specific Christian denominations. One is still able to take account of the inevitable particularity of the various Christian churches—e.g., the special feeling of being a Roman Catholic rather than a Baptist—without thereby posing a threat to the overall unity of the body of Christ. The latter, as Lee points out so well, is grounded in the common appropriation of the Jesus-event as foundational for what it means to be Christian in the modern world.

BIBLIOGRAPHY

Bracken, Joseph A. *Christianity and Process Thought.* Philadelphia: Templeton Foundation, 2006.

———. *The Divine Matrix: Creativity as Link between East and West.* Maryknoll, NY: Orbis, 1995.

———. *Does God Play Dice? Divine Providence for a World in the Making.* Collegeville, MN: Liturgical, 2012.

———. *The One in the Many: A Contemporary Reconstruction of the God-World Relationship.* Grand Rapids: Eerdmans, 2001.

———. *Society and Spirit: A Trinitarian Cosmology.* London: Associated University Presses, 1991.

———. *Subjectivity, Objectivity and Intersubjectivity: A New Paradigm for Religion and Science.* West Conshohocken, PA: Templeton Foundation, 2009.

Cobb, John B. Jr., *The Structure of Christian Existence.* Philadelphia: Westminster, 1967.

Copleston, Frederick. *A History of Philosophy*, Vol.II, Part 2. New York: Doubleday, 1962.

Griffin, David Ray. *Two Great Truths: A New Synthesis of Scientific Naturalism and Christian Faith.* Louisville: Westminster John Knox, 2004.

Lee, Bernard, SM. *The Becoming of the Church: A Process Theology of the Structure of Christian Experience.* New York: Paulist, 1974.

Lonergan, Bernard J. F. *Insight: A Study of Human Understanding.* 3rd ed. New York: Philosophical Library, 1970.

Rahner, Karl. *Foundations of Christian Faith: An Introduction to the Idea of Christianity.* Translated by William V. Dych. New York: Crossroad, 1978.

Ratzinger, Joseph Cardinal. *The Nature and Mission of Theology: Approaches to Understanding Its Role in the Light of Present Controversy.* Translated by Adrian Walker. San Francisco: Ignatius, 1995.

Teilhard de Chardin, Pierre. *The Phenomenon of Man.* Translated by Bernard Wall. New York: Harper & Row, 1963.

Whitehead, Alfred North. *Process and Reality: An Essay in Cosmology.* Corrected Edition. Edited by David Ray Griffin and Donald W. Sherburne. New York: Free Press, 1978.

3

A Protestant Perspective
Grace as Enablement

—Marjorie Hewitt Suchocki

EDITOR'S INTRODUCTION

Although philosophical theology is more widely welcomed in Catholic than in Protestant circles, theological interest in process philosophy arose in a Protestant context. The resulting theology has developed there for a century, and since World War II, the influence of Whitehead has played the largest role. Process theology has long been recognized as one option for liberal or progressive Protestants alongside others. Usually other options have been far more mainstream, but they have come and gone. Process theology, although still generally marginalized, has been the most enduring. In some denominations it has played a significant role, and some ideas that were once associated chiefly with it are now part of a progressive consensus.

Often process theology is presented in Protestant circles primarily in terms of the issues dealt with by Rabbi Artson in the first chapter. Most of what Bracken reports Lee as saying about the church and sacraments can also be appropriated by Protestants. But more central to the distinctiveness of Protestant theology have been questions of grace and responsibility, sin and salvation, and Suchocki has chosen these. Instead of reporting on what others have said, she has written an original essay. She observes a broad theological tendency in the past half century to shift focus from divine omnipotence to divine omnipresence, and she sees this as determining that the way God works in the world is now understood as grace. Whitehead provides a rich and rigorous articulation of this grace, and Suchocki works out a Protestant theology in these terms.

THROUGHOUT DIVERGENT FORMS OF Protestant Christianity several themes constantly emerge, resonating in the diverse communions. These themes are not unique to Protestantism—far from it! But within Protestantism they receive a distinctive emphasis, making them characteristic of its many forms. These themes are the grace of God, the application of grace to the human need for forgiveness of sin and growth in holiness, and the ground of grace in the very nature of God as omnipresent love. My thesis in this article is that each of these emphases not only strongly correlates with a Whiteheadian interpretation of existence, but that each is enhanced by such an interpretation. By using Whitehead to clarify these traditional themes, we can see anew their distinctive powers and possibilities for reinvigorating Protestant forms of the Christian church.

I proceed first by some clarification of each of the concepts, beginning with the notion of God's omnipresence, which I hope to show actually underlies the doctrines of grace. I then move to the Whiteheadian parallels with the concepts of God and grace, together with a process/Protestant indication of that which grace addresses, the issue of sin. Weaving these concepts together suggests the vitality of a contemporary and progressive Christianity.

THE OMNIPRESENCE OF GOD

Protestantism, like all of Christianity, has held to the three traditional attributes of God's being as omnipotence, omniscience, and omnipresence. Omnibenevolence often took its place as a fourth essential characteristic of God, but more often than not, the first three took center stage in discussions of God's being. Theoretically, each of these "omnis" had equal weight with the others, but in practice, omnipotence was clearly the dominant category, interpreting the others. God's power was understood as a magnification of the kind of power that could be held by an absolute ruler, controlling all things according to the ruler's good pleasure. And since God was considered omnibenevolent, God's good pleasure was indeed the good, defining the good. Insofar as God controlled all things, God also knew all things—for not to know all things would challenge the fullness of the divine power.

Knowing all things and controlling all things created something of a problem in the area of human evil and natural disasters, of course, so theologians argued that among the goods that God willed was the good of human freedom. This provided an escape clause of sorts against the threatened omnibenevolence of God, since human freedom allowed the possibility of human choices for that which was against God's will, or evil. Nonetheless, even this fit in with God's good pleasure, since God in omnipotent control could exercise judgment against evil, balancing it with punishment or tempering it with mercy, according to God's good pleasure. Thus, redemption on the one hand provides a corrective for human evil, and also preserves the omnibenevolence of God without challenging the omnipotence of God.

But where is omnipresence in this scenario? In a sense, it was the background characteristic, overshadowed by an omnipotence that included omniscience and omnibenevolence. An omnipotent God who knows and controls all things must also in some sense be present to all things. Omnipresence thus functioned as an extension of God's omnipotence, without contributing materially to what omnipotence meant.

In the past several decades, however—and possibly in the past century—omnipresence has emerged as a central insight into the nature of God, not as an extension of omnipotence, but more as a dominant category in its own right, with implications for revising how we understand God's power, knowledge, and goodness.

South American liberation theologies began the shift to omnipresence as the central expression of God's nature. This shift originated within Catholicism, but it was picked up by South American Protestants and successively adapted in the United States to African American experience, Latino/a experience, and also feminist experience. Ostensibly, the shift was necessitated by the burdens of oppression—how is suffering compatible with an omnipotent deity whose will is restrained by nothing other than its own nature? Without directly confronting this issue of theodicy, liberation theologians focused on the sense of God's presence among the poor and oppressed. "God's preferential option for the poor" became the watch cry, along with social protest against conditions of injustice. God's presence with the marginalized was not to endorse their marginalization, but to call for their release. This call operated through the energizing power of the Spirit as marginalized peoples mobilized to confront the systems that oppressed them.

In Black Christianity, the emphasis on God's presence with and among Black people was represented through the Black Christ: God is incarnate as a Black man, suffering with them, crying for freedom. In feminist theology (often expressed as the-alogy) figures of the Christ appeared: a woman on the cross, God with us, incarnate and crucified as a woman. Black Womanists combined both tropes, God incarnate as a Black woman. In all three forms of United States theology, the omnipotence of God apart from human action plays little if any role. God's power, exercised through God's presence, is manifested as an energizing power impelling us to actions for justice. If we look to a more traditional naming of this energizing power, it goes by the name of "grace." A stress on the omnipresence of God is at the same time an emphasis upon grace as the mode of God's power.

This movement within liberation theologies toward the dominance of omnipresence rather than omnipotence is implicit rather than explicit. The only challenge to traditional theology is a loud and clear critique of its silence on the issues of social oppression. But underlying this critique is the shift from an understanding of a God who has the power to determine all human action, to an understanding of a God whose power flows from God's energizing presence. One could argue that the implicit nature of this move actually pushed some feminist theologians away from notions of God at all. God had been so identified with patriarchal power that the rejection of patriarchal power led as well to a rejection of the concept of God altogether. Yet the residue—an omnipresent power toward the good—remained, albeit often without explicit identification as the power of God.

Liberation theologies are not the only forms of theology emergent in the twentieth century that shifted toward omnipresence rather than omnipotence. Powerful paradigm shifts in the scientific understanding of the physical structure of the universe led eventually to paradigm shifts in theology as well. The essential interconnectedness of all forms of existence, the increasing evidence concerning the evolutionary nature of all life on our planet together with the knowledge that the earth is not "finished," but is constantly in the process of creation, and scientific revelations of the immensity of the universe, and the small nature of our place within it, affected theological expressions of God's omnipotence. On the one hand,

God the Creator took on massive overtones, given the vastness of the universe. But in the process, notions of a God somehow "outside" that which has no "outside" led to a sense of God's creating from "inside" rather than "outside." That is, God's creative presence as a "withness" throughout creation began replacing the sense of a Jupiter-type God who tossed creation into existence. Relational theologies began emerging in the twentieth century—certainly in process theologies, but also in continental theologies such as Moltman's "theology of hope" and the political theologies of Ernst Bloch and Dorothee Soelle. Again, omnipotence is too well entrenched to be challenged directly. Rather, there is simply an implicit move to relational theologies that depend far more upon the creative presence of God rather than an all-controlling power of God. And the shift to omnipresence as the defining characteristic of God that shapes God's power and God's knowledge pushes to increasing emphasis of that which has always been a strong force in Protestant theologies: the emphasis on grace. For a God of presence operates not simply occasionally from outside creation, but necessarily operates continually within creation. A God of presence is a God of grace.

GRACE IN PROTESTANT THEOLOGY

Grace usually refers to the unmerited favor of God, whereby God, on the basis of God's own nature, rather than on the basis of human merit, chooses to save humans from their self-inflicted chaos of sin for a salvation that will lead them to holiness of life. The epitome of God's grace is God's incarnation in Jesus who, as the anointed one of God, suffers death for or from human sin, and is resurrected to new life. In most Protestant theology this death expresses the justice of God, which requires that sin shall have its consequences, and the mercy of God, whereby persons joined to Christ by faith share in his death and resurrection, thus escaping the consequences of sin.

Grace is perhaps the most dominant theme in all Protestantism. It is hardly unique to Protestantism, for throughout the Christian tradition profound attention has been given to expositions of the grace of God. But the Reformation's cry of "justification by grace through faith" was structured as an opposition to a perceived corruption of Christianity through "works righteousness." A careful analysis of two, towering pre-Reformation figures—Thomas Aquinas and Augustine—would reveal not only the pre-Reformation importance of grace, but actually many parallels between medieval notions of grace and that of the Reformers. The difference was one of emphasis.

The tension that arose was on the place of works. In pre-Reformation theology, the gracious gift of salvation was given by God through the sacrament of baptism, usually administered to infants. Clearly, the infant is a passive recipient of grace, which presumably fits the child for a life of faith. What, then, of the inevitable sins that occur along life's way? In the pre-Reformation church, such sins were dealt with sacramentally through penance. A part of penitential living required acts of penance on the part of the sinner, and these acts were considered meritorious. Given the assumption of a rather tier-like structure of post-earthly life, acts of merit performed in penance helped to fit one for ever-higher tiers in the afterlife. Dante's *Divine Comedy* beautifully illustrates the system, both through the downward spirals leading toward absolute hell, the in-between space of limbo, and the upward spiral leading from purgatory toward total conformity to God, which was the highest heaven.

In the popular understanding (though not the actual theology), one worked toward one's salvation through various acts of penance, which would purge sin from one's soul, and equip one for degrees of heaven. These various works of penance were meritorious, building up the righteousness that would shorten one's time in purgatory, and fit one for heaven. The system, of course, was ripe for corruption, since the giving of money could be counted a meritorious act fitting the soul for salvation. Against this piety and practice, the Reformers thundered out that salvation was not through works, but through faith, which itself was the gracious gift of God.

Precisely how grace operates within the soul was a debated question. Baptism itself became an issue. Is baptism a witness to grace received, and hence to follow upon confessions of faith? Or, as in the long tradition, is grace actually bestowed in baptism, incorporating infants into the body of Christ and launching them into a life of faith as they are nurtured within the church? If the latter, was the church once again thrown into the thorny issue of post-baptismal sins—of which there would be many? Was penance still a necessary sacrament? If so, wouldn't the temptation arise again to embrace the notion of "works righteousness"?

Thus there was a "Radical Reformation" that became the root of denominations holding to baptism as a witness to grace received and confessed. The grace of God instigated a response of faith through which the believer was then made one with Christ, and therefore a member of the body of Christ, the church. Baptism followed as a witness to this event.

Reformers such as Luther, Calvin, and those who followed them retained the notion of infant baptism during which the grace of God was received, initiating faith. But questions arose: Did everyone who had been baptized receive the grace of God? Unfortunately, it did not appear evident that Christian living necessarily followed Christian baptism. Was the grace of God ineffective in such cases? But how could it be that an omnipotent God should be ineffective in any way at all?

Responses differed. Calvin held to notions of predestination that were consistent with the notion of God's absolute power. From eternity, God predestined some to salvation as witnesses to the mercy of God, and others to damnation as witnesses to the justice of God. But only God knew who was elected to what. Baptism, then, was an effective means of grace for those whom God had elected to salvation; but for those elected for damnation, it was an apparent as opposed to a real baptism. And only God knew the difference.

Luther was more ambiguous on the point. Regeneration occurs in and through baptism, and God does choose those who are elected for this regeneration. Baptism, given as it was to infants who were not yet capable of choosing for themselves, was a witness to the pre-operative grace of God, who saves us apart from any worthiness or merit of our own. But Luther stopped short of saying that some were elected for damnation, despite their baptism, assigning this to the mystery of God's grace.

The Anglican Church, coming to birth several decades into the Reformation era, also saw baptism as a witness to the efficacious grace of God, working in us prior to our capacity to acknowledge this grace. Baptism was seen as the New Testament equivalent of the ancient Jewish rite of circumcision, administered to infant boys as a sign of the covenant, ratified by them at the Bar Mitzvah when they entered puberty. Confirmation in the church was in a sense a completion of the baptismal rite, whereby the baptized one, now instructed in the faith, confessed the faith as his or her own. Grace received was grace evidenced.

If baptism and/or confessions of faith were signs of the grace of God, they were inaugurating signs, not signs complete in and of themselves. Grace is for the sake of holy living—or, in the medieval phraseology, the initiating grace of condignity is for the sake of the lifelong grace of conformity. Reformers tended to name grace after that which it accomplishes: prevenient grace, or the grace that precedes us, drawing us toward repentance; justifying grace (or regenerating grace), whereby God's dealing with sin in Christ is applied to the human; and sanctifying grace, through which we are led in this life to greater and greater conformity to God. There is a fourth mode of grace, "glorifying grace," that refers to the final heavenly state of the redeemed soul, now made fully conformable to the image of God.

In post-Reformation Protestantism, John Wesley emphasized all modes of grace, but his distinctiveness lay in the strong role he saw in sanctifying grace. For Wesley, sanctification is the process whereby Christians are restored to the image of God. Prevenient and justifying grace are preludes to the real work of God in the Christian, which is sanctifying grace. But for Wesley, the power of grace is precisely its enabling effects. That is, whereas grace in the Reformers sometimes seemed as if it were external to the believer, operating "from above" in a determinative way, so that persons were elected to salvation or damnation independent of their own choices, for Wesley grace was effective insofar as it enabled choices to be made. Grace invites and enables human response. Whereas, the Reformers feared that any human cooperation with grace would lead once again to "works righteousness," and so virtually eliminated any sense of human freedom in connection with salvation; Wesley thought that the whole point of grace was to lead us to righteous works. Righteous works, in turn, were not set duties or penances, but were all actions and attitudes that fostered love. And love was more than an emotional state to be attained; rather, love was living in the image of God, and participating in God's own love for the world. Love was any act that cared for the well-being of creatures. Such love was *enabled* by grace, but enacted by the recipient of grace.

Could a person refuse this grace? Wesley's answer was a profound—and sorrowful—"yes." If grace enables a response, then it does not determine the response, but instead waits to see what the response will be. All grace is toward communal well-being, in whatsoever form is appropriate to the context. Thus all grace is toward the good, inviting participation in the good. To participate in the good is to participate in the love of God. Hence in and through grace, humans are invited and enabled to join in God's love, which is God's care for the world. For this reason, acts of mercy as well as acts of piety run throughout Wesleyan discussions of grace.

So then, in Methodist forms of Protestantism, prevenient grace as the grace that prepares us for salvation is given in baptism, but not exclusively so. Baptism becomes a witness to the prevenience of God's grace, always going before us, always preparing us for that which is good. Prevenient grace is a preparatory grace, leading us to desire conformity to the image of God. Justifying grace is, for Wesley, the pardon of God based (as in the Reformers) on the merits of Christ, applied to sinners. He sometimes called justifying grace the doorway to the real point of it all, which is sanctifying grace: growth in love, or "Christian perfection."

Throughout Protestant forms of Christianity, the distinctions made in the understanding of grace have to do primarily with whether grace works apart from human agency, or whether it enables human agency. While there is theological differentiation between the two, in actual practice there tends to be the assumption that God graciously calls us not only to a moment of salvation in Christ, but to a lifelong salvation whereby we actively cooperate with the grace of God to become a loving community of people: the body of Christ.

GRACE IN A PROCESS PERSPECTIVE

Process thought tends to interpret God's power and knowledge in and through its distinctive understanding of God's presence. It's not that process thinkers rationally compared omnipotence, omniscience, and omnipresence, deciding upon omnipresence as the main category! Far from it. The notion of God in process thought emerges from the understanding of God's relation to the world. Each and every single actual occasion that emerges within existence does so through three distinctive powers.

First is the power of the past, which determines to a large extent the parameters within which the nascent occasion may become. Some process thinkers regard the past as having an evocative power: each completed occasion has an efficacious appetition for that which will follow it, and the appetitions of many occasions necessarily evoke successors. Other process thinkers consider completed occasions inert—"stubborn facts" whose agency is depleted with the satisfaction of becoming. But in both cases, the past defines the parameters within which new occasions can become relative to that past.

Second is the power of the future. Every occasion represents a novel point in the universe, a convergence of actualities and possibilities never before encountered in precisely this way. In answer to the question of the "whence" of the novel possibilities—unaccounted for in the past—Alfred North Whitehead posited an actual entity whose primordial nature was the ground and the unification of all possibilities whatsoever. God, feeling all the occasions of a nascent occasion's past, feels as well the new possibilities now available for a future. God's feeling for the future is also evocative, calling that future into becoming.

Third, the new occasion comes to birth through its emerging responsiveness to feelings of past and future, integrating these feelings in such a way as to create itself in the present moment. Then, its own appetition toward successor occasions joins with the appetitions of its contemporaries to evoke yet a new present. And the process of past/future/present continues over and over again, ad infinitum. In effect, then, there are three creative powers: the finite past, the infinite future, and the selective integration of past and future in the becoming actuality, which is the present. Creation is a complex act rife with alternatives and ambiguities, with each decisive moment changing that which is possible in successor moments.

The parallels with the notions of grace outlined above—especially the sense of enabling grace particularly emphasized by Wesley—should be clear, along with the consequences for reformulating the traditional "omni's" of God. I will lift up the implications for omnipresence first, following this with explication of the implications for grace.

If creation is as complex as process suggests, then the power of God is neither unilateral nor solitary. "Omnipotence," as the power to act independently of any other action, is totally outside the process conceptuality, a surd without reference. In its place, God's power to act is always a power that is at once a responding power and an initiating power, stemming from the omnipresence of God. Neither can the power of God be said to originate from somewhere outside the universe—apart from the omnipresence of God, there is no divine power to speak of.

The reason for this follows from the nature of existence per se. If, as discussed above, what we call "existence" is a vast and dynamic succession of actual entities that in various combinations create strands of entities that yield the complexity of what we call matter in its multitude of forms, then the creative power of God as the future must be continuously operative within the system. Each occasion must experience in its own way within its own context the creative call of God toward its becoming. But considering the immensity of the universe, there is no number conceivable that is large enough to account for all the actual entities that go into making up a world, let alone a planetary system or galaxy or universe. Unless God is pervasively at work throughout the universe, there would be no becoming at all. A God somehow "outside" the universe is non-sense, since God's reception of every entity's past and provision of every entity's possible future demands an intensity of God's presence to each and every entity whatsoever. By definition, a process world is a world of divine omnipresence. There is no "outside."

Omnipresence, then, re-envisions the power of God from an "out there" to an "in here." It is an ultimate power of "withness," which is essentially an enabling power. The implications for grace are obvious, but there are also deep implications for how we understand the knowledge of God—omniscience. In a process-relational world, the old riddles of whether or not God knows the future before it happens are category mistakes, like asking whether or not God can make a stone so heavy that God cannot lift it. Rather, because of omnipresence, and a power working through omnipresence, God knows each and every entity and all states of entities precisely as they are and precisely as their immediate successors might be, along with various possible/impossible and probable/improbable scenarios into the foreseeable future. This is a perfect knowledge, knowing the actual as actual, the possible as possible, and the probable as probable. The power of God depends upon this precise knowledge, and both divine power and divine knowledge depend on the omnipresence of God. Because God is present to all things, God knows all things as they are. Relative to every becoming entity, God, knowing its entire past as well as its contemporary context, knows what is now possible for the entity, influencing it toward that possibility. A nascent occasion, receiving the possibility along with its past, is enabled to become, according to its own decisions concerning what it will do with the creative powers it has received.

Clearly, this process context deepens the traditional Protestant emphasis on grace. Grace is simply another name for the creative, enabling power of God, meeting each becoming entity in its context, calling each entity toward its good. As an enabling rather than a forcing power, God's grace works with the freedom of each entity. It's not that God *allows* an entity to be free, as if somehow God had hands tied behind the divine back that, at will, God could untie in order to force a preferred result. Rather, freedom is simply woven into the structure of existence: to exist is, by definition, to respond to a past in terms of a possible future. Everything that becomes has a responsive power to do so; it is part of the "why" of its becoming just as it does. The enabling, gracious power of God works with the responsive, free power of the becoming present. God's power is not some opposite to freedom; rather, power—all power—works with some degree of freedom. The degree, in turn, depends upon the variables of when, where, and how an entity becomes. Freedom takes place within the parameters of the actual and the possible, the past and the future. Grace enables responses that maximize freedom toward a good. Grace is the creative power of God, inviting and enabling human response.

Since grace is contextual, the theological language of "prevenient," "justifying," and "sanctifying" holds good. "Prevenient" names the enabling power of God who comes to us with our possible future; "justifying" and "sanctifying" bespeak the contextual power of God. What God offers us depends upon our need within our context. But even to talk of justifying and sanctifying forms of grace takes us beyond the enabling power of God given to every actual entity, into the world of everyday experience, for we do not talk theologically about an "actual entity" being justified or sanctified, but "persons" being justified or sanctified. A person consists of the succession of human experiences from birth to death, and these are intricately interconnected with the other actual entities that make up the body.

EVIL AND SIN IN PROCESS PERSPECTIVE

Persons develop historically through birth, growth, and death within contexts such as familial, cultural, social, political, and economic systems. Given the interrelatedness of all things, personal existence depends upon and affects myriad others. Each personal intent to thrive interacts with many other personal intents to thrive, creating the necessity of the give and take of social interaction. It is impossible, in such a situation, to avoid rhythms of enrichment and impoverishment, help and harm. That which might work to the good for some could work toward the ill of others, and this is inevitable.

God's gracious call as experienced by persons will always be toward what good is possible in any given situation. These goods are, of course, limited by the situation—and given the complexities of personal and social existence, the limitations can be considerable. On the simplest level, life lives through taking life: we must eat in order to live. While it is quite good to nourish one's body, to do so can hardly be considered good from the perspective of the cattle or chickens or fish that we eat. On more complex levels, seeking to satisfy some obligations can lead to disappointment with regard to other obligations. Without belaboring the point further, it is not possible for even the most responsible persons to live without causing some degree of harm as well as some degree of good to others.

If this were the entirety of the problem of human responsibility for harm, we might consider it simply the price of being alive—we are fragile creatures, living in an interdependent world where some harm is inevitable. Unfortunately, the situation is hardly this simple. If the issues named above are a kind of necessary violation of the good for some creature, we humans have been adept at devising numerous unnecessary forms of violence that we inflict upon one another. Sometimes these intentional acts are to shore up one's sense of safety in a vulnerable world; sometimes they are to increase one's advantage over others; sometimes they stem from a cultivated insensitivity to the well-being of those beyond one's self; sometimes they simply express rage against perceived powerlessness and vulnerability. It is impossible to list the variations of unnecessary violence we have devised against one another. Protestants, and indeed most Christians, condense them all under the name of "sin," with its corollary, guilt.

In a sense, Protestantism has consolidated all guilt by considering it guilt before God for sins against God. There is a deep sense in a process world where this is appropriate, for if God is omnipresent, then God experiences all the effects of our actions and nonactions, insofar as inaction causes harm. But there is also the possibility of obfuscation if we focus solely on the fact that all sins are against God. Sins are against God precisely because they are first of all against the individual and communal good of creatures. It is the creature—whether animate or inanimate, self or other—who is violated, the creature whose good is undone, the creature who suffers loss through the violation experienced, and therefore the sin is primarily and directly against the creature and only derivatively against God. Because God feels the creature, God experiences the creature's experience. Sin against the creature is also against God, derivative of the fact that the omnipresent God feels what happens in the world, and therefore suffers with the world.

Because of the omnipresence of God, sin is not simply that which we direct at fellow humans. God cannot feel the world selectively, drowning out all pain other than human. When we create intolerably cruel living conditions for animals we intend for food, when we intentionally destroy the habitat upon which the life of wild things (and our own!) depends, when we slaughter animals simply for the thrill of killing, we create pain and suffering that God as well as the animals must feel. We sin against God because we first sin against our fellow creatures. The guilt we accrue from sin is not only guilt before God, but also guilt before all the earth and its inhabitants.

Guilt accrues not only from intentional acts of ill will; but also from what might appear to be more passive acts of backing away from the good, choosing lesser alternatives than those God graciously makes available to us. God enables the good in every moment, offering a real possibility for that which we might truly become in the continuous developing of ourselves. But this gracious enabling is invitation, not compulsion. We are invited into our best becoming. And we experience the reality that there are occasions when we do not choose the good, but a lesser alternative. The loss of what might have been is not always readily apparent, and the continuing grace of God works with our lesser choice just as God would have continued to work with our higher choice. Unlike the immediate effects of vicious acts, these quiet refusals of a greater good can be unnoticed. But the losses entailed in such refusals reverberate, because in this interwoven web of existence an individual refusal of a higher good results in loss of better "might have beens" for myriad others. Though the sin is unnoticed, it is nonetheless real. It is sin against the self, because of the lessening of what one can be; it is sin against others whose lives are responsive to our own, and it is sin against God, who alone knows the magnitude of the loss—what might have been, over against what is.

The sense of guilt in these cases is a pervasive conviction that we ought to have chosen otherwise, or that we ought to have been able to avoid the harm we have caused.

SALVATION IN PROCESS PERSPECTIVE

Justification speaks to the condition of guilt. Acknowledgment of our refusal of the good, whether singular or habitual, and recognition of harm we have caused through intentional or unintentional acts, can paralyze us, miring us in a sense of fault that keeps us from moving beyond guilt toward an openness for the good in spite of the inevitability of failures. Justification—salvation—is considered God's mode of getting us beyond the impasse of sin and guilt.

Just as the Protestant Christian tradition has consolidated all guilt into guilt against God, even so this tradition has also absorbed all human evil into the representative figure of the Christ on a cross, whose death then represents a multi-nuanced response to human evil. Often Protestants have configured the cross as a consolidated divine punishment of evil; sometimes they read it as emblematic of the ultimate consequence of evil, which always drives toward destruction; sometimes Protestants view the cross as a sacrificial appeasement of divine wrath against that which works ill-being. Christ on a cross is a thick symbol, embracing many meanings, but ultimately connoting a resolution to evil that takes us beyond its clutching tendrils. This "beyond" is a sense of divine forgiveness, a releasing from the impeding guilt of sin in order to live more adequately toward the good.

A process interpretation of the cross tends to see it as revelatory in a multiple sense. First, it reveals the destructiveness of sin: sin is, by definition, an intentional (and sometimes unintentional) undoing of the good. The ultimate destructiveness of evil is intentional death; hence, the intentional death of Christ on the cross is revelatory of the disastrous results of evil. But insofar as we understand Christ to be a revelation of the nature of God within the conditions of finitude, the cross is also a revelation that all sins against the creature are also sins against God. "God was in Christ," we say, and the ultimate illustration in history of God experiencing the effects of our evil is God in Christ on the cross. Third, the cross is revelatory of the saving love of God. This occurs through the actions of the dying Christ: the words attributed to him indicate compassion for his fellow sufferer, care for his mother and his disciple, forgiveness for those who were killing him, and continued trust in God even in the midst of pain and the sense of God-forsakenness. The cross reveals that the God who experiences our sin and guilt nonetheless continues to offer enabling grace through compassion, forgiveness, care, love. Such love in the midst of death is stronger than death: hence Easter, resurrection, new life, new hope.

"Justifying grace," then, refers to the enabling grace of God exhibited on the cross, flowing from the very nature of God. Openness to and reception of that grace can free us from debilitating guilt for the sake of more freely contributing toward the well-being of self and others. This openness and reception are what process thinkers call "faith."

One of the primary New Testament texts used to express grace is Eph 2:8: "For by grace you have been saved through faith, and that not of yourselves, it is the gift of God." What is this faith that appropriates the grace of God? Too often it has been understood popularly to be "correct belief," as if Christian faith and Christian life could be reduced to assent to particular doctrines apart from any attention to their historical contexts. But in a process context—and indeed, in the biblical context—faith is far more tied to "faithfulness" than to correct belief. In its simplest form, faith is openness to the influence of God. This openness may indeed be mediated by preaching, baptism, Christian education, biblical study, or the like, and it is certainly an openness that is shaped by its particular social location. Openness does not mean uninfluenced receptivity. But "influenced receptivity" is hardly negative, since all influences are affected by the totality of one's situation in time and space. Precisely within one's context, usually in conformity to the terms of one's denominational affiliation, one learns a reliance on the ever-present gracious guidance of God. This reliance is itself an openness to God's enabling grace, a sort of "clearing the channel" for the flowing of enabling grace into the self or, corporately, into the faith community. One is therefore "saved by grace through faith, and that not of yourselves, it is the gift of God."

Justifying grace impels us to name the sins that bind us, confessing our guilt to those we have harmed—creature and God—and to live from the freeing power of forgiveness toward the good. It moves us directly into the process of sanctification, for it is the enabling power of God not only to free us from the blockages of sin, but to guide us into ever deeper conformities to the love of God for all creation. Sanctifying grace, like justifying grace, addresses us in our need and in our context. It is equally dependent for its effectiveness on the openness, the faithfulness, or the faith of the recipient. It does not free us from the capacity to do wrong—that would be to free us from freedom, or to free us from existing! But responsiveness to sanctifying grace increases the desire for a many-faceted goodness within self and society, with greater conformity to God's own desire for the forms of goodness that are possible and feasible within the infinitely varied contexts of existence as a whole.

This discussion of grace cannot conclude without some attention to the fourth form of grace, "glorifying grace." Because it refers to the final consummation of Christian life within the everlastingness of God, beyond our individual deaths, there is an increased speculative nature to any discussion of glorifying grace. Primarily, it refers to our final and full conformity to the love of God, the culmination of life's journey beyond death. Images of glorifying grace in the Protestant tradition abound—often in contrast to what is considered its opposite, hell. "Flee from the wrath to come" was a frequent Wesleyan exhortation, and Jonathan Edwards unfortunately gained his most widespread fame through his sermon, "Sinners in the Hands of an Angry God," depicting God as a great spider holding its victims over the flames of hell, ready to drop them in. Contrasting images of heaven tended to be glorious cities, replete with angels, golden streets, and crystal streams.

But the most profound images of glorifying grace eschew such concrete images of heaven or hell, and focus instead upon the fullness of love unimaginable, pervasive and full, finally filling all in all. It is as if finite life can only bear so much love, constrained as we are by limited capacities. But God, who is unbounded love, fits us gradually through the various modes of grace in this life to be more and more open to love—an active care for the well-being of all creatures, within the intricacies and compounded social networks of our finite existence. Death is like a graduation to a new form of existence where we finally participate fully in God's love. Sometimes images of glorifying grace, or heaven, have been used in a negative way to contrast with our ordinary lives, as if these are but small things of little worth in contrast to that unimaginable fullness that awaits us. But such denigration of ordinary existence is contrary to the very love of God that it seemingly exalts, for glorifying grace fits precisely the stuff of this mundane life for the full love of God. It is this life, in all its ambiguities, that is so valued by divine love that it is finally made a full participant in that love.

Process thinkers have their own musings on the nature of glorifying grace. Some focus so entirely upon the rich intricacy and intimacy of creaturely existence that "glorifying grace," if used as a term at all, bespeaks the glory and wonder of our experience of the universe, finitude and death notwithstanding. "Objective immortality"—the sense that our influence continues on earth through those who follow us, and that God remembers us fully and unfadingly forever—satisfies the sense of meaning and fulfillment often suggested by glorifying grace. Others work with the sense of "subjective immortality," also suggested by Whitehead, developing the sense that God so fully feels each actuality that God feels—and re-enacts—its subjectivity within the divine nature, so that each subject is destined to become a part of the divine nature. Given the peculiarities of "concrescence"—that coming together into complex unity that applies to every actual entity—this integration into God is not without judgment and consequences, for in God each finite occasion would experience God's experience of the consequences of everything it had done. Persons in God would experience the results of everything they had ever done, and this is both a form of judgment and a form of salvation, for the everlasting context is now the infinite experience of the infinite love of God. Integration into God would be the growing experience of ultimate conformity to the love of God, participating with God in the ongoing love of the world. Since it is unique persons who are thus being conformed more and more fully to the nature of God, the conformation is not uniform, but multifaceted—infinite variations of the inexhaustible grace and love of God. Glorifying grace is the ultimate glory that is a multidimensional, multifaceted conformity of all things to God within God's own everlasting becoming.

God's efficacious omnipresence, working as an enabling influence toward greater goods, is interpreted within Protestant circles as prevenient, justifying, and sanctifying grace, all with intimations for their fuller form in glorifying grace. The terms are rooted in the Protestant tradition, reflecting that tradition even in their process interpretation. Progressive forms of Christianity, of course, recognize the particularity rather than universality of these interpretations. This volume is itself a witness to the ways different faith groups can utilize the relational interdependence of a process worldview to express their own communal experience. There is richness in learning from one another, along with delight in discovering differences as well as commonalities. Deepened insight into our common human experience is the reward.

4

An Islamic Perspective
Theological Development and the Problem of Evil

—Mustafa Ruzgar

EDITOR'S INTRODUCTION

Whitehead's philosophy has not been unknown in the Islamic world, but appropriation of Whiteheadian categories for dealing with issues in Islamic theology has been very rare. Mustafa Ruzgar is, therefore, plowing quite new ground. He has chosen one of the issues also discussed by Rabbi Artson, the problem of evil, as his focus. And at one level, his treatment is similar. However, the Qur'an is quite different from Jewish Scriptures, and the subsequent history of Islamic thought is also quite distinct. Accordingly, any argument that Muslims can gain from Whitehead's thinking must be developed in a distinctively Islamic way.

Because non-Islamic readers are likely to be less familiar with Muslim literature and the way in which the Qur'an is interpreted than with Jewish and Christian traditions, this chapter will prove both of special interest and of special difficulty. Many Jews and Christians have viewed Islamic thought as too deeply authoritarian and rigid, and too committed to divine omnipotence, to allow for incorporation of processive categories. Ruzgar shows that this is not the case. Like the other Abrahamic traditions, its theologians have sometimes moved in directions that lead to untenable results, but Islam also has the potential for a creative development with which Whitehead's thought can help. Careful study of the Qur'an shows that it is not committed to the ideas antithetical to process thought that have so often been drawn from it.

Y EARS AGO, I REMEMBER having a conversation with a friend of mine following an evening prayer. My friend, who had not received any academic education on Islam but had been a member of a popular religious movement, expressed his utter disappointment when he heard that some scholars are claiming God cannot do what is logically impossible. For him, such a statement was the result of the modern tendency to rationalize everything and was contradictory to God's absolute power. In his view, raising such questions only contaminates one's mind and faith. However, in fact, raising this issue is not the result of the modern condition; it has been subject to discussions among respectable Muslim scholars in the past.[1]

I am writing this introduction in my home town where I have been on vacation for a couple of weeks. It has been seven years since my last visit and because of this I am frequently introduced to new people. One of the reactions I constantly receive when people find out that my academic interest chiefly consists of philosophy of religion is the question of Islam's compatibility with philosophy. Sometimes, implicit in this question is the firm belief that Islam evolved its doctrinal system into a solid fixity, so that interaction with new systems of thought is a fruitless endeavor.

While these examples do not represent all Muslims, it would not be too farfetched to claim that they reflect two important characteristics about the Muslim condition today. First, there is ignorance of the historical scrutiny of issues faced by Islam and the evolution of Islamic doctrine. Second, there is little interest in contemporary problems that face not only Muslims but all peoples of faith. While the former leads to an inauthentic perception of Islam, the latter causes Muslims to lose their vitality in the contemporary world. It should be noted that the two are not independent of each other, meaning that there is often a cause-effect relationship between them.

---

1. For an example of discussions about God's power to change the logically impossible, see Leaman, *Brief Introduction to Islamic Philosophy*, 24–26, 33–36.

It is my belief that engagement with process thought can help overcome both of these limitations. It can be utilized by Muslims to revisit many strongly held doctrines in order to develop more authentic perspectives that resonate with the main outlines of the Qur'anic worldview and human experience. Process thought will also help Muslims connect with issues that are current among scholars of religion and make valuable contributions to the ongoing discussion. To substantiate my argument, I will address the problem of evil as a case study. Other fruitful topics would be prophetic revelation or religious pluralism.

THE NATURE OF THE PROBLEM OF EVIL

When faced with events that cause suffering, whether moral or natural, we inevitably try to understand their source and nature. Our effort to understand does not come to a halt when we find a satisfactory answer to these questions. Most of the time, we also try to understand the *reasons* for suffering. The two sets of questions are intertwined, but for members of theistic religions, it is the "why" question that inherently relates to God. Why, the believer often asks, does God allow evil? Implicit in this question is the hypothesis that God's perfect power and goodness are incompatible with such evil occurrences.

Since ancient times, philosophers and theologians have tried to resolve this alleged incompatibility by proposing a variety of answers. The term *theodicy* specifically identifies this genre of literature. In the Western literature on theodicy, it is possible to identify several paradigmatic[2] positions. John Hick distinguishes the Augustinian theodicy, the Irenaean theodicy, and the process theodicy.[3] Islamic thought has not developed comparable paradigms on the issue.[4] This is perhaps because the Qur'an provides a number of perspectives to explain the meaning and source of suffering, each of which satisfies the needs of a different audience.

This does not mean that Muslim theologians and philosophers have paid no attention to the issue, as suggested by some Western authors.[5] Indeed, one may find considerable attention among both theologians and

2. Yaran, *Evil and Theodicy* [Kötülük ve Theodise], 17.

3. For brief information on these three types of theodicies as addressed by Hick, see his *Philosophy of Religion*, 42–56. For more detailed information, see Hick, *Evil and the God of Love*, 43–272.

4. Yaran, *Evil and Theodicy*, 17.

5. Ibid., 110.

philosophers to the problem, and some of them even claimed that only Islamic thought has been able to resolve it.[6] In the next section, I will analyze some of the prominent answers provided by Islamic authorities and question whether these have successfully solved the problem. I will discuss the Qur'an, Islamic theology, and Islamic philosophy.[7]

PROBLEM OF EVIL IN THE QUR'AN, PHILOSOPHY, AND THEOLOGY

As a general rule, the Qur'an does not deal systematically with theological or philosophical issues such as free will and predestination. Its interest is in correct belief and actions. It is pragmatic, trying immediately to capture the hearts and minds of people towards their creator. One can even discern a negative attitude towards heavy theological and philosophical issues.[8] The problem of evil is no exception. Rather than trying to solve this problem, the Qur'an focuses on the kinds of reactions/attitudes (mental or physical) people should have when they encounter evil.

Cafer Sadık Yaran, the author of the book, *Evil and Theodicy*, summarizes the Qur'anic responses to evil in four categories. First, the Qur'an suggests that God creates evil as a means of promoting spiritual growth. It tests one's faith and moral virtue. Its existence, when confronted appropriately, creates opportunities for the betterment of the individual who is directly or indirectly (i.e., as observer) subjected to suffering. Second, evil occurs as a result of free will when free will is used in inappropriate ways. Here, human beings are the direct source of evil; God is involved only indirectly. Third, suffering is created by God as a punishment of corruption. Last, the Qur'an suggests that suffering on this earth is temporary and that ultimate justice will be provided in the Hereafter.[9]

In all of these answers, the Qur'an is either implicitly or explicitly inviting human beings to use evil as an opportunity to strengthen their faith and to improve themselves morally. The flexibility of the Qur'an in providing several perspectives on suffering reveals its practical purpose. Although the source of evil can be ultimately linked to God, it is fair to

6. Ibid.

7. This suggestion of three sources is partly inspired by Yaran, *Evil and Theodicy*, 113–72.

8. Armstrong, *Islam*, 6.

9. Yaran, *Evil and Theodicy*, 132–33.

suggest that evil does not appear in the Qur'an as a theological problem to be solved by reflection about God's power and goodness.

This conclusion is shared by Abdulaziz Sachedina, who argues that according to the Qur'an, "it is ultimately faith in the transcendent God rather than the rational understanding of the philosophy of evil that can bring about confidence in the divine wisdom."[10] Sachedina further notes that "[t]he Qur'an is engaged in treating suffering as a divinely ordained temporary situation, rather than in estimating it as an ethical problem for the just and compassionate God that needs vindication and rationalization."[11] But this does not mean that the problem does not exist. Indeed, Muslim theologians and philosophers, being aware of the problem, proposed several solutions. I shall next address some of these responses.

Among Muslim philosophers, there is no unanimously-agreed solution to the problem. In fact, one can distinguish a variety of answers, such as evil as a privation of good, evil originating from the imperfection of matter or human free will, evil as a necessary concomitant of a greater good, evil being necessary to appreciate the good, and evil as an unsolvable problem left to the mystery of divine wisdom.[12] In general, one could observe that the majority of the philosophical responses have been highly indebted to the Greek philosophical systems, especially the privation theory of evil and evil as a necessary concomitant of the good.[13] These two philosophical responses are shared not only by philosophers but also by other scholars in different disciplines. Sachedina, for example, argues that "[t]he notion of evil as a necessary concomitant of good was an important theme in the theological, mystical and philosophical literature in Islam."[14] Employment of such philosophical concepts can be found in Qur'anic interpretation as well.

To illustrate the impact of philosophical views, consider, for example, Sachiko Murata and William C. Chittick's analysis of the two terms relevant to the topic, "Sharr" and "Khayr," which can respectively be translated as "evil" and "good." They argue that " . . . good is light, and evil is darkness. Just as darkness is nothing but the absence of light, so also evil is nothing but the absence of good,"[15] which resonates with the privation

10. Sachedina, "Can God Inflict Unrequited Pain on His Creatures?," 66.

11. Ibid., 67.

12. Yaran, Evil and Theodicy, 133–53.

13. Ormsby, Theodicy in Islamic Thought, 14, 27.

14. Sachedina, "Can God Inflict Unrequited Pain on His Creatures?," 74.

15. Murata and Chittick, Vision of Islam, 109.

theory of evil. They further suggest that, in the Qur'anic context, both of these terms are often used to imply a statement "about the benefit or loss that something brings" without "usually imply[ing] a statement about right and wrong."[16] Based on this observation, they argue that the meaning of evil depends on the perspective of the person who encounters it. Consequently, "[w]hat is evil for you is good for someone else, and vice versa. In the same way, what appears as evil today may turn out to have been good in the long run."[17]

While some passages in the Qur'an certainly express this perspective, such relativism cannot be posed as the ultimate solution to the problem as the type of evil that the topic demands is "genuine," not "apparent."[18] It is one thing to say that the Qur'anic context usually points out the inaccuracy of people's perception of what good and evil are, and it is another thing to reduce the entirety of evil to the relativity of human perception, especially after noting that "[m]odern sensibilities often find [God's measuring out good and evil] particularly offensive. How can a supposedly good God parcel out evil?"[19] This question implies that the type of evil they refer to here is genuine evil.

In the same vein, after recognizing the practical nature of the Qur'an, Sachedina provides a solution that he attributes to *some* scholars without naming them. The solution consists of the privation theory of evil, according to which, "evil [does not exist] in the world in the real sense of the word."[20] He further continues that "[g]oodness is identical with being, and evil is identical with non-being; wherever being makes its appearance, non-existence is also implied. Thus, when we speak of poverty, ignorance or disease we should not imagine that they have separate realities . . ."[21] He adds that the same judgment can be made about afflictions and misfortunes that are considered as evil and the source of suffering. "They, too, are a kind of loss or non-being, and are evil only in the sense that they result in the destruction and non-existence of something other than themselves."[22]

---

16. Ibid., 108.

17. Ibid.

18. For a fuller explanation of the distinction between genuine and apparent evil, see Griffin, "Creation Out of Chaos and the Problem of Evil," 103.

19. Murata and Chittick, *Vision of Islam*, 108.

20. Sachedina, "Can God Inflict Unrequited Pain on His Creatures?," 68.

21. Ibid.

22. Ibid.

The privation theory of evil goes back to Plotinus, and is supported not only by Muslim philosophers such as Ibn Sina, but also by Western theologians such as Augustine and Aquinas.[23] I support the general Qur'anic perspective to inspire believers towards developing a fruitful approach when they encounter suffering. But the attempt to solve the problem based on Greek thought is not successful. As Eric L. Ormsby paraphrases Ernst Topitsch's criticism, for example, the privation theory of evil "cannot withstand the touch of experience."[24] Moreover, this theory seems to deny the existence of genuine evil, and hence it does not address the *real* issue inherent in the problem.

Likewise, the philosophical view that considers evil as a necessary concomitant of a greater good seems to reject the genuineness of evil. Because of this, Mehmet S. Aydın rightly observes that ignoring the genuineness of evil does not solve the problem; rather, it complicates the theological considerations.[25] In other words, we observe both genuine goodness and genuine evil in the world. Rejecting the genuineness of evil will require rejecting the genuineness of good.

As a general observation, we could say that these philosophical responses to the problem of evil do not reflect the Qur'anic approach. Perhaps being aware of the very problem itself, the philosophers generally seem to distance the source of evil from God by relating natural evil to matter and body, and moral evil to free will.[26] In so doing, they are primarily influenced by Greek thought, whose influence could be observed in the philosophies and theologies of other religions. In his critique of the philosophic responses, Yaran rightly observes that linking evil only to nature and human beings will create further theological problems because a god who is distanced from evil would be significantly distanced from good as well.[27] Moreover, each theory can be questioned in terms of its success in solving the problem. As we already mentioned, some of them seem to contradict our perception of some evil as genuinely evil. The strategies that deny the genuineness of evil avoid the problem without solving it.

The influence of Greek thought can be observed in theological responses of Muslims as well, especially the Mu'tazilite insistence on reasons

23. Ormsby, *Theodicy in Islamic Thought*, 14.

24. Ibid., 15.

25. Aydın's observation is quoted in Yaran, *Evil and Theodicy*, 140.

26. Ibid., 178.

27. Ibid., 179.

and its role in explaining "the ways of God reflected Hellenistic influences."[28] Sachedina observes that "[f]rom the ninth century on, translations of the full Greek philosophic and scientific heritage became available in Arabic. The result was the development of a technical vocabulary and a pattern of syntax that reflected theological terminology substantially similar to some familiar positions in the Judeo-Christian theodicy."[29]

Muslim theologians, like the philosophers, provided a variety of answers to the problem. The two important theological schools, the Mu'tazilites and the Ash'arites, provided solutions parallel to their general worldviews, the former leaning towards reasoning and human freedom, the latter emphasizing God's power and providence.[30] The Mu'tazilites related moral evil to human free will while relating natural evil to God.[31] The Mu'tazili insistence on God's justice played the primary role in their promulgation of free will.[32] Although they related natural evil to God, due to their insistence on the primacy of reason, they thought that human reason is able to recognize "good and evil without any aid from revelation," which amounts to saying that there is a divine purpose and wisdom that could be understood by reason.[33] This general perspective led them to regard natural evil as not being really evil and even being possibly good for humans.[34]

In contrast, as a reaction to the Mu'tazilites, the Ash'arites leaned towards God's power and providence as allowing both evil and goodness. But, according to them, God cannot be judged with human reasoning because God's ways are mysterious.[35] Although the Ash'arites do not "deny the evil aspects of pain, incapacity, illness or poverty," as a result of "the doctrine of trust in God's will, a form of optimism underlies the belief that disease, destitution, social inequity, and the like are right and just."[36] Regardless of what they think about the genuineness of evil, because of their insistence on the limited role of reason, the Ash'arites ultimately argued that good and evil can be known only by revelation, not from

---

28. Sachedina, "Can God Inflict Unrequited Pain on His Creatures?," 75.

29. Ibid.

30. Yaran, *Evil and Theodicy*, 154.

31. Ibid., 153.

32. Sachedina, "Can God Inflict Unrequited Pain on His Creatures?," 76.

33. Ibid.

34. Yaran, *Evil and Theodicy*, 153–54.

35. Ibid., 154.

36. Sachedina, "Can God Inflict Unrequited Pain on His Creatures?," 77.

nature.[37] Moreover, although God decrees both good and evil, God cannot be judged with this limited human reasoning.[38]

Al-Ghazali's famous "best of all possible worlds" theodicy reflects mainly the sensibilities of the Ash'arites in terms of protecting God's power and goodness. When this theory is dissected, it would be observed that it includes several supporting arguments, some of which are not much different than the ones already mentioned. Yaran divides these supporting arguments into two categories: a priori and a posteriori. Two of the a posteriori arguments are (1) the perfection of the natural and social order and (2) the relativity of evil and its contribution to a greater good. [39] While the best possible world argument does not necessarily neglect the genuineness of evil, the supporting arguments either ignore it or deny it. Thus, my earlier criticisms apply to them as well.

In general, theologians and philosophers follow the Qur'anic theodicy in their affirmation that both goodness and evil originate from God.[40] But, as Yaran rightly observes, there is a difference of emphasis between the two camps. While philosophers try to distance evil as much as possible from God, theologians, especially the Ash'arites, who have dominated the theological discussion, try to solve the problem by emphasizing God's knowledge and power.[41] Both approaches have problems; hence it is difficult to say that the problem of evil is successfully solved in Islamic thought.

Recognizing that the problem of evil is not convincingly solved in the Qur'an, Islamic philosophy, or Islamic theology, some Muslim authors express the insufficiency of existing responses to the problem. After rejecting the view that the Muslim insistence on submission to the will of God "would remove untenable contradictions inherent in Muslim belief about the benevolent and omnipotent God,"[42] Sachedina asks the following question, which goes to the heart of the problem: "[i]n view of God's regenerative mercy (*rahma*) on all His creatures, regardless of whether they believe in Him or not, can one explain illness as a specific evil simply by contending that it is nothing more than the lack of the good state of being

37. Ibid., 76.
38. Ibid., 77.
39. Yaran, *Evil and Theodicy*, 157–69.
40. Ibid., 177.
41. Ibid., 178.
42. Sachedina, "Can God Inflict Unrequited Pain on His Creatures?," 74.

that is health?"[43] Although at times he seems to hold the privation theory of evil, Sachedina does not provide a convincing answer to the question he raised. He meticulously surveys different perspectives on the topic, but the reader is left with an impression that there is no convincing response by either Muslim or non-Muslim thinkers.

The same feeling is shared by Yaran. After presenting two opposite views with regards to the success of Islamic thought in solving the problem, first, one claiming a lack of interest among Muslims in theodicy and, second, one claiming the full interest of Muslims and their success, Yaran agrees with Ormsby, who holds a middle position, arguing that although the justice and goodness of God was an important issue among Muslim intellectuals, for a variety of reasons, the relevant issue of evil did not interest them much.[44] Accepting this comment, Yaran further explicates that the lack of interest in the problem of evil was due, not to lack of intellectual creativity, but to Muslim responses and strategies that made this problem not an irresolvable one.[45]

In his final analysis, however, Yaran admits that when the problem of evil is considered only as a philosophical or rational problem, no solution can be found to satisfy everybody. It was a problem in the past, and it will continue to be a problem in the future. However hard people try to explain evil, Yaran argues, there will always be mystery about this problem, meaning, there will be no ultimate solution.[46]

PRELIMINARY REMARKS ON GOD'S POWER AND GOODNESS IN THE LIGHT OF GOD'S GUIDANCE

The problem of evil is intricately related to two important attributes of God: omnipotence and justice/goodness. Because these two attributes are held dearly by the traditional theologians, the solution has been generally sought, not in reformulating these two attributes of God, but in modifying the notion of evil, mostly by rejecting its genuineness or significance. When the problem is related to God, rather than questioning God's power or goodness, writers simply affirm that God's ways remain for us a mystery. This shows that both philosophers and theologians were aware of the problem that when God is recognized as the cause of genuine evil, either

43. Ibid.
44. Yaran, *Evil and Theodicy*, 111.
45. Ibid.
46. Ibid., 190.

God's power or God's goodness is undermined. For example, the underlying reason for the Ash'ari rejection of any objective basis for evil was their concern that divine power would otherwise be undermined.[47]

Likewise, Al-Ghazali's "the best of all possible worlds" formula created such controversy that debates about it continued among Muslim thinkers until the nineteenth century.[48] At the heart of the debate was the concern that this doctrine leads "to 'a restriction of the divine omnipotence' . . . in the critics' views and so must be rejected."[49] In Ormsby's words, the concern about the divine omnipotence was "in fact the crux of the problem; for if nothing in possibility is 'more wonderful,' or more perfect, than what actually exists here and now, then God's omnipotence seems severely compromised."[50]

From a different perspective, such awareness proves that the solution of the problem of evil can be provided only if God's power or goodness is reformulated. A reformulation is not the rejection of the attributes of power and goodness, but a new perspective, perhaps more accurately describing God's relation to the world. No theist is willing to undermine the goodness of God because this would undercut His/Her relevance to the world. A god who does not care about the welfare of humans and the entire world would not be the God of the three monotheistic religions. A god who enjoys the suffering of sentient beings would be a vicious god quite different from the God worshipped by Muslims.

According to Islam, the entire prophetic history and revelation, one of the essential aspects of the Muslim faith, reveals God's genuine concern for humanity. God sends prophets in order to guide human beings in the right direction. This coincides with one of the central names of God, the Guide, *al-Hadi*, which could be interpreted in a variety of ways, ranging from God's creation of human beings in a perfect manner to God's guidance for their happiness.[51] However differently interpreted, Muslims do agree that there is an intrinsic relationship between God's guidance, and mercy and love,[52] which, in essence, is based on God's genuine interest

47. Ormsby, *Theodicy in Islamic Thought*, 17, 24.

48. Ibid., 3.

49. Ibid., 33.

50. Ibid.

51. Topaloğlu, *Belief in God* [Allah İnancı], 97.

52. For the relationship between prophethood and God's mercy, see Rahman, *Major Themes of the Qur'an*, 80; Murata and Chittick, *Vision of Islam*, 152. For the relationship between God's love and prophethood, see Watt, *Islam and Christianity Today*, 53.

in humanity. Indeed, the Qur'an establishes this relationship between guidance and mercy in 2:157, which reads: "They are those on whom (descend) blessings from their Lord, and mercy, and they are the ones that receive guidance." [53] Since God is the ultimate source of guidance, even prophets are considered as mere representations of this central act of God. Likewise, the Qur'an calls itself as guidance for mankind,[54] again explaining the ultimate reason for revelation.

Any attribution of evil to God would be in tension with this central idea of God's guidance and mercy as exemplified in prophethood and revelation. If there is an Islamic solution to the problem of evil, this solution needs to recognize fully this central Islamic teaching. Since other theistic religions also insist on the perfection of God's goodness, love, and beauty,[55] a god lacking such perfect features would not be the god of the theists. Because of their strong conviction about God's goodness, Muslim scholars generally thought of the problem of evil in relation to God's power, not goodness. In other words, even if God is asserted to be the source of genuine evil, direct or indirect, the immediate threat would be to God's power, not goodness, because a less-than-perfectly-good-God would be unimaginable.

Since God's goodness is not negotiable, a solution to the problem of evil can be found only in re-thinking God's power. Since the god of theists is generally thought as having "[s]upreme, perhaps even perfect"[56] power, and since Islam unequivocally emphasizes God's power, any solution to the problem of evil has to affirm God's power in order to do justice to the Muslim conception of God. However, the traditional approaches to the power of God generally tend to undermine the power of entities other than God in order to secure the absoluteness of God's power. Therefore, the proper solution of the problem lies in reformulating God's power in such a way that non-divine entities are conceived as more than passive respondents to God.

Such a reformulation, as mentioned before, is aimed at neither undermining God's power nor imposing philosophical analyses into religious dogma. Moreover, it is not a mere strategic maneuver at the expense of Muslim belief. In order to be philosophically and religiously sound, this new perspective needs to meet at least two criteria. First, both God's power

---

53. Translation is quoted from Abdullah Yusuf Ali's *Meaning of the Holy Qur'an.*

54. 2:185.

55. Griffin, *Reenchantment without Supernaturalism,* 166.

56. Ibid.

and the power of other entities need to be affirmed in a philosophically sustainable way. Second, it needs to be in harmony with the main perspective of the Qur'an.

It is my strong conviction that process thought provides a perspective that meets the first criterion. In terms of its understanding of God's power, the power of other entities, and the God-world relationship, process thought provides illuminating insights that are philosophically sustainable. In order to see whether the process insight could be held by Muslims, we need to explore its basic ideas and see if they are promoted by the Qur'an.

My thesis is that the tendency of Abrahamic theology to elaborate divine power in a way that denies creaturely, and especially human, power has been dangerously one-sided. The better balanced process view of divine and creaturely power is closer to what the Qur'an ultimately promotes. Process thought about God and the world better supports Islamic convictions about the centrality of revelation and prophethood together with God's interest in the world.

At the heart of the process theodicy lies the contention that God must not monopolize power to the detriment of the power of other entities. This means that God does not possess the totality of power. Otherwise, our "power" of self-determination and decision making would be rendered vacuous, being nothing more than mere words without actual content. As a result of this reasoning, God, who does not have the monopoly of power, works persuasively, not coercively. The existence of moral good or evil, then, is related to the free choices of human beings; it is not something supernaturally imposed or eliminated by God.

The persuasive working of God makes more sense in the light of prophecy because it reveals more fully and realistically the merciful and compassionate aspect of God, two central attributes that are repeated in every Muslim's daily prayer. Of course, the traditional views insist on retaining these two aspects as well. But unless a proper relationship that allows certain amount of power to us is established between God and the world, logical discrepancies and ambiguity remain in the attempts to reconcile our power and freedom with the depiction of God as having all the power. The views that attribute such a totality to God, such as the traditional view, jeopardize a full appreciation of God's goodness, mercy, and compassion.

In explaining God's power, Fazlur Rahman criticizes the "modern writers" for their replacement of God's "merciful justice" with "justice tempered with mercy."[57] He states that "many a Western scholar (through a combination of ignorance and prejudice) has depicted the Qur'anic God as a concentrate of pure power, even as brute power—indeed, as a capricious tyrant."[58] Rahman rejects this view by arguing that the Qur'anic description of God harmoniously integrates "orderly creativity, sustenance, guidance, justice, and mercy fully . . . as an organic unity."[59] God's power, creation, and mercy, he says, are "not only fully co-extensive but fully interpenetrating and fully identical."[60] The reason God is conceived by some as a capricious tyrant is their failure to recognize this harmonious integration between God's power and mercy.

I agree with the central theme of Rahman's argument—the Qur'an reveals a merciful, not a despotic, God. However, the misrepresentation of Qur'anic teaching cannot be attributed only to Western prejudices. Indeed, Rahman recognizes that Muslims themselves commit comparable mistakes. The problem of achieving a proper balance can be observed in the examples of the later Mu'tazilite and the Ash'arite theologians. "[T]he former made man the sole agent and denied God's role totally in order to make men 'completely responsible,' while the latter denied any power to man in order to safeguard the 'omnipotence of God.'"[61] A similar observation is made by Majid Khadduri with regards to the Mu'tazilite perception of justice, which led Khadduri to asking the following question: "Did God, the Merciful and Compassionate, create man only to leave him alone without Divine care . . . until the Last Day—the Day of Judgment?"[62]

This insight into the necessity of both God's role and human responsibility coincides with the general Qur'anic approach. The Qur'an, as stated earlier, does not provide systematic arguments in order to solve theological issues. The same could be said about the topic of freedom and predestination. While there are passages that seem to affirm the full freedom of human beings as if God is completely out of the picture, there are other passages that strongly urge God's role in everything, seeming to depict human beings as devoid of free will. These seemingly paradoxical passages show, again, the practical purpose of the Qur'an, which is to inspire human beings into correct belief and praxis.

57. Rahman, *Major Themes*, 1.

58. Ibid. The same point is repeated on p. 15 in more detail.

59. Ibid.

60. Ibid., 6.

61. Ibid., 15.

62. Khadduri, *Islamic Conception of Justice*, 53.

Because of the Qur'an's insistence on both human freedom and God's agency, any theory that is religiously plausible needs to retain both. The traditional view fails to do so because of some of the sub-arguments it strongly holds. Precisely at this point, process thought provides a rationally sustainable outlook. Next, then, I shall outline the basics of process thought relevant to the problem of evil.

PROCESS THOUGHT AND THE PROBLEM OF EVIL

At the heart of the process solution lies the worldview that satisfies the two concerns of Rahman with regards to the Mu'tazilite denial of God's role and the Ash'ari denial of power to human beings. While process thought's affirmation of God's creative activity as well as God's persuasive working agree with the Muslim sensibility of God's care for the world, and ultimately of God's goodness, its acceptance of our self-determining power as well as the power to influence others agree with the Muslim insistence on human responsibility and divine judgment.

The traditional formulation of divine omnipotence has informed, and been informed by, the doctrine of creation out of nothing. Process thinkers prefer to think that there has always been a plurality of actualities. These non-divine actualities have always had their own power. This helps us to see that the existence of genuine evil is compatible with God's power and goodness, because God's control over non-divine actualities does not work against the natural order of things.

As David R. Griffin observes, there is no textual basis in the Bible for the traditional doctrine of creation out of nothing. It has worked to reinforce an equally non-biblical doctrine of divine omnipotence, according to which, God's power essentially has no limitation except for, perhaps, logical impossibilities and divine self-limitation.[63] By perpetuating such a totalistic conception of power,[64] this doctrine involves denial of the two-fold power (self-determination and the power to influence others) to non-divine actualities by making them *completely* contingent upon God's volition. While denial of human power renders religious responsibility incongruous, *complete* contingency endangers God's goodness. Since absolute power promotes the idea of God's supernatural intervention in the natural order of things at any moment, the occurrence of genuine evil leaves no option but relating it to goodness, not omnipotence.

63. Griffin, "Creation Out of Chaos and the Problem of Evil," 103.

64. Ibid., 101, 104.

By affirming that power is inherent to all actualities, including non-divine ones, process theodicy secures God's goodness, which is exemplified in God's persuasive, rather than coercive, working in the world.[65] Although God is indirectly responsible for the existence of evil due to creation, God is not directly responsible.[66] God's persuasive working is directed toward the maximizing of goodness in the world. This reflects many of God's attributes, one of them, in Christian theology, being love.[67]

After this brief explication, we can highlight some of the central premises that are essential to process theodicy. I will consider four:

1. Accepting the doctrine of creation out of chaos/pre-existing materials instead of the doctrine of creation out of nothing.

2. Rejecting attribution of the totality of power to God in such a way as to deny power to non-divine actualities.

3. Recognizing the power of self-determination and the power to influence others in non-divine entities as being inherent in all things, which, in the case of human beings, constitutes the basis of free-will and religious responsibility.

4. Explaining evil as a result of the necessary order of things that are subject to irreversible metaphysical principles, which, consequently, secures God's power and goodness.

It is my conviction that some of these premises are central to the worldview of Islam, and the others are not fundamentally incompatible. In order to substantiate my conviction, I shall next address some of the issues that are raised by these four principles in the following order: creation out of nothing, omnipotence, free will and religious responsibility, natural laws and the God-world relationship.

Before examining these issues, a general observation is in order. Since all four of them closely relate to theology, they are intensively investigated by Muslim theologians. It would not be misleading to say that almost every logically possible position on each topic has managed to find advocates. Over time, certain positions have been marginalized losing their vitality for the masses, while others have emerged as the dominant. This process of solidification of ideas, of course, was not free from political and philosophical influences.

65. Ibid., 106.

66. Ibid., 110.

67. For a perfect analysis of how God's love is expressed through God's creative activity, see Cobb and Griffin, *Process Theology*, 41–62.

This influence is not necessarily bad. Recognition of such influences can free us to reassess the resulting doctrines in terms of their congruity with the basic Qur'anic worldview, reason, and human experience. The fact that certain doctrines have been victorious in historical competition does not necessarily mean that they agree with the Qur'an.

On the basis of this observation, I agree with the argument of Daud Rahbar, (not necessarily with his particular findings) in the following statement: "When [my book] says that the Qur'an is silent on the subjects of God's Eternity, Self-subsistence, Omniscience, Omnipotence, and His being the Only Reality *as conceived by Muslim Theology*, it does not mean that the Qur'an rejects these ideas. It only means that these ideas are beyond the scope of the Qur'an. They are sophisticated theological ideas that have been read *into* Qur'anic phrases."[68] Rahbar further clarifies that his argument "does not mean that as Muslims we should not believe in God's Eternity, Self-Subsistence, Omniscience, Omnipotence, and His being the Only Reality; but having recognized that the Qur'an is reticent on the subjects, such a belief shall be on quite different grounds."[69] These grounds, I reiterate, must be consistent with the Qur'anic worldview, reason, and human experience.

THE FOUR ISSUES THAT RESONATE WITH THE PROCESS THEODICY

All that is necessary for reaching a decision on the relevance of process thought to Islam through the discussion of the problem of evil is to discuss the way Islam addresses the four above-mentioned issues that are extracted from the four principles of process theodicy. A close inspection of the four principles would reveal that they are integrally related to each other. While the doctrine of creation out of nothing leads to the concept of absolute power, the latter seems to constitute the primary ground upon which the discussions of the God-world relationship and human freedom occur.

The issue of human freedom, for example, has been meticulously discussed by Muslim theologians in the past, often with a reference to God's absolute power. The school that became most famous in advocating free will is undoubtedly the Mu'tazilite school. Their main argument was the

68. Rahbar, *God of Justice*, XIV, first italics are mine.
69. Ibid.

claim that human beings are the authors of their own acts, just or unjust.[70] This thesis was a reaction against those who held to predestination or hybrid-free-will defenses.[71] The Muʿtazilite view was ultimately based on the necessity of religious responsibility of human beings, a central idea in the Qurʾan. They asked: "if all human acts were predicated by God, as the Jabarites maintained, how could man be held responsible for acts over which he had no control?"[72] They reasoned that "God would be committing an injustice, were He to punish man devoid of responsibility, since such act is inconceivable according to Reason and contrary to Revelation in which it is stated that 'God is never unjust unto His servants . . .'"[73]

For a variety of reasons, this defense of free will was not welcomed by many theologians. One such reason was the firm belief that "God has created everything on Earth and all motions in the universe."[74] This concern about creation was nicely expressed by the Ashʿarites, who held the view that "[j]ustice . . . is not subject to man's free will . . . because God is the creator of 'everything.' . . ."[75] Another reason for the unwelcome was, perhaps, the concern that the Muʿtazilite emphasis on God's justice and their denial of the capacity of injustice to God due to God's very nature seemed to undermine God's omnipotence.[76] Rahman explains that the orthodox considered the Muʿtazilite view of freedom as "bondage for God."[77]

The Muʿtazilite view on free will is illuminating for its consistency with religious responsibility. The reaction against the Muʿtazilites in terms of creation and omnipotence relates to my earlier argument for the integral relationship among the four principles. If, for the sake of argument, the doctrine of divine power is reconstructed in the light of a different view of creation, then perhaps the complications attributed to the Muʿtazilite view would not arise.

---

70. Khadduri, *Islamic Conception of Justice*, 41.

71. The Jabarites, for example, argued that human acts have been created by God. Al-Hasan al-Basri held to a hybrid defense of free will by attributing good to God and evil to man. For further information, see ibid.

72. Ibid., 42.

73. Ibid.

74. Ibid. This idea of God's creation, in Khadduri's book, was referenced to several verses of the Qurʾan. For a list of these verses, see ibid.

75. Ibid., 56.

76. Ibid., 45. It should be noted that the Muʿtazilites rejected God's capacity to do the unjust and the unreasonable. See, for example, Rahman, *Islam*, 89.

77. Ibid.

Likewise, the discussions about the God-world relationship are not free from the impediments caused by the doctrine of omnipotence. Apart from Muslim philosophers, the general contention has been the idea that, except for perhaps logical inconsistencies, God holds the totality of power to the extent that God can overrule natural laws. The traditionalist view on God's absolute power finds one of its clearest expressions in Al-Ghazali, who, according to Oliver Leaman, suggested that God "must have the power to act in whatever way he wishes," implying that God could "even intervene to change natural events on particular occasions."[78] In the same vein, the concept of miracles has been generally understood "as a result of God's direct intervention in his creation."[79]

The insistence on God's absolute power was sometimes carried to such a level that even ordinarily inconceivable possibilities have been thought within the power of God, coming close to betraying Al-Ghazali's reservation for the logical impossibilities. Although this extreme position does not constitute the norm, it is possible to find examples, such as Ibn Hazm, who proposed that "if God so wills, He could reward evil and punish good,"[80] or Salih Qubba, who said that "it is possible that fire be brought into contact with wood many times and yet God create no burning in it," or "that God might cause a man to burn in fire, and still not experience any pain but instead pleasure," or that "[God] might create (in man) perception . . . alongside blindness and knowledge alongside death."[81]

It is quite instructive to observe that not only those who were opposed to free will but even those who insisted on free will, reason, and God's justice, such as the Mu'tazilites, were not able to create a consistent worldview according to which free will and the God-world relationship were successfully reconciled. The primary reason for this failure was the concern to preserve God's absolute omnipotence. This observation is based on Majid Fakhry's brilliant argument on the paradoxical nature of the Mu'tazilite view of free will.

Fakhry argues that the Mu'tazilite admission of "free will in the domain of consciousness and will" was "no more than a verbal avowal" because they rejected "man's right to exercise any jurisdiction on the outward deed, which they referred mediately or immediately, to the initiative

---

78. Leaman, *Brief Introduction to Islamic Philosophy*, 25.

79. Ibid. For further explication of this idea of miracles, see ibid., 35.

80. Pavlin, "Sunni Kalam and Theological Controversies," 109.

81. Fakhry, *Philosophy, Dogma and the Impact of Greek Thought in Islam*, 100.

of God."[82] Some of the Mu'tazilite teaching, Fakhry says, surpassed "in its extremeness the teaching of their avowed antagonists, the Ash'arites, and is inspired by precisely the same theological motive: namely, the safeguarding of the absolute and unqualified omnipotence of God."[83] Although the Mu'tazilites, in general, believed in "man's prerogative to choose freely," this prerogative, argues Fakhry, "was emptied of any content through their adherence to an occasionalist metaphysics of atoms and accidents, and likewise their interest in safeguarding the unity of God and his transcendence."[84] The concern to preserve the traditionally understood concept of omnipotence that finds its most concrete exemplification in the general affirmation of God's supernaturalistic intervention in the natural order of things, called "miracles," constitutes one of the primary reasons for the paradox Fakhry attributes to the Mu'tazilite view.

There are, however, good reasons for not subscribing to such a concept of power:

1. The primary reason is to do justice to the general perception of the Qur'an about God-world relationship, which is neatly summarized by Rahman in the following words: ". . . there is undoubtedly 'natural causation.' . . But this does not mean that God creates nature and then goes to sleep; nor, of course, does this mean that God and nature or God and the human will . . . are 'rivals' and function at the expense of each other; nor yet does it mean that God operates *in addition to* the operations of man and nature."[85] It should be noted, however, that Rahman's observation on God's operation within the natural laws appears to be due to God's imposition of those laws on nature, not to irreversible metaphysical principles.[86] This suggests the possibility of supernaturalistic intervention if God so wished.

2. The second reason is that the Qur'anic notion of divine power does not necessarily coincide with the doctrine of omnipotence as formulated by the theologians. After examining many passages in the Qur'an, Rahbar argues that the passages where the Qur'an alludes to God's power or the Qur'anic phrase which is often translated as "God is the possessor of power over everything" do "not give metaphysical demarcations of the extent of God's power. [They] are always

82. Ibid., 96.
83. Ibid., 95.
84. Ibid., 108–109.
85. Rahman, *Major Themes*, 4.
86. Ibid., 6–7.

rhetorical."[87] The fact that the speculations of Muslim theologians were not free from Greek influences strengthens the suggestion that other interpretations are possible. However, Rahbar weakens the implications of his argument by using only logical impossibilities as examples of what the Qur'an does not mean. "We know that when the Qur'an says 'God is the possessor of power over everything,' it does not mean that God can create another God, or that He can annihilate Himself permanently or temporarily, or that He can say that two and two make five and yet feel happy."[88] He forgets that these examples would not be accepted by even the majority of Muslim theologians who subscribe to the idea of absolute divine power.

3. Part of the third reason is the difficulty of reasonable reconciliation between some other theological doctrines and the idea of absolute power. I have discussed the problem of the reality of genuine evil at length. The idea of predestination which follows from divine omnipotence is in profound tension with free will and divine justice. The other part is the availability of a worldview that provides a reasonable reconciliation. Process thought exemplifies such a worldview.

4. The fourth reason is the existence of certain Islamic systems of thought that affirm some of the most fundamental premises of process thought, such as the centrality of constant creation of events, and ascribe the power of self-determination to non-divine entities. Muhammad Iqbal and Mulla Sadra are two such examples within the Muslim tradition.[89] Iqbal's belief in the power of self-determination in finite egos leads him, for instance, to the following reasoning: "[n]o doubt, the emergence of egos endowed with the power of spontaneous and hence unforeseeable action is, in a sense, a limitation on the freedom of the all-inclusive Ego."[90]

As I noted with regards to Rahman and Rahbar, all of these good reasons, however, are crippled because of the authors' implicit adherence to the doctrine of creation out of nothing, which, because of its denial of the possibility of the necessary existence of some non-divine actualities and metaphysical principles, supports the doctrine of absolute power. This

---

87. Rahbar, *God of Justice*, 40.

88. Ibid., 47.

89. In order to see more detailed information on the relevance of Iqbal and Sadra to process thought, see Ruzgar, "Islam and Process Theology," 601–11.

90. Iqbal, *Reconstruction of Religious Thought in Islam*, 80.

is true to some extent even of Iqbal, although he goes far to show that the existence of creatures implies that God's power is somehow limited. He asserts that "[a]ll activity, creational or otherwise, is a kind of limitation without which it is impossible to conceive God as a concrete operative Ego," and that "[o]mnipotence, abstractly conceived, is merely a blind, capricious power without limits," which goes against the Qur'anic idea of God's wisdom and goodness. Iqbal shows that the extreme idea of omnipotence is incompatible with the existence of any world whatsoever, but he still supposes that the existence of a world is God's choice. He conceives the limitation on God's power posed by the existence of a world as being "born out of His own creative freedom whereby He has chosen finite egos to be participators of His life, power, and freedom."[91]

With regards to the problem of evil, Iqbal asks the following question: "[h]ow is it . . . possible to reconcile the goodness and omnipotence of God with the immense volume of evil in His creation?"[92] In his answer, he takes refuge in the limitation of our knowledge by suggesting that "[w]e cannot understand the full import of the great cosmic forces which work havoc, and at the same time sustain and amplify life."[93] However, he does not deny the possibility of "man's eventual victory over evil" on the basis of his description of the Qur'anic worldview as "meliorism" that "recognizes a growing universe."[94]

Should Iqbal and others not have presupposed the doctrine of creation out of nothing, they would not necessarily cripple their own arguments. Especially in the case of Iqbal, such a rebuttal would make more sense because his organic perception of the universe is better sustained and enriched with a view that admits non-derivative power to the finite egos. After all, there are, yet again, good reasons to question the endorsement of creation out of nothing by the Qur'an.[95] There is the strong possibility of foreign influences upon Muslim theologians on this issue.[96] There is also good semantic evidence for the non-existence of this doctrine in the Qur'an as evidenced by Shinya Makino's meticulous analysis of the Qur'anic verses relevant to the creation of human beings and nature. He

91. Ibid., 80–81.

92. Ibid., 81.

93. Ibid., 82.

94. Ibid.

95. For a brief discussion of the doctrine of creation out of nothing, see Ruzgar, "Islam and Process Theology," 610–11.

96. Yücedoğru, *Creation from the Perspective of Science and Religion*, 88–89.

concludes that "throughout the Qur'an, the creation of nature as well as that of man is by no means seen as the creation of anything out of nothing, but it is always conceived that everything was created out of something pre-existing."[97] Makino's findings about the Qur'an closely resemble to those of David R. Griffin about the Bible. Both argue that the texts affirm creation as God's act of ordering materials pre-existing in a chaotic state.

It is quite illuminating to observe the frequency of logical inconsistencies in some of those who interpret the Qur'anic text to imply creation out of nothing. In his book on creation, for example, Tevfik Yücedoğru commits the mistake of using a circular logic when he endorses this doctrine as Qur'anic. On the one hand, he suggests that one of the many meanings of the three words used by the Qur'an to designate creation (*halk*, *fatr*, and *bed'*) is creation out of nothing. He bases this judgment on his assumption that when these words are used in the context of creation of the universe in the Qur'an, they mean creation out of nothing. On the other hand, when it comes to explaining particular verses in the Qur'an where these words and their derivatives are employed, he simply suggests that those verses refer to creation out of nothing because the words used there to explain creation, such as *halk*, means creation out of nothing.[98]

As this discussion reveals, the likelihood that the doctrine of creation out of nothing is not Qur'anic constitutes the fifth reason for not subscribing to the traditionally conceived view of omnipotence. When all of these reasons are thought cumulatively, there is a reasonable case for interpreting the Islamic doctrines that relate to God, world, and God-world

97. Makino, *Creation and Termination*, 22.

98. Yücedoğru, *Creation from the Perspective of Science and Religion*, 27–47. Not only this and similar inconsistencies but also bad examples of judgment are abundant in Yücedoğru's work. For example, he suggests that "if creation was out of something, the Qur'an would clearly tell what this thing was" (46). However, he ignores the possibility that the same judgment could apply to creation out of nothing as well precisely because, as he himself admits, "the Qur'an never explicitly tells that creation was out of nothing" (32, 104). Another example of bad judgment can be found in his suggestion that although God has given a minimal amount of some of his attributes to human beings, such as power, knowledge, etc., God has never shared the act of creation with others, even minimally. "The fact that human beings are able to invent things can in no way be comparable to God's act of creation" (16–17), says Yücedoğru. Implicit in his suggestion of non-comparability of human invention with God's creation is the assumption that other human features (power, knowledge, etc.) have generally been understood to be comparable to God's corresponding features. Yet, even the most traditional accounts would not agree with such a comparison.

relationship in congruence with the process worldview which offers a religiously and logically satisfactory solution to the problem of evil.

CONCLUSION

I started this chapter by narrating two personal anecdotes. In the first one, I introduced one of my friends who was highly critical of discussions about God's power and logical impossibilities. In the second anecdote, I mentioned the suspicion of several Muslims about the relevance of philosophy of religion to Islam. Such criticisms by lay Muslims and their suspicions of certain discussions and topics result partly from their lack of knowledge about the historical evolution of Islam's doctrinal system. They also result partly from their conviction that, since the fundamental doctrines of Islam have now been perfectly fixed and completed, there is no need to engage with contemporary streams of thought to re-explore them. Furthermore, this conviction may be shared even by some Muslim intellectuals who have studied the history of Islamic theology.

Although I acknowledge that everyday Muslims may find some of the arguments detailed in this chapter difficult to follow, I believe that the discussion is relevant to them on a number of grounds. Three of them are especially important:

1. First, the history of the efforts of Muslim scholars to explore almost every logical possibility to resolve the problem of evil, shows that Islamic thought has evolved through creative efforts to find the best explanatory framework. Therefore, Muslims today, especially lay Muslims, need not worry about discussing these issues further. On the contrary, such discussions will enrich Islamic thought and perhaps help develop it further.

2. Second, contemporary philosophies can be brought into such discussions just as Greek thought has been utilized by Muslim scholars in the past. This will not only strengthen the relevance of Islamic thought to current discussions but also energize Muslims' intellectual creativity. Indeed, some of the traditional issues may closely relate to contemporary discussions in theology and philosophy. To illustrate this, I argued that various aspects of process thought are highly relevant to the discussions of the problem of evil among Muslims. Therefore, Muslims today do not need to fear engagement with foreign philosophies and theologies.

3. Third and most important, I hoped to demonstrate in this chapter that, despite my Muslim friends' convictions, many doctrines of Islamic thought have developed over time with multiple voices. By re-addressing these doctrines in the light of contemporary discussions, Islamic thought can be developed further. I believe that this process of creative thinking must not be left to a handful of specialists. Lay Muslims, like my friends, should participate in this process because their participation will not only make the discussions more relevant to daily religious experiences but also provide checks and balances to this open-ended adventure.

BIBLIOGRAPHY

Ali, Abdullah Yusuf. *The Meaning of the Holy Qur'an*. Beltsville, MD: Amana Publications, 2006.

Armstrong, Karen. *Islam: A Short History*. New York: Modern Library, 2002.

Cobb, John B. Jr., and David Ray Griffin. *Process Theology: An Introductory Exposition*. Philadelphia: Westminster, 1976.

Fakhry, Majid. *Philosophy, Dogma and the Impact of Greek Thought in Islam*. Aldershot, UK: Variorum, 1994.

Griffin, David Ray, "Creation Out of Chaos and the Problem of Evil." In *Encountering Evil: Live Options in Theodicy*, edited by Stephen T. Davis, 108–44. Atlanta: John Knox, 1981.

———. *Reenchantment without Supernaturalism: A Process Philosophy of Religion*. Cornell Studies in the Philosophy of Religion. Ithaca, NY: Cornell University Press, 2001.

Hick, John. *Evil and the God of Love*. New York: Harper & Row, 1966.

———. *Philosophy of Religion*. Englewood Cliffs, NJ: Prentice-Hall, 1983.

Iqbal, Sir Muhammad. *The Reconstruction of Religious Thought in Islam*. Lahore: Shaikh Muhammad Ashraf, 1944.

Khadduri, Majid. *The Islamic Conception of Justice*. Baltimore: John Hopkins University Press, 1984.

Leaman, Oliver. *A Brief Introduction to Islamic Philosophy*. Cambridge, UK: Polity, 1999.

Makino, Shinya. *Creation and Termination: A Semantic Study of the Structure of the Qur'anic World View*. Tokyo: Keio Institute of Cultural and Linguistic Studies, 1970.

Murata, Sachiko, and William C. Chittick. *The Vision of Islam*. St. Paul: Paragon, 1994.

Ormsby, Eric L. *Theodicy in Islamic Thought: The Dispute over Al-Ghazali's "Best of All Possible Worlds."* Princeton: Princeton University Press, 1984.

Pavlin, James. "Sunni *Kalam* and Theological Controversies." In *History of Islamic Philosophy*, edited by Seyyed Hossein Nasr and Oliver Leaman, 105–18. London: Routledge, 2001.

Rahbar, Daud. *God of Justice: A Study in the Ethical Doctrine of the Qur'an*. Leiden: Brill, 1960.

Rahman, Fazlur. *Islam.* Chicago: University of Chicago Press, 1979.

———. *Major Themes of the Qur'an.* Minneapolis: Bibliotheca Islamica, 1980.

Ruzgar, Mustafa. "Islam and Process Theology." In *Handbook of Whiteheadian Process Thought Volume 1*, edited by Michel Weber and Will Desmond, 601–11. Frankfurt: Ontos, 2008.

Sachedina, Abdulaziz. "Can God Inflict Unrequited Pain on His Creatures? Muslim Perspectives on Health and Suffering." In *Religion, Health and Suffering*, edited by John R. Hinnels and Roy Porter, 65–84. London: Kegan Paul International, 1999.

Topaloğlu, Bekir. *Belief in God* [Allah İnancı]. İstanbul: İSAM Yayınları, 2008.

Watt, W. Montgomery. *Islam and Christianity Today: A Contribution to Dialogue.* London: Routledge & Kegan Paul, 1983.

Yaran, Cafer Sadık. *Evil and Theodicy* [Kötülük ve Theodise]. Ankara: Vadi Yayınları, 1999.

Yücedoğru, Tevfik. *Creation from the Perspective of Science and Religion: From Past to Present* [Geçmişten Günümüze İlim ve Din Açısından Yaratılış]. Bursa: Emin Yayınları, 2006.

5

A Hindu Perspective
Mutual Transformation of Cosmologies

—Jeffery D. Long

EDITOR'S INTRODUCTION

*I*N THE ABRAHAMIC TRADITIONS *each has a clearly defined Scripture, and in no case is the Scripture philosophical or cosmological. Each tradition must ask how to relate this nonphilosophical, and generally unsystematized, Scripture to critical reflection and especially to philosophy. The questions the theologian addresses are determined by the beliefs derived from Scripture and life in the community based on it. Those writing chapters for this book believe that Whitehead's conceptuality is helpful in answering some of these questions.*

The religious literature that was formulated in India is quite different. Much of it is highly philosophical and cosmological. The cosmological philosophy of Whitehead resembles this literature. Hindus are accustomed to a diversity of philosophical and cosmological schools. Whitehead adds another voice. Hindus ask whether it is worthwhile to engage a new philosophy coming out of a modern Western context. Many answer negatively, convinced that their existing views are quite sufficient and remembering painfully the way that other systems of Western thought have been imposed upon them.

Long is a faithful Hindu and also an appreciative student of White-head. He believes that a dialog between Hindus and Whitehead is, indeed, fruitful for both parties, and he spells out in detail specific ways in which each side can benefit the other. For example, naming the world of appearances in which we necessarily live "maya" has tended to depreciate its value, although there are Indian traditions that do not understand maya negatively. Whitehead can strengthen the positive view of the reality and importance of the world. The long and rich history of Hindu worship demonstrates that the process rejection of divine omnipotence is in no conflict with religious devotion to God.

INTRODUCTION

Process thought has had to fight something of an uphill battle in its efforts to gain widespread acceptance in Christian theological discourse, and it remains a novel system of ideas among both Jewish and Islamic thinkers. Other articles in this volume will no doubt attest to these facts—as, in a sense, does the volume itself, premised as it is on the understanding that process thought can benefit all of these religious traditions, but also on the assumption that a case needs to be made yet in order for this understanding to take root and flourish.

The situation is somewhat different for Buddhism, and, as I shall argue in this essay, for Hinduism. Indeed, Whitehead himself perceived quite early in the development of his metaphysical system that it "seems to approximate more to some strains of Indian, or Chinese, thought, than to western Asiatic, or European, thought."[1] This is not to say that process thinkers have no challenges to face in arguing for the relevance of this system to these traditions. But the challenges are different from those posed by the Abrahamic traditions.

In the case of the Indic religions, such as Buddhism, Jainism, and the complex of traditions that has come to be called by the singular title, "Hinduism," a great variety of issues arise when one engages particular systems in a dialogue with process thought, depending on the specific details of the systems in question. An Advaita Vedāntin will have a different set of

---

1. Whitehead, *Process and Reality*, 7.

agreements and disagreements with process thought than a Jain will. And both will engage with a different set of issues than, say, a Dvaita Vedāntin.

But, speaking generally, and more abstractly, the process thinker rooted in an Abrahamic religious tradition is likely to be struck by the broad agreement between the overarching worldview of Hinduism—by which I mean the nexus of views shared by various Hindu systems, despite other things on which they may disagree—and process thought. Ideas like a deity who is immanent and subject to change have long been widespread in Hindu traditions. To persuade fellow Hindus of their usefulness is not particularly challenging.

Although a tendency to think in terms of substance rather than process is as pervasive in Hindu traditions as it is in the Greek-inspired theologies of the West, it is also the case that there is a set of fundamental metaphysical structures shared by Hinduism and process thought: a dipolar divine reality, with both personal and impersonal aspects, and a cosmos of experiencing entities existing in relations of mutual dependence with that divine reality (although the degree of that mutuality varies among traditions). Both Hinduism and process thought are panentheistic, seeing divinity as all pervasive. And both Hinduism and process thought reject the idea of *creatio ex nihilo*, conceiving of creation as ongoing, and having no definite beginning or end, but also as being punctuated by cosmic epochs (called *kalpas* in Sanskrit) that do have a finite, though vast, temporal extent.

The basic metaphysical structure of reality posited in process thought is thus not at all outlandish from a mainstream Hindu perspective. This is in contrast with mainstream Christianity. The challenge for the Hindu process thinker is therefore not so much to persuade fellow Hindus of the validity of process thought in its broad outlines as to identify specific Hindu concepts that correlate with process concepts and engage in the work of translating these concepts into a Hindu idiom, and vice versa. The aim of this translation work is to share ideas between Hinduism and process thought, and so to utilize process thought in the service of Hinduism while enriching process thought with Hindu insights.

As in the translation of languages, the translation of concepts from one system to another is rarely, if ever, a simple matter of one-to-one correlation. Inevitably, taking an idea from one system and correlating it with an idea from another, especially when the two systems of thought have arisen in very different cultural and linguistic settings, involves distortion.

But rather than being frustrated by this fact, or seeing it as a barrier to showing the mutual relevance of process thought and Hinduism, one should see it, in the spirit of Whitehead, as an occasion for "creative transformation"—as a creative distortion—in which a third, new, hybrid system can arise: a Hindu process theology, which sheds new light on both Hinduism and process thought. By engaging skillfully with the subtle (and sometimes not so subtle) differences between the ideas of these two systems, one may, in the process of seeking to correlate these ideas, spark new insight into both. Whitehead's concept of God, for example, is close, though not identical, to the Vedāntic concept of Īśvara. By correlating these two concepts, by bringing a little bit of Īśvara to God and a little bit of God to Īśvara, we can advance toward a deeper understanding of the divine actuality to which both concepts point. By building a third concept from the mutually compatible insights of both, the asymptotic progress of philosophy towards truth is advanced; and both systems of thought thereby benefit.

In this essay, the specific ways in which I shall argue that process thought can be of benefit to Hinduism are:

- To aid in the recovery of the Tantric concept of *māyā* as "creative trans-formation," to supplement its Advaitic sense as 'illusion,' which has been emphasized by academic scholarship.

- To aid in the articulation of the doctrine of the *jīva*, or soul, by means of the process affirmation of ontological monism with structural dualism.

- To aid in the articulation of the religious pluralism of the Ramakrishna tradition with the process concept of the three ultimate realities.

On the other hand, I will also argue that Hinduism can benefit process thought, by shedding light on specific process concepts and concerns. Specifically:

- Hinduism sheds light on the process understanding of soul development by affirming that souls have, like God and the world, always existed.

- The Hindu emphasis on the fundamental unity of existence complements the emphasis of process thought on change and difference.

- Hinduism demonstrates that a non-omnipotent deity can be worshiped with intensity and devotion, contrary to the claims of proponents of classical Christian theology.

Given the aforementioned fact that a tendency to think in terms of substance rather than process is as pervasive in Hindu traditions as it is in the Greek-inspired theologies of the Abrahamic traditions, one might be surprised not to find a move to correct this tendency in my list of ways in which process thought can benefit Hinduism. While I do see this as one way in which process thought can be of use to Hindu thinkers, a task implicit in much of what follows, I also think it is the case that substantialism has not been as detrimental to Hindu thought as in the Western traditions. I see this as being due, first of all, to the heterogeneous nature of Hinduism, and to the absence of any centralized institution to enforce specific doctrines as 'orthodox.' In fact, no less than six orthodox systems of philosophy are traditionally listed in classical Hindu thought, with varying degrees of commitment to a substance-based ontology, and varying understandings of what a 'substance' is. It is also the case that Hindu thought had to come to terms early in its history with a very strong set of critiques from what could be called, broadly speaking, a process perspective—namely, that of Buddhism. Buddhism "has been included, assimilated, superseded, and at the same time excluded and disregarded by Hindu thought,"[2] the reaction to it depending upon the Hindu school of thought in question. Hindu formulations of the concept of substance therefore similarly vary in the degree of their sensitivity to process critiques, some being relatively amenable to a process re-interpretation, and others less so.

Finally, the emphasis on the primacy of Scripture in pre-modern Hinduism, and of experience in modern Hinduism, have both tended to militate against strong philosophical dogmatism. Given the diverse ontological interpretations to which the Vedic Scriptures are amenable, as will be discussed below, a strong emphasis on one particular metaphysical concept—such as unity in Advaita Vedānta, or, just the reverse, diversity in the case of Dvaita Vedānta—tends to meet with criticism from other schools of thought that place their emphasis on other concepts and other parts of the Vedic Scriptures where those concepts are more prevalent. And the emphasis on the primacy of experience in modern Hinduism has similarly led to a move away from metaphysical reductionism, and toward a both/and rather than an either/or approach to the nature of reality, as in the Ramakrishna tradition's claim that the relative and the absolute are both valid modes of conceiving of reality.

2. Halbfass, *India and Europe*, 191.

POLITICAL ISSUES: IDENTITY AND AGENDA

As a tradition practiced predominantly by a people who have, again and again, been subjugated by a succession of imperial powers—first by powers that professed an Islamic ideology, then by powers that professed a Christian one[3]—Hinduism has suffered greatly. It has suffered not only from their imperial policies but also from the depiction of Hinduism at the hands of the scholars of the imperial powers. In recognition of the distortions introduced by this scholarship, the label "orientalism" has now been applied to it.[4] Even the term "Hinduism" is a product of Orientalist objectification of Indic traditions.

One who wishes to engage in a mutual translation of Hindu and process thought involving the kind of "creative distortion" just described must therefore be cautious of the potential misuse of one's work, as well as being very open and candid about one's presuppositions and agenda. For this reason, I always make it a point to disclose my own identity and agenda in pursuing comparative theological work of this kind, in which I presume creatively to engage with the concepts of both process and Hindu systems of thought.

Though I am not of Indian descent, I identify myself as Hindu—specifically, with the modern or 'Neo' Vedānta tradition associated pre-eminently with Sri Ramakrishna and Swāmī Vivekānanda. Though some non-Indian members of this tradition do not identify themselves as Hindu, I choose to do so.

I identify myself as Hindu for several reasons. Generally speaking, I find that in order to communicate my beliefs and spiritual practices to others, a handy label—one of the big 'isms' from among the widely known world religions—is useful. Though raised a Roman Catholic Christian, my beliefs and practices differ sufficiently from those of the Catholic—or

---

3. My word choice—that these powers *professed* Islamic and Christian ideologies—is deliberate. I do not intend to imply that the religious self-understanding professed by these powers was *authentically* Islamic or Christian, but that this was how these powers understood themselves—or at least described themselves rhetorically. I differ from my Hindu nationalist co-religionists in wishing to see imperial activity as *incompatible* with an authentic Islamic or Christian self-understanding, and not as *intrinsic* to such a self-understanding. The suspicion of these two traditions runs deep among many Hindus.

4. For detailed accounts of the unpleasant political ramifications of orientalist scholarship, see Inden, *Imagining India* and Sugirtharajah, *Imagining Hinduism*. The term *orientalism* for Western imperial scholarship on the non-Western world was famously coined by Edward Said in *Orientalism*.

any Christian—tradition for a self-identification as Christian to be both distorting and deceptive. I could simply say that I practice Vedānta, as many adherents do, but this would inevitably involve having to explain what Vedānta is, which would itself involve the use of the term 'Hindu,' unless I wanted for some reason to conceal the cultural point of origin of this tradition.[5]

Given the widespread idea that all Hindus are Indian, identifying myself as Hindu also involves some explanation. However, this is relatively easy to address simply by stating that I am Hindu because I find the philosophy of Hinduism to be compelling and its cultural, ritual expression attractive. I am sometimes asked why I did not become Buddhist—a religious identity that does not, in the minds of most, involve an ethnic identification. My short answer is that theism is central to my worldview as it is not in Buddhism.

In short, I believe in reincarnation, meditate daily, and perform *pūjā* to Hindu deities. I formally became a Hindu through a ceremony performed by a priest of the Ārya Samāj. I have a Hindu wife whom I married in a Hindu ceremony. I have a guru who is a member of an ancient order of Hindu monks. And, on one occasion, I was the officiating priest at a Hindu wedding. If I am not a Hindu, then, I ask, who is?

The purpose of all this self-disclosure is to allay the concerns of any Hindus who may be alarmed at the prospect of a Westerner presuming to do Hindu theology—to whom even the word *theology* sounds suspiciously Christian—and claiming that Hindu traditions might have something to learn from something as Western—and Christian—sounding as 'process theology.' I am therefore stating at the outset that this theological project is carried out in the service of Hinduism, by a thinker who identifies himself as Hindu, and not by a covert Christian missionary engaged in

---

5. Many adherents of modern Vedānta, or *Vedāntists*, are quite insistent that Vedānta is a universal philosophy, not confined to any particular religious tradition, including Hinduism. While I also hold that the fundamental truths of Vedānta can be found anywhere, I note also that the articulation of Vedānta is in a cultural idiom that is overwhelmingly and indisputably Hindu. We chant Sanskrit mantras, we read the *Upaniṣads* and the *Bhagavadgītā*, as well as numerous other *sūtras* and *śāstras*, the order of our monks and nuns is based in India, and so on. To downplay all this in the name of promoting the universality of Vedānta philosophy strikes me as deceptive. My suspicion is that the urge to de-emphasize the specifically Hindu dimensions of Vedānta as a practice stems from the same urge that de-links yoga, in many Western settings, from its Indic roots, promoting it simply as a universal wellness practice. This is a holdover from old racist, imperialist attitudes that see Hinduism as too exotic to identify oneself with, but that still appropriate attractive aspects of the tradition.

acculturation in order to facilitate the conversion of Hindus to Christianity—a concern of many Hindus today.

In fact, I see process thought not as a Christian metaphysical system, but as a secular philosophy. Its main founding figure, Alfred North Whitehead, was distinctly uncomfortable with organized religion.[6] Though Christian theologians have profitably engaged with this system of thought in order to articulate Christian concepts in ways more coherent with reason and experience than is classical, Greek-informed Christian thought, and though David Ray Griffin has said that process thought "can largely be regarded as one more attempt to explicate a biblical vision of reality," it is certainly in sharp tension with traditional orthodoxy.[7]

Indeed, the affinities of process thought are greater with Hinduism than with orthodox formulations of Christian theology. And as Griffin explains, the notion that process thought is an attempt to explicate a biblical vision of reality "plays no role in the attempt of process philosophy to make its case. That is, there is no claim that process philosophy is true *because* it is based on revealed ideas." Its claims, rather, "stand or fall . . . by their success in the interpretation of life."[8] And to assume that its historical connections to 'a biblical vision of reality' must make process thought inimical to Hinduism is of course to beg an important question, for it assumes that a biblical vision of reality is incompatible with Hinduism.

But is this necessarily the case? In fact, as mentioned above, one of the central Vedāntic teachings to which I hope to show process thought can contribute is its doctrine of religious pluralism: that many paths, including biblically-based paths, contain truth and can lead, in practice, to God-realization (and must not, therefore, be fundamentally inimical to Hinduism).

Finally, my claim that not only can process thought be helpful to Hinduism, but also that Hinduism can be helpful to process thought, should allay Hindu concerns that I might be embarking upon an imperialist project, or claiming that Hinduism needs process thought to 'rescue' it. I see Hinduism and process thought as *mutually* relevant.

---

6. He says, for example, that "There is always in religion an element of brutality, and it is generally the work of sincere men trying to conserve a state of society." Price, *Dialogues with Alfred North Whitehead*, 160.

7. Griffin, *Reenchantment without Supernaturalism*, 362.

8. Ibid.

DISCERNING THE BASIC VEDĀNTIC MODEL OF REALITY

The first difficulty one faces when seeking to correlate process and Hindu ideas is the internal variety that constitutes the family of religions and philosophies that goes by the name *Hinduism*. I briefly alluded earlier to the fact that the use of the term *Hinduism* to designate a unitary tradition is a product of scholarly objectification and reification of many diverse traditions in such a way as to create an artificial sense of unity—a sense that makes it easier to conceptualize and engage with these traditions, but that also lends itself to distortion and marginalization of particular Hindu voices.

It has also lent itself to a political program—*Hindutva* or Hindu nationalism—which asserts Hindu identity over and against other, minority—for the most part Muslim and Christian—identities in India in a politically divisive way akin to the rhetoric of the Christian Right in the United States. Scholars critical of this stance have pointed out the extent to which it marginalizes not only non-Hindus, but also Hindus who are, for a variety of reasons, uncomfortable with it.[9] In the name of combating this "syndicated Hinduism," and preserving the variety of the tradition, some scholars have gone so far as to eschew the use of the term "Hinduism," claiming, in effect, that Hinduism does not exist.[10]

But other scholars, myself among them, take the view that this is an extreme position. All ancient and widespread religious traditions are internally diverse. If Hinduism does not exist, then neither does Christianity or Islam. In fact, there are shared assumptions, texts, and practices that do unite most Hindu traditions.[11]

The important thing to note in one's work, as I am doing right now, is that, when one speaks of Hinduism in the singular, it should always be understood that there are a great many voices in the Hindu conversation, and universal agreement on any given topic is quite rare. The generalizations that follow are just that—generalizations—and I make them in the full awareness that many Hindus would not agree with them, or even cast the issues in question in the particular way that I have. But I make them because they *do*, in fact, represent a wide swath of Hindu traditions, as I

9. Recovering the voices of these 'alternative Hinduisms' is a large part of the project of Wendy Doniger's most recent work, *The Hindus: An Alternative History*.

10. A collection of essays, many of which articulate this perspective is Sontheimer and Kulke, eds., *Hinduism Reconsidered*.

11. A volume of essays, some of which express this view, is Llewellyn, ed., *Defining Hinduism*.

have seen these represented in texts and lived in practice by the Hindus I have met.

The shared worldview and set of practices that gives cohesion to the collection of traditions called *Hinduism* can be called, broadly, either Vedic or Vedāntic. "Vedic" is a term that refers to the *Veda* (sometimes rendered in the plural as *Vedas*), the ancient collection of texts, of indeterminate date, that most Hindus regard as śrūti, or divinely revealed.[12] "Vedānta" is a term with a variety of meanings. Meaning, literally, 'the end of the *Veda*,' this term is sometimes used to refer to the last portion of the *Veda* to be composed: a set of texts more widely known as the *Upaniṣads*. But it is also taken to refer to the philosophy articulated in these texts, and conceived by its adherents as the 'end' or ultimate goal toward which earlier Vedic texts and prescribed practices point. And in the modern period, in the tradition of Sri Ramakrishna and Vivekānanda, it is taken to be the universal philosophy underlying all religions and philosophies, as well as modern science. For *Veda* originally means knowledge, or wisdom, and, as Swami Vivekānanda writes, "All scriptures, all truths are Vedas in all times, in all countries, and these truths are to be *seen*, and any one may discover them."[13]

Broadly speaking, one could say that, in terms of praxis, Hinduism is Vedic, in the sense that what defines orthopraxis is a set of norms based, ultimately, on Vedic authority. The practices of the Brahmins, those tasked with preserving the Vedic way of life, and Brahmanical literature, much of which is commentary on the *Vedas*, are the norm against which correct practice, or *dharma*, is measured.

To be sure, a great deal of Hindu practice deviates from any allegedly 'pure' Brahmanical or Vedic tradition that one could reconstruct from the most ancient layers of text. But the *idea* of the Veda is nevertheless a powerful one, in terms of which Hindus conceive practices ranging from the worship of the deities to the day-to-day rituals of home and family life.

The emphasis of the Vedic tradition, though, as I hope my language has indicated, is *practice*. In terms of worldview—and the kinds of issues

12. Modern academic scholarship locates the *Ṛg Veda*, the earliest extant Vedic text, between 1500 and 1200 B.C.E. Traditional Hindu scholarship places it much earlier, sometimes as early as 6500 B.C.E. A possible 'middle path' is the idea that particular *Ṛg Vedic* concepts date to an earlier period, as the Hindu tradition suggests, but that the text took the specific form it now has around the time suggested by academic scholarship.

13. Swāmī Vivekānanda, *Complete Works*, 7:9.

with which a process thinker might be engaged, it is more accurate to describe Hinduism as *Vedāntic*.

The Vedānta tradition, though it is closely related to, and arguably derived from, the Vedic, is yet distinct from it. The Vedic tradition, as represented by the orthodox Pūrva Mīmāṃsā system of Hindu thought, is largely agnostic regarding such issues as the existence of God or the afterlife. Its main concern is the correct performance of ritual and, by extension, correct behavior in general in one's daily life (concepts that are both encompassed by the term *dharma*). Even the existence of the Vedic deities, which, it might be presumed would be taken for granted in a system that is based on ritual offerings to such deities, is "purely hypothetical" in this system of thought.[14]

Vedānta, however, is a worldview, and the predominant one that unifies at least the mainstream of Hindu tradition. The textual sources that Vedānta regards as of the greatest importance are not the ritual injunction or *karma kāṇḍa* texts that I have called *Vedic*, but three sources called the *prasthāna traya*, or 'triple source': the *Upaniṣads*, the *Bhagavadgītā*, and a set of aphorisms called the *Brahma* or *Vedānta Sūtras*.

It is difficult, but not impossible, to discern a singular, coherent worldview in this collection of texts, which I shall call here the basic Vedāntic model of reality. But it is also here that one immediately steps into an ancient intra-Hindu controversy; for a variety of revered Vedāntic teachers, or *ācāryas*, have written authoritative commentaries and established teaching lineages, or saṃpradāyas, in order to perpetuate their views of this model of reality. Though the teachings of these lineages overlap considerably, their differences are of great importance to their adherents.

In the West, the most famous of the Vedāntic ācāryas is Śaṅkara (788–820 C.E.). He developed an interpretation of Vedānta known as non-dualist, or *Advaita* Vedānta. On this interpretation of the Vedāntic texts, the sole reality is *Nirguṇa Brahman*: infinite being, consciousness, and bliss, with no limiting qualities, and utterly beyond time and space. The rest of existence, on this view, is a product of ignorance—a result of *māyā*, a term that is often translated as 'illusion'—and is superimposed on the reality of *Brahman*. Realizing the unreality of ego and the subject-object distinction—seeing that *Brahman*, the universal self, and *Ātman*, the individual self, are one—and perceiving *Brahman* as the sole reality is the condition for liberation, or *mokṣa*: freedom from the otherwise endless cycle of birth, death, and rebirth into a state of limitation and suffering.

14. Laurie Patton, personal communication.

Śaṅkara's insistence on *Brahman's* being the sole reality is closely tied to his acceptance of a substantialist metaphysics—a metaphysics widely assumed in Hindu thought of the classical period. "The idea of a substance," as John Cobb explains, "is of something that exists in itself independently of everything else and has in itself no differentiating attributes."[15] Because 'differentiating attributes' include number, Śaṅkara concludes—as Spinoza would do centuries later and a continent away—that only one substance can exist. The conclusion that all entities other than the one substance are illusory follows from the fact that, "In human experience . . . only the attributes [of a substance] are given." The substance itself, as it is in itself, is not perceived in our ordinary experience—though, for Śaṅkara, the ultimate goal is, indeed, to perceive *Brahman* as it truly is, as one's very self—to realize the identity of *Brahman* and the self, or *Ātman*—and thereby become liberated. "We have, then a contrast between the reality, i.e., the substance, and appearance, the world of attributes. Appearance has the 'reality' of appearance, but if it is thought to be the truly real, it is misleading and illusory."[16] Thus, for Śaṅkara, appearance, which encompasses the entire realm of our conventional experience, is *māyā*—neither real nor unreal. Appearance partakes of reality inasmuch as it has a real basis, but is unreal inasmuch as it fails to apprehend reality's true nature. To use a favorite metaphor of Śaṅkara, the realm of ordinary experience is like a snake that one sees in poor light which, on further investigation, proves to be a rope.

Rāmānuja (1017–1137), in contrast with Śaṅkara, developed the system of 'qualified non-dualism' or 'non-dualism-with-difference' (Viśiṣṭādvaita Vedānta), in which the distinctions between God, self, and world are real, not appearance. In this system, *Brahman* is seen as an *organic* unity in which real internal differences and relations obtain, rather than the undifferentiated unity affirmed by Śaṅkara. For Rāmānuja, *mokṣa* does not arise from an abstract realization of an impersonal principle, as in Śaṅkara's system, but from divine grace, which is experienced in the relationship of *bhakti*, or devotion: the fundamental religious emotion of Hindu practice. One could argue that, as a system, the Vedānta of Rāmānuja bears the closest resemblance to process thought of all Vedāntic systems, with its affirmation of an organic unity with real internal differences.

Mādhva (1238–1317) developed the system of Dvaita, or dualistic, Vedānta. This view identifies Brahman wholly with the personal God (specifically Viṣṇu, 'the all-pervasive one'), and firmly rejects any view, such as

15. John Cobb, personal communication.
16. Ibid.

Śaṅkara's Advaita Vedānta, that conceives of ultimate reality in impersonal terms or sees phenomenal reality as only *māyā*. Hard-core metaphysical realists, the adherents of Dvaita Vedānta see *māyāvāda*, the teaching of *māyā*, as inimical to *bhakti*. Advaita and Dvaita mark the opposite poles of the spectrum of Vedāntic views.

The problem for an interpreter of Vedānta is that verses supportive of all three of these views can be found throughout the *prasthāna traya*—the corpus of authoritative Vedāntic texts. As in traditions of scriptural interpretation globally, the adherents of a particular school of thought typically take those verses which uphold their particular interpretation to be literally true, explaining other verses as presenting analogies, or using rules of grammar in their interpretation that will yield the desired meaning (even when this is the opposite of the plain meaning). Śaṅkara insists, for example, that Brahman is *identical* with all of its predicates, whereas Rāmānuja claims that it *possesses* predicates as all subjects do.

All these forms of interpretation insist that one cannot simply pick up and read the *Upaniṣads* or the *Bhagavadgītā*, as a modern reader might be inclined to do, in order to get at their true meaning. In order to engage in a valid way with these texts one must inhabit a tradition of interpretation, and have a living guru to guide one's interpretation. (My own interpretation, for example, is situated in Sri Ramakrishna's tradition.)

The three Vedānta traditions I have just mentioned are the best known and the most influential, at least in the pre-modern period. But they are not the only ones. Most of them try to carve out a 'middle path' between what they see as the extreme views of Śaṅkara and Mādhva. These 'intermediate' systems of Vedānta affirm both diversity and unity, or, in the case of *Bhedābheda*, both duality and non-duality (*Dvaitādvaita*).

In the modern Vedānta of Ramakrishna, the various other systems of Vedānta–as well as the other major world religions and philosophies, plus modern science—all express parts of the truth, from frames of reference appropriate to the persons who adhere to them. This idea is sometimes analogized with Einstein's theory of relativity, as a kind of religious doctrine of relativity.[17] In affirming the validity of all frames of reference, Ramakrishna's Vedānta could also be seen as one of the 'intermediate' types of Vedānta. Like these other systems, it affirms both the unity emphasized by Advaita and the diversity emphasized by Dvaita. Each view has insight into truth.

17. Swāmī Ātmapriyānanda, "Ramakrishna and Relativity."

Despite all of this diversity of interpretation, it is possible to discern that a common structure of reality is affirmed by all the Vedāntic systems. This model of reality is characterized by ten categories that are shared across all of the schools of Vedānta. These categories are: *Brahman, Nirguṇa Brahman, Saguṅa Brahman, Īśvara, Jagat, Jīva, Prakṛti, Māyā, Karma,* and *Mokṣa*.[18] Although these schools of thought differ in their use of these categories—the sharpest difference being between Advaita and Dvaita in regard to the nature of Brahman and of *māyā*—there is also broad agreement on many other issues.

PROCESS THOUGHT AND THE BASIC VEDĀNTIC MODEL OF REALITY

What is the basic Vedāntic model of reality? And how does it correlate with process thought? The primary category of Vedānta is the category of *Brahman*. The first verse of the *Brahma Sūtras* is *athāto brahmajijñāsa*— "Therefore now [we begin] an inquiry into *Brahman*." This verse, as understood in all of the Vedāntic systems, essentially defines Vedānta as an inquiry into the nature of *Brahman*.

What is *Brahman*? *Brahman* could be defined as existence itself or the totality of Being. Also called 'the Real' (*sat*), Brahman is coextensive with reality as such. It is that which is real pre-eminently, and from which the existence of all other entities is derivative and in which they participate. It is that, by knowing which, all things are known.[19] It is also the ultimate object of religious aspiration, of the ancient Upaniṣadic prayer, "Lead me from the unreal to the real, from darkness to light, from death to immortality."[20] It is eternal. "It is immortal; it is *Brahman*; it is the Whole."[21] As a word, *Brahman* literally means "the expansive" or "that which makes things great."

At this point, a process thinker might recall Whitehead's characterization of the ultimate reality as 'creativity,' to which I would argue *Brahman* corresponds. On Whitehead's account, this ultimate reality "is actual in virtue of its accidents. It is only then capable of characterization

---

18. A host of terms—indeed, an entire linguistic structure—is shared across these systems. I have simply isolated these ten as particularly central to the metaphysical concerns that these systems share with process thought.

19. *Chandogya Upaniṣad* 6:1.

20. *Asato mā sad gamaya, tamaso mā jyotir gamaya, mṛtyor mā-amṛtaṁ gamaya.*

21. *Bṛhadaranyaka Upaniṣad* 2:5.

through its accidental embodiments, and apart from these accidents it is devoid of actuality."[22] It is an ultimate principle that takes on a concrete reality *as* the actual entities making up the world. Whitehead goes on to say that, "In monistic philosophies, Spinoza's or absolute idealism, this ultimate is God, who is also equivalently termed 'The Absolute.'" This is quite similar to Brahman's being the ultimate object of religious aspiration. But, Whitehead continues, "In such monistic schemes, the ultimate is *illegitimately* allowed a final, 'eminent' reality, beyond that ascribed to any of its accidents."[23] If anything, this would seem to point to a radical *disjuncture* between Vedānta and process thought; for what is Brahman but a supremely real reality, from which all other things are held to be derivative, and which is regarded as God? Is Vedānta not another form of monistic absolute idealism?

We must recall here the various systems of interpretation that exist within the broad framework of Vedānta, as well as Whitehead's own distinction between creativity and God. For Whitehead, God is not creativity and creativity is not God. Creativity is, again, "an ultimate which is actual in virtue of its accidents."[24] It is actual inasmuch as it is manifested in and as the realm of time and space. But God is creativity's "primordial, non-temporal accident."[25] God is, for Whitehead, logically (although not ontologically) *derivative from* creativity, the supreme embodiment of creativity, "a stable actuality whose mutual implication with the remainder of things secures an inevitable trend towards order."[26]

Vedānta, too, makes a distinction *internal to Brahman* between what Whitehead calls the principle of creativity and God. This distinction is associated most prominently with Śaṅkara, the first *ācārya* of the Advaita

22. Whitehead, *Process and Reality*, 7.

23. Ibid., emphasis mine.

24. Whitehead's use of the term 'accident' should, of course, be differentiated from the use of this term in substantialist metaphysics. As John Cobb points out, "Apart from God there is no creativity. It is true that the 'notion' of God is not in the Categoreal scheme and is derivative from that. But ontologically, God's existence is as necessary to creativity as creativity is to God" (personal communication).

25. Ibid. Whitehead's use of the term 'non-temporal' here can lead to confusion, and is regarded by some process thinkers as unfortunate. He does not mean that God is outside of time and space (and so non-actual)–though the primordial nature of God does meet this description—but that there is no time in which God is not (the consequent nature of God). Unlike other temporal entities, God has no beginning and no end. As we shall see, in Hinduism, there are many such 'non-temporal'—i.e. perpetually existing—entities—including the souls of all living things.

26. Whitehead, *Adventures of Ideas*, 115.

tradition. Śaṅkara draws a distinction between *Nirguṇa Brahman*, mentioned earlier—Brahman as it is in and of itself, with no limiting qualities—and *Saguṇa Brahman*, or Brahman *with* such qualities. One could see *Nirguṇa Brahman* as equivalent to Whitehead's idea of creativity in its unmanifested, 'deficiently actual' state, and *Saguṇa Brahman* as creativity manifested as both God and the world of actual entities, which is how Śaṅkara sees it as well—though for Śaṅkara, it is the manifested, *Saguṇa Brahman* that is deficient. The views of Whitehead and Śaṅkara, one could say, mirror one another: sharing a common structure, but reversing their respective valuations of its primordial and actualized dimensions.

Saguṇa Brahman, for Śaṅkara, is how *Nirguṇa Brahman* is perceived prior to one's attainment of true knowledge, or *jñāna*—the knowledge that leads to liberation from the cycle of rebirth. It is the snake that is really a rope. It is a product of ignorance, projected by us on the true reality of Brahman. It is *māyā*—neither real nor unreal. It is not wholly real, because we do not perceive it as it truly is, as *Nirguṇa*, or without limiting qualities. But it is also not wholly unreal, for Brahman is its basis. *Saguṇa Brahman* is *Nirguṇa Brahman* as seen through the obscuring veil of *māyā*.

The chief difference between process thought and Advaita Vedānta, then, is not in the basic structure of reality that they posit—with an unmanifest ultimate reality that manifests in time and space as God and the world—but in the relative valuation that each places upon these manifest and unmanifest forms. In this sense, the philosophy of Śaṅkara *is* very much like Western monistic philosophies—such as that of Spinoza, or of absolute idealism—which Whitehead mentions as contrasts with his own system in that, "One side makes process ultimate; the other side makes fact ultimate."[27] The structure of reality posited by process thought and systems of absolute idealism, such as Advaita Vedānta, is basically the same. But which *dimension* of that structure is seen as most real—the eternal, nonactual, and unmanifest or the temporal, actual, and manifest—is reversed.

If Advaita Vedānta were the only system of Vedānta, then there would appear to be a chasm between Vedānta and process thought similar to that which exists between process thought and the Western substantialist classical theologies and philosophies against which it is a reaction.

In India, however, the reaction against the concept of an impersonal, non-actual absolute occurred much more quickly than in the West: a mere two centuries after Śaṅkara, in the form of Rāmānuja's qualified non-dualism. As mentioned previously, for Rāmānuja, Brahman is an *organic* unity

---

27. Whitehead, *Process and Reality*, 7.

which encompasses both the relative and absolute 'poles' of existence, and which includes both God and the world of actual entities. Similarly, the various other 'intermediate' systems of Vedānta affirm that Brahman is *both* the non-actual, ultimate ground of being—much like Whitehead's unmanifest creativity—*and* the totality of actual existence, including both God and the world. The basic Vedāntic model of reality, when one takes into account these various non-Advaitic perspectives, is therefore close to the worldview of process thought.

How does this work? Brahman/creativity is the basic nature of existence, with an unmanifest or non-actual/*Nirguṇa* dimension as well as a manifest/*Saguṇa* dimension, the latter of which consists of God and the world—the totality of actual entities which are manifestations or concrescences of their unmanifest, atemporal substratum. Process thought and the mainstream of Vedānta are at one in affirming the reality of actual existence—of God and the world—and in rejecting the notion of absolute idealism (and of Advaita Vedānta) that the non-actual, unmanifest dimension of reality must be pre-eminent. Process thought, much like the Neo-Vedānta of Ramakrishna, affirms the necessity and mutual dependence of *both* the manifest and unmanifest dimensions of Brahman, which authors in this tradition generally refer to as 'the relative' and 'the absolute,' respectively.

To give Śaṅkara his due, however, it was he who first developed the idea of the twofold structure of Brahman accepted by most other systems of Vedānta—the main exception being Dvaita. And the degree to which Śaṅkara's insistence on the pre-eminent reality of the *Nirguṇa* dimension of Brahman necessarily issues in the claim that all actual existence is an illusion is debatable. *Māyā*, as mentioned previously, and as will be discussed in more detail below, does not only mean 'illusion,' but also means 'creativity,' a meaning with interesting implications for the engagement of Vedānta with process thought. The other systems of Vedānta also accept the term *māyā*, but define it as God's creative power—an idea not at all incompatible with process thought, with the provision that all entities, and not only God, possess such power; for all actual entities participate in the nature of reality as creativity. God's creative power is pre-eminent, but not absolute. A modern exponent of Śaṅkara's philosophy, Anantanand Rambachan, has argued that to call the whole of actual existence *māyā* is not to say that it is not real, but only that its reality is dependent upon that of *Nirguṇa* Brahman.[28] A process thinker would say this as well, but

28. See Rambachan, *The Advaita Worldview*.

would further affirm the *mutuality* of this dependence. The point is that it is possible to read Śaṅkara in a way that is not so out of step with other systems of Vedānta, or with process thought, as is generally supposed. Śaṅkara, a central figure for Hindu philosophy, can therefore be seen as in the mainstream of Vedāntic thought. To be sure, Śaṅkara's substantialism still marks his system off from process thought. But a re-valuation of the novel and changing over the static and the actual over the unchanging and non-actual can still allow his basic structure to be retained, in a new form, much as Christian process thinkers have reinterpreted Greek substantialist concepts such as the Logos and retained them in a process context.[29]

The Vedāntic concepts that correlate with the process ideas of God and world are *Īśvara* and *Jagat*. *Īśvara*, 'the Lord'—usually visualized as either Viṣṇu or Śiva—plays much the same role in Vedānta that God does in process thought: as the supreme actuality that coordinates all other actual entities and constitutes them into a coherent universe. The *jagat*, or world, correlates with the process idea of the world made up of actual entities. Interestingly, the literal meaning of *jagat* is 'flow' or 'process.'

So the world is understood in Hinduism as a flow of temporary events, in a state of constant flux, just as it is in process thought. Similarly, *Īśvara* and the *jagat* have both always existed. Although the entities that make up the *jagat* are individually of a momentary and impermanent character, the collective flow that they make up is ongoing. God is not the creator of the world *ex nihilo*, but co-exists with it perpetually in a state of mutual interaction, just as in process thought.

The world is understood in all systems of Vedānta as including both the souls of living beings, or *Jīvas*, and non-living matter, or *Prakṛti*. As will be discussed below, there is a strong dualism of soul and body in most

---

29. Cobb and Griffin make a similar move when they write, for example, that "God [as creative love] is the source of novel order and ordered novelty in the world. Although in this vision a shift has been made from static to dynamic order and from order as such to order with novelty, what is spoken of is what the Church Fathers called the Logos." Cobb and Griffin, *Process Theology*, 98. The shared structure which I affirm Śaṅkara to share with process thought is identified by Richard King, in reference to a shared structure of Advaita Vedānta and Mahāyāna Buddhist thought when he writes, "In a sense one might say that [these two traditions] are looking at the same picture from opposite sides of the mirror. Their presuppositions (and therefore their conclusions) are thus diametrically opposed. Paradoxical as this may seem, it is because of 'the directly facing nature' of the two systems that the Mahāyāna and the Advaita traditions are so often confused; in many respects their discussions and conclusions are mirrored in the views of the other. Mirror images are, of course, reversals of the things which they reflect . . ." King, 238.

Hindu traditions. But this has not given rise to the classic 'mind-body problem' as it is found in Western philosophy.

This could be for a variety of reasons, but one factor is certainly the way matter is understood in Vedānta. For, unlike the West, where matter has been defined chiefly as 'dead' and unconscious—as 'stuff'—in Hindu thought, *prakṛti* is seen as an inherently dynamic reality, consisting of a constantly shifting interplay of three basic qualities, or *guṇas*. These *guṇas* are *sattva* (lucidity), *rajas* (dynamism), and *tamas* (inertia). *Rajas* and *tamas* could be analogized with the Chinese concepts of *yang* and *yin*, respectively—positive, dynamic energy, and dark, inertial energy—with *sattva* as something like an equilibrium between them, with the stillness of *tamas* combined with the alert awareness of *rajas*. Indeed, in many texts, *prakṛti* is identified with *māyā* as the creative power that both conceals and reveals the true nature of reality. As the stuff of existence, it is identified, at least in Advaita Vedānta, with *Brahman*, which is seen as both the material and the efficient cause of the world—the material cause, in its role as matter, and the efficient cause, in its coordinating role as God. The non-Advaitic systems of Vedānta tend to reject the idea of *Brahman* as material cause.[30] But even these non-Advaitic systems, which identify Brahman as God, and so as distinct from the realm of matter, or *prakṛti*, see *prakṛti* as dynamic and not as the 'dead' matter found in Western forms of dualism and materialism.

As will be discussed below, the Vedāntic way of thinking about spirit and matter can be correlated with the process idea that actual entities can arrange themselves into two basic types of structure. They can be personally ordered—in which case one entity succeeds another over the course of time, inheriting the collective knowledge and experience of its predecessors, and thus, in some cases, evolving into a conscious entity, or 'soul.' Or they can be ordered impersonally, as non-internally related contemporaries—a grouping that Whitehead referred to as a "corpuscular society"—in which case they form, at the macroscopic level, the enduring material objects of day-to-day human experience.[31]

Central to Vedāntic soteriology—as well as to the soteriologies of its cousin traditions, Jainism and Buddhism—are the concepts of *karma*, rebirth, and *mokṣa*, or liberation from the cycle of rebirth. *Karma* is the principle of action, according to which all actions lead to corresponding

---

30. Unlike more pluralistic Vedāntic ontologies, the logic of Śaṅkara's monism requires him to posit the idea of *Brahman* as material, as well as efficient, cause.

31. Whitehead, *Process and Reality*, 35.

effects. Analogous to Newton's Third Law of Motion—"For every action there is an equal and opposite reaction"—but extended to the spiritual and moral as well as the physical realms, *karma* can be likened, in process thought, to the idea of the essential relatedness of the present to the totality of the past. *Karma* is basically the conditioning of the present moment by the decisions of the past.

Like process thought, Hinduism teaches that we are all free in the present moment to choose how we will respond to our circumstances. But that freedom is also conditioned by those very circumstances, which are themselves an effect of all past choices: our own, as well as those of all other entities. *Mokṣa*, or liberation, the ultimate salvific goal of all the systems of Vedānta, can be seen as a state of maximal freedom with respect to the past. The strategies for attaining it vary from system to system, with Advaita emphasizing a state in which we do not identify with our temporal, ever-changing subjectivity, but with Brahman, or creativity, itself. The theistic systems, on the other hand, affirm a state of ongoing participation in the life of the divine—a loving union with God.

THE MUTUAL RELEVANCE OF PROCESS THOUGHT AND HINDUISM

Having briefly delineated the basic Vedāntic model of reality, and having brought it into conversation with process thought, we can now turn to the various ways in which process thought can benefit Hinduism, and Hinduism can also benefit process thought. To review these, the various ways in which process thought can benefit Hinduism are:

- To aid in the recovery of the Tantric concept of *māyā* as 'creative trans-formation,' to supplement its Advaitic sense as 'illusion,' which has been emphasized by academic scholarship.

- To aid in the articulation of the doctrine of the *jīva*, or soul, by means of the process affirmation of ontological monism with structural dualism.

- To aid in the articulation of the religious pluralism of the Ramakrishna tradition with the process concept of the three ultimate realities.

The ways in which Hinduism can benefit process thought, by shedding light on specific process concepts and concerns, are that:

- Hinduism sheds light on the process understanding of soul development by affirming that souls have, like God and the world, always existed.

- The Hindu emphasis on the fundamental unity of existence complements the emphasis of process thought on change and difference.

- Hinduism demonstrates that a non-omnipotent deity can be worshiped with intensity and devotion, contrary to the claims of proponents of classical Christian theology.

I shall now turn to each of these in succession.

RECOVERING MĀYĀ AS CREATIVE TRANSFORMATION

As the foregoing discussion shows, it is Śaṅkara who first introduces the distinction between *Nirguṇa* and *Saguṇa*—unmanifested and manifested—Brahman. While, like monistic philosophers in the West, Śaṅkara locates pre-eminence in the unmanifested aspect of the absolute—the reverse of Whitehead's valuation of the concrete aspect—the basic structure Śaṅkara establishes is not fundamentally different from that of process thought. Śaṅkara and Whitehead both see God not as identical to the unmanifest absolute, but as dependent upon it[32]—and so like the rest of the world, as being subject to time, change and relationality. *Saguṇa* Brahman encompasses God and the world, which the other systems of Vedānta affirm are organically related, as a soul is related to a body.[33]

It is also significant that *māyā*, which makes Brahman appear as the God-world complex,[34] can be translated as 'illusion,' but also as 'creativity'—an aspect of *māyā* given special emphasis in Goddess-based Śākta, or Tantric, Hinduism.

Process thought, very much like Tantric thought, accepts the basic structure of the relative and the absolute that Śaṅkara develops, but reverses the relative value that Śaṅkara places on these. According to Tantra, it is only *through* the relative that the absolute can be realized. A process thinker might say it is only as actualized—i.e., "in virtue of its accidents"[35]—that

32. Though again, for process thought, this dependence is mutual.

33. Rāmānuja introduces this particular image to the tradition to illustrate the God-world relation.

34. I have elsewhere dubbed the God-world complex the *theocosm*. Long, *Vision for Hinduism*, 84–85.

35. Whitehead, *Process and Reality*, 7.

creativity can be known. In Tantra, both the relative and the absolute, the many and the One, are affirmed:

> Like Advaita Vedānta, most schools of Tantra also maintain that the ultimate Reality is singular. However, they tend toward the view that the Many actually and not merely apparently evolve out of the One (while still being contained within the One as the eternal backdrop of cosmic existence). They reject any metaphysics of illusionism. This emanationism is technically known as *sat-kārya-vāda*, which denotes that the effect (*kārya*) is preexistent (sat) in the cause: the world could not come into existence if it did not already exist in potential form in the ultimate Being.[36]

Of course, if one simply correlates *māyā* with the process idea of creativity in its ultimate sense—which has already been correlated with Brahman—one loses an important distinction. Māyā, for Śaṅkara, is not simply equal to Brahman. It both is and is not Brahman, 'Neither real nor unreal.' It is the *appearance* of the reality that is Brahman, as perceived by non-enlightened beings.

In process thought, too, the concept of appearance plays an important role. As Cobb explains:

> If we give up the idea of substances, the distinction between appearance and reality remains, but it functions differently. Both appearance and reality are highly differentiated. Neither can be identified with creativity as such, i.e., not qualified by the primordial nature of God. The reality is what actual entities are in their own subjective immediacy. Appearance is the way they are apprehended in sense experience. In human experience, there is the visual appearance of the face of the other and the sound of the voice, on the one side, and there are the emotions, purposes, and ideas subjectively entertained on the other. Whitehead thinks that there is some continuity between the two, but a great deal of difference as well. He hopes that there is some connection between the way the green grass appears to me and how the cells in the grass themselves feel. But of course the difference is enormous. Again, the appearance, (māyā?) is very important, contributing greatly to the lives of all who can enjoy it, but it cannot be identified with reality.[37]

---

36. Feuerstein, *Tantra*, 66–67.

37. Cobb, personal communication.

It would seem then, that *māyā* might best be translated into process thought as the idea of *appearance*—on its reformed, process interpretation, as described by Cobb, rather than the substantialist interpretation with which this idea is associated in substantialist ways of thinking, both Indic and Western.

But of course one then risks losing the alternative meaning of *māyā* as a kind of creative power, which is central both to Tantra and to the theistic, non-Advaita systems of Vedānta, such as Viśiṣṭādvaita and Dvaita.

The process concept, I think, that best corresponds to *māyā*, in both of the senses that this term traditionally conveys, is neither creativity nor appearance, but *creative transformation*. Creative transformation, according to Cobb and Griffin, is the situation of pre-existing elements of reality within a new and wider context that endows these elements with a new meaning, purpose, and function:

> Creative transformation is the essence of growth, and growth is of the essence of life. Growth is not achieved by merely adding together elements in the given world in different combinations. It requires the transformation of those elements through the introduction of novelty. It alters their nature and meaning without suppressing or destroying them.[38]

Creative transformation, then, is a dynamic process, much like *māyā* in its Tantric sense. *Māyā* unfolds and actualizes the infinite possibilities of creativity in its static, non-actual sense. The relationship between *māyā* and Brahman is depicted iconographically in the Śākta tradition as the Goddess Kālī dancing on the inert form of her husband, Śiva. Śiva is pure consciousness, the envisioning of infinite possibilities. Śakti, as Kāliā, is *māyā*: the dynamic enactment of those possibilities, or creative transformation.

Māyā as creative transformation encompasses the notion of creativity, but also the idea of appearance. As Cobb says, on a process understanding, there is a difference between appearance and reality: namely, the difference between how we might perceive a given entity and the subjective immediacy of that entity as it experiences itself. There is the green grass that I see, and how the grass cells feel themselves. These are not unrelated, but they are clearly very different. However, my perception of the green grass is not *only* an appearance; for my experience of green itself becomes part of the *reality* of my concrete existence. It is an element of *my* subjective immediacy. It therefore becomes a novel element to be realized by any future

38. Cobb and Griffin, *Process Theology*, 100.

actual occasion, in the ongoing process of emergence and concrescence. As in the concept of *māyā*, appearance may be deceptive, but it is also intrinsic to the creative process, the process of creative transformation. Future entities are free to actualize it as they choose, for good or for ill.

This analysis of appearance reflects the Tantric understanding of *māyā* as well. The Śākta tradition distinguishes between two aspects of *māyā*: *vidyāmāyā* and *avidyā māyā*, or the *māyā* of wisdom and the *māyā* of ignorance, respectively. These are not really two different aspects of *māyā*, much less two different *māyās*. Rather, they refer to two different ways in which living beings encounter and engage with the one *māyā*. *Avidyā māyā* corresponds to *māyā* as conventionally translated in academic scholarship on Hinduism—as illusion, which keeps us from seeing the true character of reality, which is, in turn, essentially relational and organically unified. *Vidyā māyā*, however, the *māyā* of wisdom, connects us more closely with the meaning of the word *māyā* as 'creative power.' *Vidyā māyā* is when we perceive reality in such a way that it does not conceal, but rather reveals, its true nature: again, as essentially relational, organically unified, and creatively transformative. The same experience can lead one person to despair or destructive self-indulgence and another to greater insight, helping her to advance on the path to enlightenment; for *māyā* both conceals and reveals the true nature of reality. For the Śākta tradition, *māyā* is the great Goddess—Mahādevī—who is also called Śakti, which also means, significantly, creative power.

One potential contribution of process thought—a very important one, I think—to Hinduism is for it to make common cause with the Śākta tradition, and to contribute to the larger project of the re-valuation of the natural world that is important not only to human well-being and wholeness, but also to combating the major ecological crisis that the sense of nature as 'mere' matter, or as subservient to the arbitrary whims of a wholly transcendent God, has facilitated. As Nicholas F. Gier writes of Śākta theology, "The worship of the Goddess appears to require that we view matter, as did the ancients and Indians today, as dynamic, organic, interrelated, and alive."[39]

It is also significant, I think, that for Christian process theologians, the prime symbol of creative transformation is Christ.[40] But if the prime symbol for creative transformation in the Hindu traditions is the Goddess, this suggests an interesting set of possibilities in terms of interreligious

39. Gier, *Spiritual Titanism*, 136.
40. Cobb and Griffin, *Process Theology*, 98–101.

dialogue and the appropriation of the divine feminine in Christianity. The symbolisms of the crucifixion and of Mā Kālī have important resonances, and not only because both are, at first glance, bloody and terrifying—particularly for outsiders to their respective traditions. Both involve surrender of the ego and acceptance of the will of a higher power, a willingness to be a channel for that higher power for the creative transformation of reality. Jesus allows himself to be sacrificed so his followers may have a new life. The devotee of Mā Kālī sees the head of the decapitated demon that the Goddess is holding as his *own* head, the symbol of the ego, which he freely offers in order to be liberated. Kālī and Christ are both radical symbols of creative transformation, which, when contemplated in their full, shocking detail, invite their devotees to embrace the new and the unknown without fear.

ONTOLOGICAL MONISM WITH STRUCTURAL DUALISM

But though the Tantric understanding of *māyā* and the Vedāntic view of *prakṛti* give reason for seeing the material world as a sacred space—the field of divine activity and the arena in which the search for enlightenment occurs—there is also, as mentioned earlier, a strong dualism of soul, or *jīva*, and body (*śarīra* or *deha*) in the mainstream Hindu traditions. In the *Bhagavadgītā*, God, in the form of Kṛṣṇa, argues that his good friend, the warrior Arjuna, should not fear death—his own or those of others—because it is only the body that dies, while the soul continues on, not at all diminished by the destruction of its bodily vehicle:

> Just as the embodied one experiences childhood, and youth, and old age, in this body, in the same way he enters other bodies. A wise man is not disturbed by this. Just as a man discards worn-out clothes and gets others that are new, so the embodied one discards worn-out bodies and enters others that are new. For death is certain for anyone who has been born, just as birth is certain for anyone who has died. Since this condition cannot be avoided, you should not mourn.[41]

This dualism would appear at first glance, particularly to thinkers from a Western cultural background, to be at odds with a positive valuation of matter. However, as mentioned earlier, this dualism of soul and body, which forms the basis of the Hindu doctrine of rebirth, has not

41. *Bhagavadgītā* 2:13, 22, 27 (Thompson, trans., 9–11).

led to quite the same version of the 'mind-body' problem that has been a prominent part of philosophical discussion in the West on the nature of consciousness.

The basic problem with Cartesian dualism is the issue of how it is that two completely unlike entities—one purely spiritual and conscious, and the other purely material and unconscious—can be associated with one another in such a way as to give rise to our conscious, embodied experience as we know it. Also embedded in this discussion is an assumption that unconscious matter precedes conscious spirit, thus giving rise to the question of how a conscious entity can evolve or arise from one that is not conscious—i.e. from 'dead matter.'

Again, this problem has not arisen in this particular way in Hindu traditions because *prakṛti* has always been seen as a dynamic reality, rather than a 'dead' one. In fact, the Western conception of 'dead' matter correlates more closely to the Hindu idea of the *tamasic*, or inertial, manifestation of *prakṛti* than it does to *prakṛti* as a whole.

One of the most ancient Hindu accounts of the division of soul and body sees this division not in terms of a drastic binary split between a wholly spiritual entity and a wholly physical one, but one which views spirit as residing within a series of gradually more and more physical emanations or 'sheaths' (*kośas*). These sheaths or 'subtle bodies' exist in varying locations on a spectrum between what one could call purely physical and purely spiritual 'poles.'[42]

The implicit idea here seems to be one that process thought can tease out and make more explicit with its understanding of different orderings of actual entities: a deeper monism underlying the plurality of spirit and matter (and the various grades of subtle body between them). Particularly in the Advaita tradition, with its affirmation that *Brahman* is both material and efficient cause of actual existence, one can see that, beyond the duality of soul and body, there is an underlying unity. But what is the relationship between the underlying unity and the evident duality? An Advaita Vedāntin might say the duality is a mere appearance, an effect of *māyā*. But process thought can spell out this relationship more explicitly and in greater detail.

Process thought is basically monistic, in the sense that it affirms that there is but one type of metaphysical entity: the actual entity, which is a concrescence of possible qualities inherited either from the past or from

42. In Vedānta, the *kośas* are five sheaths made of food, breath, mind, consciousness, and bliss.

the coordinating mind of God, and of the experiences of lived actuality of those past entities that the actual entity incorporates. But it also affirms, as mentioned earlier, that actual entities can arrange themselves in distinct ways. They can be personally ordered—in which case one entity succeeds another over the course of time, inheriting the collective knowledge and the past experiences of its predecessors, thereby evolving into a conscious entity, or 'soul.' But they can also be ordered in an impersonal way, as non-internally related contemporaries, in which case they form, at a macroscopic level, the enduring material objects of day to day human experience.

David Ray Griffin aptly calls this view an ontological monism with a structural dualism. This view dispenses with the difficulties involved both in Cartesian dualism—with its problem of interaction between two completely disparate types of entity—and Western-style materialism, with its question of how a conscious entity can be derived from one that is not conscious. Instead, it affirms, at bottom, the existence of actual entities that have the character of units of experience, but arranged in such a way as to account for the duality of conscious and non-conscious beings that we encounter in our lived existence.[43]

This model can be very useful to Hindus in the encounter with contemporary Western thinking about mind-body issues. The *jīva* can be understood as a personally ordered society of actual entities whose interactions with other levels of reality can be accounted for by the fact that those other levels, or 'strata,' are also made up of the same type of fundamentally relational entities. Physical objects can similarly be seen as corpuscular societies. And the idea of *kośas*, sheaths, or 'subtle bodies' (*sukṣma śarīra*), with intermediate degrees of 'spirituality' or 'physicality' can be accounted for in the same way.

PROCESS THOUGHT AND HINDU RELIGIOUS PLURALISM

The third area in which process thought can be useful to Hinduism is in helping to articulate the idea—associated pre-eminently, though not exclusively, with the 'Neo' or modern Vedānta of Sri Ramakrishna and Swāmī Vivekānanda—of the harmony of religions. Also known as religious pluralism, this is the view that there are many true and effective

43. Griffin argues extensively for this model in *Parapsychology, Philosophy, and Spirituality*, 96–149.

paths to salvation—that there are many true religions, and that all of these can help one to reach *mokṣa*.

This is an idea that has received extensive criticism in the West, particularly in the forms it has taken in the work of Christian theologians and philosophers of religion such as John Hick, Wilfred Cantwell Smith, and Paul F. Knitter.

Process thinkers have weighed in on this issue a great deal—not as opponents to the essentially liberal and open-minded approach to religious difference that religious pluralism expresses, but as friendly critics, who see that expressions of pluralism often do not do justice to the rich diversity that actually obtains among the world's religious traditions.

Specifically, there is a tendency to conceive of many religions as leading to the same basic goal, which is quite often presented as a non-dualistic realization of an impersonal ultimate reality, much like the goal of Śaṅkara's Advaita Vedānta. Other types of religious fulfillment, such as a loving union with a personal deity—as in the theistic traditions of Hinduism, as well as the Abrahamic religions—or the cultivation and affirmation of harmony with and within the cosmos—as in nature-based traditions such as Shinto, Neo-Paganism, or the various indigenous traditions found globally—are then subordinated to this goal. David Ray Griffin has called this approach to religious pluralism "identist" because its advocates claim an identity of ultimate religious goals.[44]

Process thought, however, allows for the development of a non-reductive, or 'deep,' religious pluralism, in which the various ultimate goals of the different types of religious practice can co-exist in a coherent, systematic worldview, without being reduced to one another. The impersonal ultimate reality of traditions like Buddhism, Daoism, and Advaita Vedānta can be well correlated with the unmanifest principle of creativity in process thought. The personal deity of theistic religions can be correlated with the God of process thought. And the cosmos of inter-relating beings found in the nature religions can be correlated with the relational world of actual entities. Religious pluralism is thus shown to be perfectly consistent with a process worldview.

As we have seen, each of these three ultimate realities of process thought can also be correlated with fundamental structures of the basic Vedāntic model of reality. Unmanifest creativity is *Nirguṇa Brahman*. God is *Īśvara*, the coordinator of the world of finite beings. And the world of finite beings, the *jagat*, or flow of existence, is the world of actual entities.

44. Griffin, "Religious Pluralism," 3–38.

By mapping process thought onto the basic structure of reality affirmed in the Vedānta traditions, one draws attention to its various dimensions: the impersonal, the personal, and the cosmic. Vedāntic religious pluralism can thus be demonstrated quite easily to be a logical entailment of the larger structure of reality that Vedānta affirms. The various paths to *mokṣa*, to maximal freedom with respect to the collective effects of the past, or *karma*, can each be seen to orient themselves around different structures of existence. The differences among these paths can therefore be accommodated with less distortion than if all are seen simply as paths to the realization of *Brahman* without qualities, or to loving union with God. Though there are certainly differences between *Nirguṇa Brahman*, Buddhist *śūnyatā*, and the Eternal *Dao*, or between Viṣṇu and Allah and Yahweh, the idea that these differences may be more of an effect of varied cultural expressions is more plausible than if both personal and impersonal forms had to be correlated with the one impersonal ultimate reality, or alternatively, with one personal God.

And yet, the saving experiences associated with all of these realities can still be seen to be experiences of the realization of *Brahman*, because, as we have seen, the category of *Brahman* encompasses *both* the personal and the impersonal, *both Nirguṇa* and *Saguṇa*. The idea is to maintain both poles of this both/and affirmation, reducing neither to the other, nor giving one pre-eminent reality over the other.[45]

"THERE NEVER WAS A TIME WHEN I DID NOT EXIST, NOR YOU"

Turning now to ways in which Hinduism can be of benefit to process thought, the first of these is with regard to the topic, discussed earlier, of the relationship of soul and body. We have already seen that process thought elucidates the Hindu view of the distinction between soul and body with its idea of the different types of structure that are formed by actual entities.

45. As John Cobb has suggested, this can also be seen as a contribution of Hinduism to process thought. "Whereas Western traditions tend to oppose the three goals to one another, Hinduism shows how they can be complementary within a wider community. The process vision seems less abstract and idealistic when located in the Hindu context than when considered against the background of religion in the West" (personal communication). This is the gist of my argument for Hinduism as a model for global inter-religious relations in *A Vision for Hinduism*.

As Griffin argues, the Hindu doctrine of rebirth—or reincarnation—which I have mentioned earlier, but have not yet discussed in any depth, is wholly compatible with process thought.[46] For a Hindu process thinker, an important contribution of Hinduism to process thought regards the origin of souls—that, like God and the world, they simply have always existed—and that the reasons for their associating themselves with bodies, for rebirth, have to do with lessons they need to learn, with their search for that state of freedom from the conditioning of the past—from *karma*—that is their ultimate goal.

As Kṛṣṇa famously states in the *Bhagavadgītā*: "[I]n fact, there never was a time when I did not exist, nor you, nor any of these other lords. And there never will be a time when we do not exist."[47]

Process thought is compatible with a wide array of views about the afterlife. The traditional Abrahamic idea of a heaven or hell, as well as the view that there is no conscious survival after the death of the body, can both be accommodated on a process understanding. In his process exploration of parapsychology, Griffin suggests that a variety of scenarios may actually be playing out in the world: that some souls have been reincarnated, while others may be consciously existing in a state of immortality, and that others have passed out of conscious existence completely at the time of death.

To be sure, Griffin's assessment is based on available (and quite controversial) evidence from the field of parapsychology, and not on the claims of a single religious tradition. But the highly detailed and elaborated views of the Indic traditions provide, I think, a good deal of food for thought for process philosophers and theologians with regard to the nature and purpose of conscious existence. If all the souls in the universe have, in fact, always existed, and will always exist, then the idea of souls as co-creators and co-participants in the life of the divine gains a certain degree of purchase.

In the Jain tradition, it is held that souls begin as barely conscious beings called *nigodas*, which are similar in some respects to actual entities at their most basic—centers of experience, but not necessarily with conscious awareness as we would recognize it. But at a certain point they begin to aspire instinctively to a higher order of experience. They therefore begin to associate with bodies, at first of a very simple kind, and then with gradually greater and greater levels of complexity, which thus enable

46. Griffin, *Parapsychology, Philosophy, and Spirituality*, 184–208.
47. *Bhagavadgītā* 2:12.

them to maximize the intensity of experience of which they are capable. When they reach a point at which they are able to conceptualize the nature of existence and can begin to understand the true nature of reality, they develop the aspiration for *mokṣa*, or spiritual liberation—which, as maximal freedom, has all along been the impetus for the evolution they have undergone. Many contemporary Hindu thinkers correlate the process of biological evolution with this process of soul evolution, seeing the two as interrelated dimensions of a larger universal process of God-realization: of reality transforming itself in a creative way in order to realize its own true nature.

This is a conversation to which process thought can contribute and from which it can also learn, particularly with its concept of creativity as the fundamental character of being. The idea of a universal process of spiritual evolution, involving an ongoing engagement of souls with the material world as the field of soul development, fits very well with the Whiteheadian idea of the cosmos as a process of ongoing intensification of and sharing of experience among actual entities and between actual entities and the divine.

The important caveat, of course, needs to be added that the soul, conceived as identical over time, even within a single lifetime, is an abstraction in process thought. Much as in Buddhism, the sense of personal identity arises, according to process thought, on the basis of the shared inheritances of actual entities in a series. But it is the actual entities, and not the series that they form, that are the concrete realities. Hindu *jīva*, or soul, language can be retained on a process understanding, just as personal identity language can be retained on a Buddhist understanding, only on the condition that such an entity is not seen as metaphysically ultimate, but as provisional and abstract. Here, again, Śaṅkara, typically seen as the Vedāntic thinker in the greatest tension with process thought, can be of help; for in Advaita Vedānta, as in Buddhism, the sense of personal identity is seen as not reflecting the ultimate nature of reality, and as something to be overcome in the quest for *mokṣa*. Process thought can be of assistance in this regard, just as process thought can be enriched by the specificity and concreteness that Hinduism lends to its idea that actual entities have always had an experiential character.

THE FUNDAMENTAL UNITY OF EXISTENCE

As mentioned earlier, the chief distinction between process thought and absolute idealism is the value that process thought places on the realm of actuality—of change and difference—as opposed to the unmanifested aspect of the absolute. To cite Whitehead once again, "One side makes process ultimate; the other side makes fact ultimate."[48]

The Vedāntic systems, however—with the exception of Dvaita—have tended to give emphasis to *Brahman* as the underlying unity of existence. Advaita does this, one could say, to the extreme. But the intermediate systems, such as Rāmānuja's, also give emphasis to this idea of a unity underlying plurality, and connecting diverse entities as elements in a pluralistic, yet ultimately singular, system.

This idea of an underlying unity is, I think, one that could have value for the process tradition. For though Whitehead does ascribe ultimate value to process, to the relative world of change, he also values the idea of unity, without which his system provides "absolutely no reason why the universe should not be steadily relapsing into lawless chaos."[49] It is of course for this reason that his system must include a supreme actuality—God—to ensure an underlying unity to existence: to ensure that the multitude of actual entities are coordinated in such a way as to constitute a universe. Whitehead does not name this unity which God, like Viṣṇu, preserves, though he does speak of the necessity of what he calls "Law" or "a certain smoothness in the nature of things," apart from which "there can be no knowledge, no useful method, no intelligent purpose."[50]

This notion of Law correlates well with the Hindu idea of *dharma*, mentioned earlier, which is definitive of correct moral behavior, but which also includes such ideas as cosmic order and the laws of nature. The existence of God ensures the basic stability of existence—the fact that things proceed in an orderly fashion, according to *dharma*.[51]

But what ensures the existence of God? A process thinker might reply that God, as conceived in process thought, is a logical necessity of the metaphysical system. But what is logical necessity but the interrelationship of ideas in a coherent, *unitary* system of thought? Logic, one could

48. Whitehead, *Process and Reality*, 7.

49. Ibid., *Adventures of Ideas*, 115.

50. Ibid., 109.

51. This is the main function of God as personified by Viṣṇu, the preserver of the cosmic order from the forces of chaos, or *adharma*, themselves personified as various demonic beings that Viṣṇu must combat.

say, is a manifestation of unity, in the sense of an underlying, necessary interconnectedness of things. Unity *precedes* logic, being, as Whitehead says, ontologically 'primordial.'[52]

Brahman, one could then say, is not *logical*, but is logic itself: the transcendental condition for any system of thought or of any reality whatsoever. Brahman is Law. Brahman is *dharma*. Brahman is universal order: the meta-foundation of the system of reality described in process thought. It is what Whitehead calls the primordial nature of God.

NO OMNIPOTENT DEITY: NO PROBLEM!

The God of Dvaita Vedānta, and of Hindu theism in general, is omniscient in the sense of knowing all actuality and all possibility, and is also supremely benevolent, being the pre-eminent locus of all good qualities (*guṇāśraya*).

But, while being supremely powerful, God is *not* understood in Dvaita Vedānta as being omnipotent in the sense to which process thinkers typically object. Mādhva is at one with process thought in affirming that God co-exists in the world with numerous other free beings—the *jīvas*, or living souls. Just as in process thought, the freedom of non-divine actual entities is not an illusion, or a gift that has been shared with them by an inherently omnipotent being, with which all the power ultimately resides. Actual entities simply *are* free. Because of its affirmation of divine non-omnipotence, Dvaita scholar Deepak Sarma describes this system as a 'mitigated monotheism.'[53]

It is also the case that God is generally known in Hindu texts and ritual systems through specific personifications, or 'deities'—the gods and goddesses of Hinduism—who are not typically presented as omnipotent. As Bimal Krishna Matilal explains:

> According to received doctrine, God is supposed to be omnipotent and he should also see that justice is done in the end. But Kṛṣṇa in the *Mahābhārata* did not always claim to be omnipotent. Apart from certain inspired speeches (e.g. in the *Gītā*) he acknowledges his human limitations. He admitted before the hermit Utaṅka how powerless he was to stop the devastating war, and restore friendship between the two warring families.

---

52. Cobb, personal communication.
53. Sarma, *Introduction to Mādhva Vedānta*, 70–71.

For as he said, the war was inevitable, and he had no power to stop the inevitable.

Kṛṣṇa's own admission that he did not have any power to stop the battle or devastation either of the Kauravas or of the Yādavas (his own race) is an important evidence to show that the Hindu conception of God does not always include the attribute of omnipotence. I believe this constitutes an important difference between the Judaeo-Christian theology and Hindu theology. Words such as *Īśvara* or *Bhagavān* are often used to denote what is called "God" in the Western tradition, but these words do have a number of meanings in the Indian tradition. God in Hindu theology is not always a creator God—that is, he is not a Creator *ex nihilo*. Nor is the Hindu God always a personal being. In the case of Kṛṣṇa or Rāma, he is of course conceived as a personal being, in fact a human being with all possible human virtues and vices. Of course, it has been claimed that Kṛṣṇa (or Rāma) was mightier than anybody else, had intelligence superior to that of anybody else, but this is hardly equivalent to the claim of omnipotence or even omniscience.[54]

The greatest single obstacle to the widespread acceptance of process thought in the West has been precisely the idea of God as non-omnipotent, an idea that many believe renders God unworthy of worship. Yet this conception of God does not prevent Hindus from experiencing intense theistic devotion.

As William James famously writes, it only takes one white crow to prove that not all crows are black. The fact that Hindus display intense devotion to forms of the divine that are, though supremely powerful, not omnipotent, proves that the problematic concept of an omnipotent deity that process thought rejects is not necessary to devotional practice. This, I think, is an important contribution of Hinduism to process thought in making its case for its understanding of God as one that can, indeed, have religious relevance.

CONCLUSION

I hope I have shown here that process thought and Hinduism have a number of affinities that can facilitate an easy exchange that can enrich and benefit both systems of thought. The basic Vedāntic model of reality is, in its essentials identical to the idea of process thought that reality is a

54. Ganeri, *Philosophy, Culture, and Religion*, 99–100.

manifestation of a principle of creativity. Within this manifestation, there is a divine, supremely powerful but not omnipotent, reality coordinating the experiences of the actual entities that constitute the rest of existence. The actual entities, in turn, constitute two basic types of structure, each of which answers, broadly, to the accounts given in Hindu traditions of the soul, or *jīva*, and matter, or *prakṛti*. Distinctively Hindu concepts such as *karma*, rebirth, and liberation, can also be seen to be coherent with and interpretable in terms of the philosophy of process.

Process thought can benefit Hinduism by helping in the recovery of the concept of *māyā* as creative power, or creative transformation, rather than as a wholly negative concept of illusion. The interpretation of *māyā* as 'illusion', both among Vedānta traditions and in outsider scholarship on Hinduism, has led to a depiction of Hinduism as 'otherworldly' and unconcerned with such issues as social justice and the degradation of the physical environment. The recovery of creative transformation as a central Hindu concept can, in turn, facilitate a re-valuation of the natural world as a field of divine activity, rather than as 'mere' matter—the view that has facilitated the ecological disaster that humanity now faces, and that threatens India, in particular with many dire consequences, like the melting of the Himalayan glaciers that feed sacred rivers such as the Gaṅgā, and the immersion of other sacred sites, such as the Jagannāth temple in Pūri, under rising sea water. It can also facilitate a re-valuation of Tantra, a tradition that has been marginalized in Hindutva, or Hindu nationalist, constructions of Hinduism.

Process thought can also help Hindu thinkers engage the mind-body issue with greater clarity and detail, with its account of soul and matter as differing structures of actual entities of the same, fundamental ontological type. This, too, ties in with the re-valuation of the material world of *prakṛti*, which is often identified with *māyā* in Hindu thought.

Finally, process thought can help with the articulation of a deep Hindu religious pluralism that can address the pressing issues of interreligious conflict and violence.

Hinduism can, in turn, enrich process thought, with its understanding of souls as having always existed, thus obviating the need for an account of the emergence of consciousness, and presenting a rich and complex model of reality that takes process ideas of the cosmos as an ongoing creative process to another level of detail, a cosmic narrative that intertwines both spiritual and biological evolution as different facets of the same essential dynamic movement toward greater and greater freedom.

The Hindu emphasis on the fundamental unity of existence also addresses a trend in process thought to emphasize process and change over ultimate fact. Both of these philosophical tendencies—to emphasize either the one or the many, the absolute or the relative—should complement and balance one another, rather than either being taken to an extreme. It is not that I perceive any particular process thinker as having gone to such an extreme. But it seems that, for a Hindu process thinker, an emphasis on process *and* reality will always be central.

Finally, the fact that Hindus have long conceived of the divine as non-omnipotent, while simultaneously cultivating intense theistic devotion, expressed through temples, music, dance, poetry, and a wide variety of other classical and folk arts, assists process thinkers in the Abrahamic traditions to advance their case that the concept of God is not diminished by a process understanding. Far from being unworthy of worship, such a God has inspired a whole civilization for millennia.

Clearly, I have only begun to scratch the surface of the potential interactions of process thought and Hinduism in this essay. Further development of Hindu process theologies will no doubt reveal even more points of contact, as well as potential areas of creative tension, between process thought and the rich, vast, and complex family of traditions that go by the name of *Hinduism*.

SELECT BIBLIOGRAPHY

Process Thought

Cobb, John B. Jr., and David Ray Griffin. *Process Theology: An Introductory Exposition.* Philadelphia: Westminster, 1976.
Griffin, David Ray, editor. *Deep Religious Pluralism.* Louisville: Westminster John Knox, 2005.
———. *Parapsychology, Philosophy, and Spirituality: A Postmodern Exploration.* SUNY Series in Constructive Postmodern Thought. Albany: SUNY Press, 1997.
———. *Reenchantment without Supernaturalism: A Process Philosophy of Religion.* Cornell Studies in the Philosophy of Religion. Ithaca, NY: Cornell University Press, 2001.
McDaniel, Jay and Donna Bowman, editors. *Handbook of Process Theology.* St. Louis: Chalice, 2006.
Price, Lucien. *Dialogues with Alfred North Whitehead as Recorded by Lucien Price.* Boston: Godine, 2001.
Whitehead, Alfred North. *Adventures of Ideas.* New York: Free Press, 1967. (First published in 1933.)

———. *Process and Reality: An Essay in Cosmology*, Corrected Edition. Edited by David Ray Griffin and Donald W. Sherburne. New York: Free Press, 1978.

Hinduism

Bhagavadgītā. Translated by George Thompson. New York: North Point, 2008.
Doniger, Wendy. *The Hindus: An Alternative History*. New York: Penguin, 2009.
Feuerstein, Georg. *Tantra: The Path of Ecstasy*. Boston: Shambhala, 1998.
Ganeri, Jonardon, editor. *Philosophy, Culture, and Religion: The Collected Essays of Bimal Krishna Matilal*. New York: Oxford University Press, 2002.
Halbfass, Wilhelm. *India and Europe: An Essay in Understanding*. Albany: SUNY Press, 1988.
Inden, Ronald. *Imagining India*. Cambridge, MA: Blackwell, 1994.
King, Richard. *Early Advaita and Buddhism: The Mahāyāna Context of the Gauḍapādīya-kārikā*. Albany: State University of New York Press, 1995.
Llewellyn, J. E., editor. *Defining Hinduism: A Reader*. New York: Routledge, 2005.
Rambachan, Anantanand. *The Advaita Worldview: God, World, and Humanity*. SUNY Series in Religious Studies. Albany, NY: SUNY Press, 2006.
Said, Edward. *Orientalism*. New York:Vintage, 1979.
Sarma, Deepak. *An Introduction to Mādhva Vedānta*. Ashgate World Philosophies Series. Aldershot, UK: Ashgate, 2003.
Sontheimer, Gunther-Dietz, and Hermann Kulke, editors. *Hinduism Reconsidered*. New Delhi: Manohar, 2001.
Sugirtharajah, Sharada. *Imagining Hinduism: A Postcolonial Perspective*. London: Taylor & Francis, 2007.
Tapasyānanda, Swāmī. *Bhakti Schools of Vedānta*. Mylapore, Madras: Sri Ramakrishna Math, 1990.
Vivekānanda, Swāmī. *Complete Works*. Kolkata: Advaita Ashrama, 1989.

Process Thought and Hinduism

Gier, Nicholas F. *Spiritual Titanism: Indian, Chinese, and Western Perspectives*. SUNY Series in Constructive Postmodern Thought. Albany: SUNY Press, 2000.
Langbauer, Delmar. "Sanatana Dharma and Modern Philosophy: A Study of Indian and Whiteheadian Thought." PhD diss., Claremont Graduate School, 1970.
Long, Jeffery D. "Anekanta Vedanta: Toward a Deep Hindu Religious Pluralism." In *Deep Religious Pluralism*, edited by David Ray Griffin, 130–57. Louisville: Westminster John Knox, 2005.
———. "Can a Hindu Pan-Inclusivism Also Be a Deep Hindu Pluralism? A Response to Matthew Lopresti." *Process Studies* 36/1 (2007) 121–30.
———. "Plurality and Relativity: Whitehead, Jainism, and the Reconstruction of Religious Pluralism." PhD diss., University of Chicago, 2000.
———. "Truth, Diversity, and the Incomplete Project of Modern Hinduism." In *Hermeneutics and Hindu Thought: Toward a Fusion of Horizons*, edited by Rita Sherma and Arvind Sharma, 179–210. New York: Springer, 2008.
———. *A Vision for Hinduism: Beyond Hindu Nationalism*. London: Tauris, 2007.

————. "A Whiteheadian Vedanta: Outline of a Hindu Process Theology." In *Handbook of Process Theology*, edited by Jay McDaniel and Donna Bowman, 262–73. St. Louis: Chalice, 2006.

Lopresti, Matthew S. "Sanatana Dharma as a Whiteheadian Religious Pluralism?" *Process Studies* 36/1 (2007) 108–20.

Simmons, Ernest Lee Jr. "Process Pluralism and Integral Nondualism: A Comparative Study of the Nature of the Divine in the Thought of Alfred North Whitehead and Sri Aurobindo Ghose." PhD diss., Claremont Graduate School, 1981.

6

A Buddhist Perspective
Contributions to Ecological Ethics

—Christopher Ives

EDITOR'S INTRODUCTION

Fundamental to Whitehead's philosophy is the replacement of substance by process, of enduring objects by societies of indivisible occurrences that he calls actual occasions. The result brings his philosophy very close to Buddhism. The latter rejected the notion of sva bhava, which is much like the Western notion of substance. This led to its denial of both Brahman, the ultimate reality underlying everything, and Atman, the underlying self. In relation to most forms of Abrahamic thinking and much of Hindu thinking as well, Whitehead poses the challenge to free themselves from substance categories. In Buddhism Whiteheadians see what a tradition is like that has been purifying itself from substance thinking for two and half millennia. Buddhism provides a particularly rich opportunity for Whiteheadians to learn some of the spiritual implications of the conceptuality they have derived from a different source.

What, nevertheless, may Buddhists learn from this new form of process thought? Ives proposes how Buddhists may improve their work in ecological ethics by interacting with what Whiteheadians have written in this field.

Obviously, Buddhism received its basic shape when ecological questions and issues were marginal at best. As they have become central, Buddhists have moved into this field with rich resources. Yet, just as in Western traditions, answers to the older questions sometimes create problems for dealing adequately with new ones. Ives shows that some of the work of Whiteheadian thinkers can either be appropriated or modified so as to assist Buddhists in this important part of their new reflections.

I N RECENT YEARS BUDDHIST thinkers have turned their attention to environmental problems, drawing on, and in some cases reinterpreting, traditional doctrines and practices. They have deployed constructs from Buddhist metaphysics, epistemology, psychology, and soteriology. Especially helpful as a resource for constructing a Buddhist environmental ethic is the soteriological scheme of the Four Ennobling Truths,[1] especially when it is reinterpreted in social, political, and economic terms.[2] In particular, the psychological analysis of the "three poisons"—ignorance, greed, and ill-will—and other "unwholesome" mental states that cause suffering offers a basis for critiques of worldviews and patterns of behavior that are ecologically destructive.[3] And in terms of the path out of our morass, Buddhism provides sophisticated frameworks for ways of living that are actually richer—spiritually, morally, socially, aesthetically—than consumerist lifestyles and more supportive of the full flourishing of other sentient beings, ecosystems, and the biosphere as a whole. By mining these resources, Buddhist thinkers have made their most distinctive contributions to broader discussions of our ecological crisis.[4]

In their writings they have also engaged many of the central topics of environmental ethics, such as instrumental and intrinsic value, anthropocentrism, animal rights, and holism. Their arguments, however, have foundered at times, especially concerning interdependence, responsibility, identification with nature, intrinsic value, equality, animal rights, and the sacredness of nature.[5] The problems in their writings are not primarily the

1. Suffering, its cause, the cessation of suffering, and the path to that cessation.

2. See Ives, "Deploying the Dharma," 23–44.

3. See ibid., "Buddhism and Sustainability," 38–50.

4. See, for example, the essays in Kaza, *Hooked!*; Badiner, *Mindfulness*; Kaza and Kraft, *Dharma Rain*; Tucker et al., *Buddhism and Ecology*; and Badiner, *Dharma Gaia*.

5. See Ives, "In Search of a Green Dharma," 165–86.

result of sloppy argumentation, for in key respects they reflect limitations in Buddhism relative to environmental ethics.

Given its congruence with Buddhism on many key points, Whitehead's philosophy offers resources for addressing these limitations. Buddhist thinkers can benefit from a close look at how John B. Cobb, Jr., David Ray Griffin, Jay McDaniel, Catherine Keller, and other process thinkers have addressed issues in environmental ethics. In this essay I consider how Buddhist environmental ethicists can, without violating their tradition's central insights and principles, appropriate facets of Whiteheadian ecological ethics.

Like process thinkers and deep ecologists, contemporary Buddhist ethicists generally reject the dualism between mind and matter, humans and nature, and extend intrinsic value to non-human animals in an attempt to grant them moral standing ("considerability"), at least as moral patients if not as moral agents. In this way they have joined other environmentalists in rejecting the "speciesism" that privileges humans. With its doctrines of no-soul and emptiness, however, Buddhism[6] seems hard-pressed to come up with a basis for ascribing intrinsic value. Steven Rockefeller notes that "the concept of intrinsic value suggests the existence of some fixed essence or permanent self in things, which is contrary to the Buddhist doctrines of dependent co-arising, impermanence, emptiness, and no-self."[7] Nevertheless, Buddhism does offer possible bases for intrinsic value. Rockefeller also remarks, "It is true that some Western philosophers and theologians may try to explain the idea of intrinsic value with reference to the existence of a soul, an eternal self, or some sort of permanent essential nature, but this is not the only way to explain that other beings are subjects worthy of respect and are not mere objects or means to be used and exploited. Could the intrinsic value of all beings be explained, for example, with reference to Buddha-nature?"[8] Unfortunately, however, Buddhists historically have not agreed on either the connotation or the denotation of "buddha-nature." Some see it as a potential to become awakened, while others see it as an awakening that already exists within us. And as Lambert Schmithausen has highlighted, Indian Buddhists restrict it to sentient animals while in East Asia some Buddhists extend it to plants or even to rocks and mountains.[9]

---

6. For the sake of the argument, I am speaking of Buddhism monolithically here, even though the tradition is internally diverse.

7. Rockefeller, "Buddhism," 320.

8. Ibid.

9. Schmithausen, *Buddhism and Nature*, 22–24.

Insofar as Buddhism focuses on the suffering of sentient beings, another option is to follow the lead of ethicists like Peter Singer and argue for sentience as a basis of intrinsic value. In Buddhism, as indicated by *ujô*, "having feeling," one of the two Japanese terms that are rendered in English as "sentient being," sentience consists primarily of the capacity to feel suffering, understood in canonical sources as the suffering of physical pain, suffering due to mental dispositions, and suffering experienced when things change.[10] More broadly, as delineated in the *Samyutta Nikâya*, sentience encompasses "feeling, perception, volition, contact, attention."[11] It spans rudimentary sensation and physical pain at the lower end of the spectrum[12] all the way up to the high-level consciousness and existential anguish of humans. Although Buddhism does not elaborate in detail on the variations of sentience along this spectrum, at the very least the tradition plots different types of sentient beings across six levels of rebirth.[13] Given the core Buddhist focus on the anguish and liberation of sentient beings, we can safely argue that Buddhism ascribes value to them. But is it *intrinsic* value, which may connote buddhistically suspect notions of separate, enduring individuals who possess this value and, by extension, rights? Or are most sentient beings valued simply as objects of "compassionate regard"?

Process thought can help Buddhists think through the exact nature of sentience and its connection to intrinsic value. In Whitehead's system, all actual entities, through prehension, feel the "Many" impinging on them. That "Many" consists of the data available as the physical pole and the eternal objects presented by God in the initial aim. In concrescence, actual entities engage in "decision"[14] relative to this Many, and through creative self-determination attain satisfaction and enjoyment, especially of beauty

---

10. The historical Buddha reportedly said, "There are, friend, these three kinds of suffering: the suffering due to pain, the suffering due to formations, and the suffering due to change" (Bodhi, trans., *Connected Discourses*). John Makransky terms these three types of *duhkha* "obvious suffering," "the suffering of ego-conditioning," and "the suffering of transience" (*Awakening through Love*, 161–63).

11 Bodhi, trans., *Connected Discourses*, 535. This interpretation of these facets of "name" (*nama*) as sentience is given by Peter Harvey, *Buddhist Ethics*, 311.

12 Buddhism does not spell out exactly how far down sentience extends. To amoebas? Only to organisms with nerves?

13 In Japanese, *rokudô*: denizens of hell, hungry beasts, animals, human beings, warrior titans (*ashura*), and gods (*deva*).

14. Concrescence entails de-cision insofar as some possibilities offered by the physical pole, or by God in the form of the initial aim, are ignored.

(defined as "harmony and intensity of subjective feeling").[15] The feeling, deciding, satisfaction, and enjoyment are the core elements in the "experience" of the actual entity. And as Leslie Muray points out, "experience is the locus of value."[16] In this way, Whitehead offers a basis for intrinsic value "all the way down" the spectrum of things—or, more exactly, actual entities with their "experience," whether conscious or subconscious—that are found in nature.[17] Hence, in response to the anthropocentric attribution of intrinsic value only to humans, John Cobb can argue that "if intrinsic value lies simply in the enjoyment of being, as Whitehead believed, then there is no reason to restrict value so narrowly. On the contrary, there is every reason to assume that living things in general enjoy living and want to continue living."[18]

Similarly, Buddhist sentience is not limited to high-level human consciousness. At the very least, sentience (if not buddha-nature) exists in virtually all animals, though it may not extend to the "feeling" and "experience" that Whitehead ascribes to actual occasions all the way down to subatomic particles. But does the feeling of suffering exhaust the scope of sentience for Buddhists?

Here, too, Buddhists can draw from process thought. For Whiteheadians, as we just saw, intrinsic value derives from experience, with its feeling, creativity, satisfaction, enjoyment, and beauty. A close examination of Buddhist texts reveals that Buddhism, too, values certain positive facets of human experience. Theravâda Buddhists lift up nirvana as the ultimate "good," while also valuing such proximate goods as "wholesome" mental states, especially generosity, the antidote to the "poison" of greed; the four "divine abodes" of loving-kindness, compassion, sympathetic joy, and equanimity; and the seven factors of enlightenment.[19] The Mahâyâna tradition places special value on the six perfections[20] and, ultimately, perfection itself, or full buddhahood. Of course, Buddhist thinkers presumably would not, as mentioned above, incorporate Whitehead's notion of feeling enjoyment "all the way down," nor would they accept the primor-

15. McDaniel, "A Process Approach to Ecology," 233.

16. Muray, "Politics in Process Perspective," 220.

17. For expediency's sake, I am bracketing the debate about the exact definition and boundaries of "nature."

18. Cobb, "Thinking with Whitehead about Nature," 187.

19. Mindfulness, investigation of the Dharma, vigor, joyousness, serenity, concentration, and equanimity.

20. Generosity, moral discipline, patience, exertion, meditative absorption, and wisdom.

dial nature of God, or God's providing the initial aim and trying to persuade actual occasions to integrate the eternal objects offered in that aim.

Expanded beyond the experience of suffering to encompass such "goods" as wholesome mental states, perfections, nirvanic awareness, and full buddhahood, sentience can be designated as a Buddhist basis for attributing moral standing if not intrinsic value. As seen in critiques of Peter Singer's utilitarian standpoint, however, several issues emerge when we take sentience as the basis for intrinsic value.[21] The first is the question of painless slaughtering. Although valuation of sentient beings might appear to prescribe vegetarianism if not veganism, what about methods of slaughtering animals that are quick and painless, that cause no fear or physical pain? Second, does a moral focus on sentience not incline us to a condemnation of predation in the wild and imply that we have a duty to stop grizzlies from eating salmon as they come upstream in Alaska, or to keep wolves from hunting elk in Yellowstone?[22] Third, if we set up sentience as the cornerstone of a Buddhist environmental ethic, we confront the possibility of our ethical concern (our "ecological moral regard," if you will) getting directed more at a turkey in pain on a factory farm than at the last few members of an endangered species of wild turkey, which may be living painlessly yet facing extinction. And fourth, what does one do when protecting individual animals (such as locusts or deer) from pain undermines the protection of ecosystems, as is the case when the protected individuals grow in number to the point where they threaten the health of the system?

Even when we set up sentience as a properly Buddhist basis for ascribing intrinsic value to things, we still have to address another issue in environmental ethics: the *relative* intrinsic value of things. Like deep ecologists, most contemporary Buddhist ethicists reject anthropocentric hierarchy and argue for the commonality or identity of things, but they usually do not explore exactly how we might make moral distinctions between different types of sentient beings. Here, too, Buddhism can appropriate insights from process thought. John Cobb treats the issue of relative value in a comparison of the process perspective with that of deep ecology. Like other Whiteheadians, he argues that although experience and enjoyment extend "all the way down," there are degrees of experience and hence value. "All creatures have intrinsic value, but some have greater intrinsic

21. See Singer, "All Animals are Equal," 155; cited by Cobb, "Thinking with Whitehead about Nature," 178.

22. Buddhists can learn from McDaniel's discussion of predation in his essay, "A Process Approach to Ecology," 247–48.

value than others. That is to say, the inner life of some creatures is more complex, deeper, and richer than that of others."[23] Compared with single cells or fleas, humans have a complexity and richness of experience, and "[a]n experience that includes more of the world is of greater value than one that includes less."[24]

Buddhism offers its own basis for sorting intrinsic value. Although all sentient beings experience one or more of the three main types of suffering mentioned above, humans experience all three and, moreover, are aware that they do so, thus compounding the degree of anguish they can feel. This characteristic is one reason humans are positioned higher up on the six levels of samsaric rebirth than animals. And even though we are positioned below the realm of gods (and in most versions of the six levels we are below the realm of warrior titans as well), it is through rebirth as a human that sentient beings can practice Buddhism and attain release from the cycle of rebirth. "In the lower realms," according to Peter Harvey, "there is much suffering and little freedom of action. In the heavenly realms, life is blissful in comparison with human life, but this tends to make the gods complacent, particularly those in the highest heavens, so they may also think that they are eternal, without need of liberation. The human realm is a middle realm, in which there is enough suffering to motivate humans to seek to transcend it by spiritual development, and enough freedom to be able to act on this aspiration. It is thus the most favorable realm for spiritual development."[25] Traditional Buddhists hence celebrate the good fortune of being born as a human, an event as rare in the cosmos as a sea turtle randomly poking its head up above the surface in the center of the one floating ring, several feet in diameter, that has been drifting around the seas of the world. Further, as sketched above, human sentience can take increasingly valued forms as people cultivate virtuous mental states, perfections, nirvana, or buddhahood. And the greater value of those states is reflected in Buddhist claims that it is karmically more detrimental to harm bodhisattvas and buddhas than other beings. (Presumably, their role in liberating others also contributes to their higher value in the Buddhist scheme of things.)

In short, just as Whitehead argues that the complex experience of humans accords us greater intrinsic value, Buddhism can argue that humans have complex types of sentience—in terms of both the experience

23. Cobb, "Protestant Theology and Deep Ecology," 224.

24. Ibid., 225.

25. Harvey, *Introduction to Buddhist Ethics*, 30.

of suffering and the mental states or perfections that are crucial on the path to liberation—that are not seen in dolphins, dogs, or frogs, and hence humans have more intrinsic value. This distinction provides a basis for weighing courses of action, for engaging in what I have termed elsewhere a "calculus of suffering."[26] Of course, critics might respond that a new anthropocentrism or "speciesism" has crept back in to this analysis, or at least another privileging of humans, insofar as it is a human ethicist here who is sorting this value along a spectrum and is doing so in a way that grants humans the most intrinsic value. John Cobb has responded to this criticism: "More positive value is lost and more suffering is inflicted in killing a whale than in destroying some plankton. Of course, this is a human judgment, but that does not make it anthropocentric in the way we should avoid."[27]

Deep ecologists might also argue that insofar as I am arguing for the intrinsic value of individual beings with sentience, I am succumbing to a type of individualism, albeit with a broader array of individuals worthy of moral regard than in narrowly anthropocentric approaches. For an environmental ethic, those critics would claim, the focus also—or *primarily*—needs to be on the value (or disvalue) of individuals for the whole of which they are part, whether their species, local biotic community, or bioregion. They might even claim that we should focus not so much on the value of individuals for those larger wholes, but on the value of the wholes themselves.

Simon James addresses this issue in a recent book on Buddhist environmental ethics, where he comments that the intrinsic value sought in environmentalism is not something an entity possesses in a non-relational sense as "the value a thing has independently of its relations to anything else."[28] Rather, James notes that environmentalists construe the value of an individual as "relational, that is, a function of the habitat in which the organism lives,"[29] with the entity having value because of the ways in which it contributes to "the good of the various environmental wholes of which it is part."[30]

26. Ives, *Zen Awakening*, 138.
27. Cobb, "Protestant Theology and Deep Ecology," 224.
28. James, *Zen Buddhism*, 86.
29. Ibid., 87.
30. Ibid.

Although James makes an important point here about one type of relational value, it seems a bit of a stretch to term it "intrinsic value."[31] In this regard as well, process thinkers can prove helpful. David Griffin has sorted the various types of value by clarifying the distinction between intrinsic and extrinsic value. The latter, "any kind of value something has for something else,"[32] includes instrumental value in the narrow sense but also ecological value, "value for sustaining the cycle of life," as well as other values, such as companion value, aesthetic value, medicinal value, scientific value, monetary value, and symbolic (moral and religious) value.[33] Griffin thus provides a typology with which Buddhist ethicists can organize their assessment of value.

Buddhist thinkers can draw from and then build on this typology to arrange the different types of value along a spectrum. At one end is narrowly instrumental value, evident when things are used for human ends and in the process are transformed, consumed, and/or destroyed, as when a vein of coal is mined, a tree is turned into two-by-fours, or a bison is shot and eaten. Technically, instrumental value is also being tapped when non-human entities engage in similar activities, such as when a wolf kills an elk, a caterpillar eats a leaf, or a fungus consumes the bark of an oak tree. (Insofar as they sustain food chains and ecological balance, the elk, leaf, and bark possess ecological value as well.) Moving along the spectrum we come to subtler types of instrumental value, which beings access when they benefit from things without changing them substantially or causing them significant harm. Examples of this are the symbolic value of wilderness areas tapped when people backpack through it and the recreational value dolphins derive from the waves in which they frolic. (Critics might retort that the value in the wilderness areas or waves is a non-instrumental form of extrinsic value, yet insofar as humans or dolphins use those parts of nature for certain ends I am attributing instrumental value to them.) Further along the spectrum we shift from instrumental value to other, non-instrumental types of extrinsic value, such as the aesthetic value of

31. James seems to be using "intrinsic value" in the way that Arne Naess speaks of "inherent value." Griffin writes, "The *inherent* value of something (in Naessian discussions) *stands in contrast solely with its (perceived) value for human beings* . . . Accordingly, 'inherent value' in the Naessian sense includes most of what counts as 'extrinsic value' in the Whiteheadian usage*" ("Whitehead's Deeply Ecological Worldview," 202, emphasis in the original).

32. Or as Cobb puts it, "the value of each experience for other experiences" ("Deep Ecology and Process Thought," 119).

33. Griffin, "Whitehead's Deeply Ecological Worldview," 192–93.

a crimson sunset, or the ecological value of individuals for larger wholes, as seen in the role that trees play in transforming carbon dioxide through photosynthesis.[34] And then we come to intrinsic value, both of humans and of non-human sentient beings.

When we assess value along this spectrum, not only does our analysis shift away from an exclusive focus on sentience and the intrinsic value of individuals (human or non-human) that possess it, but we can recognize that even though humans may have more complex and valuable sentience than bacteria—or things like trees that have no sentience—and hence have more intrinsic value as well, bacteria and trees play a much more important role in larger systems and hence have more ecological value than humans do. As Griffin points out, "those species whose (individual) members have the least intrinsic value, such as bacteria, worms, trees, and the plankton, have the greatest ecological value: without them, the whole ecosystem would collapse."[35] And he continues, "By contrast, those species whose members have the greatest intrinsic value (meaning the richest experience and thereby the most value for themselves), such as whales, dolphins, and primates, have the least ecological value. In the case of human primates, in fact, the ecological value is negative . . . "[36] These points are worth bearing in mind in the Buddhist environmental ethic I am beginning to sketch here, for they serve as a counterweight to the privileging of humans that could occur if we were to set up sentience as the primary or sole criterion of value.

Of course, we should not lean too far in the other direction either. Griffin comments, "Deep ecologists and land ethicists have been focusing primarily on ecological value. Given that focus, they rightly see that those species at the base of the ecological pyramid—such as the worms, the trees, the bacteria, the plankton—are vital. If these thinkers focus exclusively on ecological value, they may see concern for the liberation of humans and other mammals from suffering as diversionary or worse."[37] Buddhist environmental ethicists, who may slip into devaluing humans as destructive and privileging non-human species or ecosystems, can learn from Griffin's reluctance to think only in terms of biocentrism. Clearly, he is pointing us in the direction of eco-justice. In a similar vein, John Cobb

34. Of course, humans and other entities indirectly benefit from that contribution insofar as it helps maintain a certain healthy balance or integrity in the current configuration of things.

35. Griffin, "Whitehead's Deeply Ecological Worldview," 202.

36. Ibid., 202–3.

37. Ibid., 203.

writes that "what is called 'deep ecology' usually begins with the condition of the earth and moves from that to the well-being of the human species and its members. This is a rational approach to be fully respected. But it is not the Christian one. Christians typically begin with the 'neighbor' who is in need."[38]

This concern for one's fellow humans should not sound foreign to Buddhists, for it accords with the four "divine abodes" and the bodhisattva ideal, though in Buddhism the plight of the neighbor has usually been interpreted in terms of existential, "religious" suffering (albeit with some attention to unmet basic needs) as opposed to the "mundane" suffering of poverty, political oppression, and other forms of injustice. And at the practical level, as Buddhists take into account different types of value in their moral analysis, they can benefit from a further comment Griffin makes: "Once we see that the total inherent value of things, the total value things have in themselves, includes both their intrinsic value and ecological value, and that these values generally exist in inverse proportion to each other, we can see these two ethical concerns as complementary, not conflictual. Both concerns are valid and need to be addressed simultaneously."[39]

In advocating that through the appropriation of process thought Buddhist ethicists should deploy sentience as a basis for attributing intrinsic value, determine *relative* intrinsic value by assessing different types of sentience, and factor in extrinsic value (in both its instrumental and non-instrumental forms), we must question whether "intrinsic value" is the right focus for a Buddhist environmental ethic, especially in light of Buddhist rejection of the possibility of atomistic entities with enduring, independent essences or unchanging value. Perhaps the better construct is simply "value," encompassing the spectrum of values I have just outlined.[40]

But even if we in this way construct a more sophisticated Buddhist formulation of value, including the value of things for larger wholes, we are still left with the question of whether, on a Buddhist basis, we can ascribe value to *wholes*, such as species, ecosystems, or the biosphere. This question throws us into the ongoing debate between animal liberationists and deep ecologists. The former look out for individuals, while the latter privilege larger wholes, such as species and ecosystems, even if their

38. Cobb, "Protestant Theology and Deep Ecology," 220.

39. Griffin, "Whitehead's Deeply Ecological Worldview," 203–4.

40. This still leaves us with the question of whether the possession of "value" grants entities certain rights, but I will leave that discussion for another time.

protection entails pain and suffering for certain individuals (hence the charge of "environmental fascism"[41]). A classic case in this debate is the culling of members of an overpopulated or exogenous species that is having a deleterious effect on an ecosystem, as seen with pine beetles in the Rockies, zebra mussels in the lakes of New England, and the mountain goats that were introduced into the Olympic Mountains by Teddy Roosevelt and are now harming alpine meadows and other fragile areas.

The metaphysics and epistemology of Buddhism does seem to compel us to direct our attention not only to individual entities but to species, local biotic communities, regional ecosystems, and the biosphere. Simon James writes that "it would seem that Zen and ethical holism show a similar awareness of the natural world as a whole,"[42] and that "[t]he teaching of universal emptiness means that to know the nature of any element of reality one must look to its context, its environment."[43] Yet in key respects Buddhism has usually not ascribed positive ecological value to larger wholes. In fact, throughout Buddhist Asia, forested and mountainous areas, while conducive to detachment from the mental afflictions exacerbated by life in towns and cities, have been seen as dangerous places, inhabited by any manner of wild beasts, powerful demons, and untamed spirits. And the overwhelming focus has been on liberating humans from suffering, securing this-worldly benefits, and memorializing the dead, not on trying to preserve nature or engage in ecologically sustainable economic practices.

Even so, Buddhist thinkers have recently drawn from holistic thinkers like Aldo Leopold, who famously writes in *A Sand County Almanac*, "A thing is right when it tends to preserve the integrity, stability, and beauty of the biotic community."[44] In an essay on Buddhist ecology, David Barnhill argues that "when we think of something as Other, then we *devalue* it: any value it may have is instrumental. But if nature is considered a community we are part of, then its value is intrinsic: both the individual beings and the system as a whole have their own integrity."[45] If we work from the

---

41. Regan, *Animal Rights*, 362.

42. James, *Zen Buddhism*, 74. James astutely adds "Zen seems to embody a concern for individual phenomena at odds with extreme holism" (75).

43. Ibid., 75.

44. Leopold. *Sand Country Almanac*, 262. In a critique of Leopold, Frederick Ferré comments, "we *simply do not know enough* about the web of life to be confident which actions will or will not enhance the 'integrity, stability, and beauty' of the biotic community ... [and] the words Leopold chose by which to define his standard of biocentric ethics are notoriously hard to understand with precision" ("Persons in Nature," 17).

45. Barnhill, "Great Earth Sangha," 188. John Daido Loori and his Zen Mountain

Buddhist formulation of intrinsic value I set forth above, however, it seems hard to concur with Barnhill's attribution of intrinsic value directly to "the system as a whole," for the system is lacking in sentience (though Barnhill may have elsewhere defined intrinsic value in a way that would support an argument for the intrinsic value of nature as a whole). But what about another type of whole: species with sentience? Though there is not necessarily any collective or meta-level sentience in such a species, it is a whole composed of members who each have sentience.

To think this through, Buddhists may be able to appropriate process thought once again. Whiteheadians see intrinsic value as only "located in individuals"[46] and reject direct attribution of intrinsic value to wholes. That being said, the whole does comes to possess value as a function of the intrinsic value possessed by the individuals that constitute it. John Cobb has written that "for process thought, the intrinsic value in the system as a whole is still located in the individual occasions. A healthy ecosystem has far more occasions enjoying complex experiences."[47] And from a Whiteheadian perspective, the health of the parts and the health of the whole are interdependent. As Cobb remarks, "For the most part, in the natural world the realization of intrinsic value by individuals and the flourishing of the system are highly correlated."[48]

Buddhists can follow suit and justifiably though cautiously argue on Buddhist grounds for the greater value—though perhaps not the intrinsic value—of at least one kind of whole, a healthy ecosystem, relative to another kind of whole, a damaged ecosystem, for while a healthy ecosystem necessarily includes the pain that occurs in predation and natural disasters, in general it supports more liberation and entails less suffering than a polluted or disrupted ecosystem, such as the global climate system, the disruption of which by all scientific accounts has been increasing human suffering as pests and diseases spread, ocean levels rise, and agriculture gets damaged by too little or too much rain (while also increasing the suffering of many non-human animals, though not all animals: pine beetles are flourishing as winters get warmer in the Rockies). And insofar as species occupy ecological niches and make important contributions to their ecosystems, they have clear ecological value as well (with the possible

Monastery echo Leopold's notion of the "land community" in their expansion of the scope of their sangha to include the sentient and insentient beings co-inhabiting its 250-acre site in the Catskills.

46. Cobb, "Deep Ecology and Process Thought," 122.

47. Cobb, comments on the first draft of this essay (August 2009).

48. Ibid.

exception of *homo sapiens*, whose ecological value, as noted above, has been negative, at least since we stopped being hunters and gatherers[49]), though, again, it seems hard to argue on a Buddhist basis that a species per se has intrinsic value.

To the extent Buddhist ethicists might consider along these lines the ways in which wholes have value or "integrity," they can better specify what the whole is that they are valuing. The whole right now, with nuclear contamination and high levels of greenhouse gases? Or the whole that existed before the Industrial Revolution, when the planet was less damaged, or some future, healthier world? To broach this point here may seem pedantic, but this issue looms large in the case of Zen Buddhists, who, construing enlightenment in part as "according" or "becoming one" with whatever actuality we encounter, run the risk of valorizing actuality—the whole we encounter—and subverting the impetus to change it to something more optimal. This issue also crops up when Buddhists wax poetic about the ecological ramifications of the vast splendor of Indra's net as described in the *Avataṃsaka-sûtra*. Simply put, looming over Buddhist celebration of wholes is the naturalistic fallacy, which Buddhist thinkers need to avoid by making sure they do not stop with affirmations of oneness and by remaining clear-eyed about the need to make distinctions, especially the kind that are crucial in environmental ethics: between a negative "is" (such as a toxic river) and the related positive "ought" and telos (cleaning up the toxic river and the clean river that will result).

This issue ties into questions that have been raised about the adequacy of Buddhist metaphysics for environmental ethics.[50] In four articles in *Religion* and the *Journal of Buddhist Ethics*, for example, Ian Harris has identified several stumbling blocks, especially concerning teleology. He claims that Buddhist theories of causality render Buddhism dysteleologic in that they allow for "no magnet at the end of history drawing events inexorably towards their ultimate goal, no supra-temporal *telos* directing events either directly or indirectly."[51] Harris further alleges that "the dys-

---

49. See Cobb, "Deep Ecology and Process Thought," 123–26, for an overview of his dialogue with Paul Shepard about the value of humans and their impact on the environment at different points in our evolution (or devolution).

50. It also ties in to the shaky argumentation when Buddhist thinkers, using "interdependence" as their rendering of *pratîtya-samutpâda* (Pâli, *paticca-samuppâda*), make claims about how everything is dependent on everything else for its well-being and how we have to take responsibility for everything that occurs. See my analysis of these issues in "In Search of Green Dharma."

51. Harris, "Causation and Telos," 52.

teleological character of Buddhist thought militates against anything that could be construed as injecting the concept of an 'end' or 'purpose' into the world."[52] And as a practical upshot of this, he writes, "It is, for example, very hard to see how a specifically Buddhist position on global warming or on the decrease in diversity of species can be made, unless of course one can appeal to the supranormal intelligence of a handful of contemporary Buddhist sages."[53] Analogous questions could be raised by process thinkers, who even without notions of a fixed end have wondered whether Buddhism offers any parallel to Whiteheadian formulations of freedom, novelty, and evolution toward greater complexity and value as the process of reality unfolds in terms of creativity.

Indeed, Buddhist metaphysics does in some respects seem lacking as a basis for environmental ethics. Interrelational arising (*pratîtya-samutpâda*) holds for all facets of reality, including damaged ecosystems. And as the mode that characterizes everything in the universe (except, in some doctrinal stances, space itself and nirvana), it is not headed toward any particular configuration in the physical realm of nature and society, toward any ecological or social telos. Moreover, Buddhism has at times seemed to argue that people can awaken within any configuration of interrelational arising, presumably even when starving, getting tortured, or struggling with a degraded environment. Further, the thrust of Buddhism as a religion may seem less toward affirmation than toward negation, primarily of our entangled mental states, excessive ideation, attachment to nature, or attachment to future socio-political scenarios.[54]

Nevertheless, we can question Harris's claims. In a response to Harris, Donald Swearer argues, "It is debatable whether or not a theory of causality (or conditionality) must be teleological in order to be environmentally viable. For instance, [Thai Buddhist] Buddhadâsa's biocentric ontology can be interpreted deontologically, or, as Buddhadâsa phrases it, nature implies certain moral maxims or duties."[55] If we were to draw on the strong suit of Buddhism that I sketched at the beginning of this essay—the focus on the eradication of Buddhist "poisons" as a basis for ecologically sustainable economic practices[56] and, by extension, for the

52. Ibid., 53.

53. Ibid.

54. Granted, the Buddhist path involves a negation of our ignorance, acquisitiveness, excess possessions, ill-will, and disregard for the harm we cause.

55. Swearer, "The Hermeneutics of Buddhist Ecology," 39.

56. Complementing Buddhist criticisms of high levels of consumption by those in "advanced" societies, Rita Gross has advanced Buddhist arguments calling into

preservation of biodiversity—we could offer such maxims as "restrain one's actions, focusing on needs not greed, and act in ways that cause no or minimal harm and help sustain healthy ecosystems and communities."

We can also challenge Harris's claims that Buddhism is dysteleologic and the only basis on which we can resist global warming is through appeals to the "supranormal intelligence" of Buddhist sages. When construed in a broad sense, teleology is not limited to ends that are somehow built into natural entities as Aristotelian final causes, to some future telos toward which the world as a whole heads with brute inevitability, or to ends that are created and then bestowed on us by a supernatural deity. That is to say, separate from metaphysical teloi there may be properly Buddhist teloi that are sufficient for an environmental ethic.

Specifically, Buddhism provides what we might call moral and soteriological teloi. Judging from Buddhist texts (and simplifying for the sake of the argument), the ultimate telos for Theravâda Buddhists is nirvana, and for those of the Mahâyâna persuasion the goal is full, perfected buddhahood, and though God is not luring us there, buddha-nature as our innate awakening or capacity to awaken sets us in that direction. From this angle a Buddhist ethicist can argue that the proximate telos of Buddhism is the reduction of suffering in all of it forms and the ultimate telos is the complete cessation of suffering (especially in its narrower, existential sense) achieved in nirvana or buddhahood.

The question then, especially at the practical level, is that of what states of affairs in society or the environment might be preferable if not optimal for reducing and eliminating suffering. Buddhist texts, thinkers, and movements (like Sarvodaya in Sri Lanka) have advocated socio-political arrangements similar to the kind of telos that Jay McDaniel envisions in his call to "create communities that are just, compassionate, nonviolent, participatory, and ecologically wise."[57] And in terms of environmental ethics, Buddhists can counter Harris by arguing that their religion implicitly calls on its followers to work to attain the telos of healthier ecosystems,[58] which relative to damaged ecosystems will cause less unnatural or unnecessary disease and pain in its inhabitants. A devil's advocate might retort,

---

question the pro-natalist positions of other religions as global population increases and exerts increasingly severe pressures on support systems. See "Population, Consumption, and the Environment," in *Dharma Rain*, 409–22.

57. McDaniel, "A Process Approach to Ecology," 241.

58. I realize that the construct of "systems" in nature connotes something more static and enduring than the more fluid and chaotic reality that many ecologists emphasize these days.

however, that a damaged ecosystem could make people more aware of suffering and more willing to let go of attachments, even to the physical world, similar to how early Buddhist texts call on monks to further their spiritual progress by meditating beside corpses and in cemeteries.

Here, too, Buddhists can appropriate process thought to work through these issues. Though Whiteheadians do not argue for any fixed goal or final telos of reality, they do argue for "an aim at increasing value in the whole, from which is derived the aim in each occasion to attain some value, alongside many other processes that reduce value."[59] And this value is construed in part as beauty. According to Jay McDaniel, "In process theology beauty is understood to be the very aim of the universe and the aim of God."[60] The process of attaining these aims is evolutionary, but not in terms of a preexisting design or fixed telos, for "God lures the universe into self-creation of new forms of order relative to what is possible in the situation at hand. Evolution is an ongoing process, not yet finished, that is prompted but not coerced by the indwelling spirit of God into newness."[61] For humans, the lure of God within us is "a lure to live well; that is, to live with beauty—with harmony and intensity—relative to the situation at hand."[62] This is to live with high levels of "enjoyment." And as Cobb and Griffin remark, "The two variables involved in the degree of enjoyment are harmony and intensity. . . . The criteria of harmony and intensity (based on variety held in contrast) are taken from aesthetics. Whitehead accordingly uses the word 'beauty' to describe the achievement of an occasion of experience that fulfills these criteria. To maximize beauty is to maximize enjoyment. God's purpose, then, can be described as the aim toward maximizing either beauty or enjoyment."[63] As one component of enjoyment, intensity is "variety held in contrast," which points to the value of diversity and complexity, both internally in experience and externally in nature.

Buddhists can appropriate this Whiteheadian approach to delineate their own ecological teloi. In addition to affirming certain types of inner complexity—especially a more purified, "wholesome" character if not nirvana or perfection (analogous to Whiteheadian "enjoyment")—Buddhism can affirm greater ecological complexity (i.e., fewer species going extinct

---

59. Cobb, comments on the first draft of this essay (August 2009).

60. McDaniel, "A Process Approach to Ecology," 229.

61. Ibid., 238.

62. Ibid.

63. Cobb and Griffin, *Process Theology*, 64–65. In this way "strength of beauty" functions as a basis for attributing intrinsic value (Cobb, "Deep Ecology and Process Thought," 117).

or ecosystems getting denuded) as generally entailing less suffering—less malnutrition and starvation, more cures discovered for diseases—and more aesthetic and symbolic value. Of course, one question to keep in mind here is whether our goal should be biodiversity per se or an optimal biodiversity. As Peter Singer has pointed out, most of us do not celebrate the net increase in biodiversity after nitrogen-rich fertilizer runs off a corn field and triggers an algae bloom in a nearby river.

With these points in mind we can argue that the goal of Buddhist environmental activism is not the promotion of some telos built into or transcendent of reality, but the telos of balance and harmony (albeit in a sense different from Whitehead's), the preservation (or restoration) of what had evolved before human destruction, and the non-obstruction of the "natural" unfolding of nature. That being said, it is important to recognize that nature at its healthiest is not necessarily a state of harmony devoid of chaos, conflict, and change. Just as nature abhors a vacuum, it hates unchanging plenums, too. Large natural wholes are not static but change cyclically within their current configuration and may even shift subtly (or in some cases dramatically) to a new configuration, though usually, even as the configuration shifts, the system maintains a certain degree of integration and homeostasis. Construing the telos of Buddhist ethics in this way, one could agree with Bill Devall, for example, that "Change, in the form of evolution, has no direction, no finality. However, evolutionary change tends to develop greater diversity. Protection of biodiversity is another precept of an ecocentric Sangha."[64]

One other resource Buddhists might be able to tap in their formulations of environmental ethics is Whitehead's notion of beauty. As Zen Buddhists—and nature writers around the world—have claimed, natural beauty can lift us out of our narrow selves and fill us with awe and wonder, even if we do not experience the enlightenment experience that Dôgen referred to as being "confirmed by the ten-thousand things." Simon James notes that for "Zen there is no clear line between a moral concern for nature and an aesthetic appreciation of it."[65] And in his discussion of Leopold's focus on "integrity, stability, and beauty," David Barnhill states that "our moral love and respect for nature is based on an aesthetic appreciation of the beauty and value of the land."[66] Or as Theravâda ethicist Padmasiri

---

64. Devall, "Ecocentric Sangha," 161.

65. James, *Zen Buddhism*, 73. To adjudicate this claim we need to look critically at such claims in light of what Zen scholars have recently labeled "reverse Orientalism."

66. Barnhill, "Great Earth Sangha," 92.

de Silva has argued, it is the "aesthetic dimension that reinforces our move toward conservation."[67] At the same time, some Buddhists have warned against getting enraptured by natural beauty, for it can become an object of attachment. And close analysis of the Zen's "love of nature" as expressed through the arts indicates that the nature that Japanese love in their aesthetic traditions is usually a miniaturized, stylized nature, not untamed nature in the wild (which, as noted above, is often seen as dangerous), and even when Buddhists travel to wilder nature or live in it as hermits, they value it instrumentally as a good place for cultivating detachment, as a teacher of impermanence, and as a source of images that are symbolic of other Buddhist doctrines. Though this valuation may provide an impetus to preserve wilder nature, the environmental track record of Japan clearly indicates that something more is needed. Perhaps Whitehead's notions of beauty and the link he makes between beauty and intrinsic value can help Buddhists integrate beauty into their formulation of environmental ethics. That exploration, however, will need to wait for another occasion.

In the meantime, as I have sketched in this essay, Buddhist environmental ethicists can draw from process thought as they begin to articulate authentically Buddhist formulations of intrinsic value, extrinsic value, the value of wholes, and the teloi for environmental ethics and activism.

BIBLIOGRAPHY

Badiner, Alan Hunt, editor. *Dharma Gaia: A Harvest of Essays in Buddhism and Ecology.* Berkeley: Parallax, 1990.

———. *Mindfulness in the Marketplace: Compassionate Responses to Consumerism.* Berkeley: Parallax, 2002.

Barnhill, David. "Great Earth Sangha: Gary Snyder's View of Nature as Community." In *Buddhism and Ecology: The Interconnection of Dharma and Deeds*, edited by Mary Evelyn Tucker et al., 187–217. Cambridge: Harvard University Press, 1998.

Bodhi, Bhikkhu, translator. *The Connected Discourses of the Buddha: A Translation of the Samyutta Nikâya.* Boston: Wisdom, 2000.

Cobb, John B. Jr. "Deep Ecology and Process Thought." *Process Studies* 30/1 (2001) 112–31.

———. "Protestant Theology and Deep Ecology." In *Deep Ecology and World Religions: New Essays on Sacred Ground*, edited by David Landis Barnhill and Roger S. Gottlieb, 213–28. SUNY Series in Radical Social and Political Theory. Albany: SUNY Press, 2001.

———. "Thinking with Whitehead about Nature." In *Whitehead's Philosophy: Points of Connection*, edited by Janusz A. Polanowski and Donald W. Sherburne, 175–96. SUNY Series in Constructive Postmodern Thought. Albany: SUNY Press, 2004.

---

67. Silva, Padmasiri de. "Buddhist Environmental Ethics," 15.

Cobb, John B. Jr., and David Ray Griffin. *Process Theology: An Introductory Exposition.* Philadelphia: Westminster, 1976.

Devall, Bill. "Ecocentric Sangha." In *Dharma Gaia: A Harvest of Essays in Buddhism and Ecology*, edited by Alan Hunt Badiner, 155–64. Berkeley: Parallax, 1990.

Ferré, Frederick. "Persons in Nature: Toward an Applicable and Unified Environmental Ethics." *Ethics and the Environment* 1/1 (1996) 15–25.

Griffin, David Ray. "Whitehead's Deeply Ecological Worldview." In *Worldviews and Ecology: Religion, Philosophy, and the Environment*, edited by Mary Evelyn Tucker and John A. Grim, 190–206. Ecology and Justice Series. Maryknoll, NY: Orbis, 1999.

Harris, Ian. "Causation and *Telos*: The Problem of Buddhist Environmental Ethics." *Journal of Buddhist Ethics* 1 (1994) 45–56.

Harvey, Peter. *An Introduction to Buddhist Ethics: Foundations, Values, and Issues.* Cambridge: Cambridge University Press, 2000.

Ives, Christopher. "Buddhism and Sustainability." In *The Spirit of Sustainability*, edited by Willis Jenkins and Whitney A. Bauman, 38–50. Great Barrington MA: Berkshire, 2009.

———. "Deploying the Dharma: Reflections on the Methodology of Constructive Buddhist Ethics." *Journal of Buddhist Ethics* 15 (2008) 23–44.

———. "In Search of a Green Dharma: Philosophical Issues in Buddhist Environmental Ethics." In *Destroying Mara Forever: Buddhist Ethics Essays in Honor of Damien Keown*, edited by John Powers and Charles S. Prebish, 165–86. Ithaca, NY: Snow Lion, 2009.

———. *Zen Awakening and Society.* Honolulu: University of Hawaii Press, 1992.

James, Simon P. *Zen Buddhism and Environmental Ethics.* Burlington, VT: Ashgate Publishing, 2004.

Kaza, Stephanie, editor. *Hooked! Buddhist Writings on Greed, Desire, and the Urge to Consume.* Boston: Shambhala, 2005.

Kaza, Stephanie, and Kenneth Kraft, editors. *Dharma Rain: Sources of Buddhist Environmentalism.* Boston: Shambhala, 2000.

Leopold, Aldo. *A Sand County Almanac: With Essays on Conservation from Round River.* New York: Ballantine, 1966.

Makransky, John. *Awakening through Love: Unveiling Your Deepest Goodness.* Boston: Wisdom, 2007.

McDaniel, Jay. "A Process Approach to Ecology." In *Handbook of Process Theology*, edited by Jay McDaniel and Donna Bowman, 227–48. St. Louis: Chalice, 2006.

Muray, Leslie A. "Politics in Process Perspective." In *Handbook of Process Theology*, edited by Jay McDaniel and Donna Bowman, 217–26. St. Louis: Chalice, 2006.

Regan, Tom. *The Case for Animal Rights.* Berkeley: University of California Press, 1983.

Rockefeller, Steven C. "Buddhism, Global Ethics, and the Earth Charter." In *Buddhism and Ecology: The Interconnection of Dharma and Deeds*, edited by Mary Evelyn Tucker and Duncan Ryuken Williams, 313–26. Cambridge: Harvard University Press, 1998.

Schmithausen, Lambert. *Buddhism and Nature.* Tokyo: International Institute for Buddhist Studies, 1991.

Silva, Padmasiri de. "Buddhist Environmental Ethics." In *Dharma Gaia: A Harvest of Essays in Buddhism and Ecology*, edited by Alan Hunt Badiner, 14–19. Berkeley: Parallax, 1990.

Singer, Peter. "All Animals Are Equal." In *Animal Rights and Human Obligations*, edited by Tom Regan and Peter Singer, 148–62. Englewood Cliffs, NJ: Prentice-Hall, 1976.

Swearer, Donald. "The Hermeneutics of Buddhist Ecology in Contemporary Thailand: Buddhadâsa and Dhammapitaka." In *Buddhism and Ecology: The Interconnection of Dharma and Deeds*, edited by Mary Evelyn Tucker and Duncan Ryuken Williams, 21–44. Cambridge: Harvard University Press, 1998.

Tucker, Mary Evelyn, and Duncan Ryuken Williams, editors. *Buddhism and Ecology: The Interconnection of Dharma and Deeds*. Religions of the World and Ecology. Cambridge: Harvard University Press, 1997.

7

A Chinese Perspective
Stimulus to Recovery of Tradition

―Meijun Fan and Zhihe Wang

EDITOR'S INTRODUCTION

Whereas in every other case, the perspective is that of a living religious community, in the Chinese case, it is that of current Chinese culture. That culture is still influenced by ancient Chinese religious traditions, but it is also influenced by nearly two centuries of efforts to overcome those traditions. This chapter is about the role of Whiteheadian thought in this, quite distinctive, context. It turns out that its role is potentially, and even already actually, much larger than it has yet been anywhere else. One might say that elsewhere its role is that of aiding in some way in the clarification or development of an ongoing tradition. In China it is participating in making possible a major cultural shift.

This shift has diverse elements within it, but one part is renewed openness to China's ancient wisdom. There will be no wholesale going back to ancient ways, but as the limitations of the first enlightenment become apparent, China can find elements of its traditions that meet the newly recognized needs. These are often insights that have been developed also by Whitehead and his followers. And because they are now appreciated by some in the

Western scientific community, commitment to modern science and technology need not discourage their appropriation. Thus Whitehead can contribute to a new cultural synthesis that is open to the contribution of ancient wisdom and religious traditions.

CHINESE TRADITION, IDENTIFIED AS "Dao thinking" in this chapter, is processive in the real sense. However, the Chinese leadership rejected this tradition in the first Chinese enlightenment as China marched toward modernization. The resulting modernization had many negative consequences, including environmental problems, an increasing gap between the rich and the poor, the imbalance between mind and body, and the loss of faith among Chinese people. In order to overcome the weaknesses of modernization, China needs a second enlightenment, in which it recovers the best of Dao thinking. Western process philosophy has played a very important role in calling people's attention to the value of this tradition. This chapter shows how Whiteheadian process thought helps to renew appreciation and acceptance of classical Chinese thought.

The paper is divided into four sections. In the section that follows we briefly summarize Dao thinking: the primacy of process, yin-yang thinking, harmonious thinking, and the principle of "following two courses at the same time." In the next section we present how this process-oriented tradition was radically rejected as trash by the First Enlightenment in China beginning with the May Fourth movement in 1919. This was deeply influenced by the Enlightenment in Europe in the seventeenth and eighteenth centuries. It notes also the negative consequences of this rejection. In the third section we explore the need for a second Chinese Enlightenment based on process philosophy, and we describe the role Whiteheadian thought has played in helping Chinese people to revalue their own process-oriented tradition. And in the last section, we examine the influence of process thought on contemporary Chinese society including its recent shift toward an ecological civilization.

THE KEY PROCESS FEATURES OF DAO THINKING

The Primacy of Process

It is well known that Chinese thought lays great stress on process. That is why Whitehead emphasized that his philosophy has a special affinity with Chinese thought compared to Western thought. "One side makes process ultimate, the other side makes fact ultimate."[1] Whitehead identifies being, which in the West has often been construed in static ways, with process and becoming. For him, "the actual world is a process, and the process is the becoming of actual entities."[2] Charles Hartshorne, another important process philosopher, also saw this affinity between the Chinese and the Whiteheadian outlook: "Chinese thought lacks the prejudice against becoming which is a weakness of Hindu and even Greek thought."[3]

The emphasis on becoming is implicitly embodied in its understanding of Dao, the concept of the ultimate in Chinese tradition. Tao is not a transcendent and self-enclosed substance, not a supernatural God, but a dynamic process, the creative advance of the world. It is becoming itself.

As a Chinese character, "Dao" (道) is made up of a head (首) and walking (辶 or 辵). Together, Dao literally means a head walks; so we may say that Dao means thinking. Later, people use Dao to indicate road, path and way (道路): law, reason and principle (道理) as well.

The word "Dao" is often translated into English as "way" or "path." In the English language these words are nouns, and English nouns are sharply distinguished from verbs, things from actions. However, in Chinese there is no sharp distinction between nouns and verbs, and a great many Chinese words serve as both. That is the reason why one who thinks in Chinese "has little difficulty in seeing that objects are also events, that our world is a collection of processes rather than entities."[4] Thus, when the Chinese speak of the Dao, they have in mind a path and an action, a way and a process, according to which everything is in process and everything is in the state of incessant transformation. This tendency toward process thinking is also found in the *Yi Jing (The Book of Changes)*, which says that everything that interacts with others is promising and prosperous. For example, since heaven and earth interact and communicate, all things

1. Whitehead, *Process and Reality*, 7.
2. Ibid., 22.
3. Hartshorne, "Process Themes," 324.
4. Watts, *Way of Zen*, 19.

in the universe are prosperous. It is the process that "binds all things into one, equalizing all things."[5]

This emphasis on process means that there is a subtle but important difference between the Dao and the traditional idea of God in the Western sense. Dao as way is not God as an absolute, transcendent creator-lawgiver who "deliberately and consciously governs the universe."[6] Such an idea of God is alien to the Chinese mind. This is not because the Dao lacks consciousness or directivity; it is described in many different ways. It is because the Dao is not transcendent in the sense of being totally outside nature, and it is not governing in the sense of being manipulative or overpowering. On the contrary, Dao according to Lao Zi, the founder of Taoism, is a naturally creative process.

> *The Great Tao flows everywhere.*
> *It accomplishes its task but does not claim credit for it.*
> *It loves and nourishes all things,*
> *But does not lord it over them.*[7]

Dao's dimension of process is one of its most important characteristics.

In Chinese thought, Dao is not simply a cosmological reality; it is also a way of living that human beings can embody: they can move within its rhythms and it can move within their way of living in the world. In this respect it may be similar to what Christians mean by the spirit of God, or Holy Spirit. As people live in the Dao, they enjoy the process of living itself. In Whitehead's words, their reward is in the immediate present. They are not in a hurry to reach destinations; the traveling itself is enjoyable. This traveling can involve being open to people of different religions, learning from them, assimilating their insights, making friends with them, being changed by them. Thus the religious life itself is a process. Tao is regarded as the indefinable, concrete process of the world, the way of life. For Chinese process thinkers and perhaps for Western-influenced process thinkers as well: "The road ('the way,' 'the Tao') is better than the inn."[8] The primacy of process lays a deep foundation for Chinese Dao thinking.

5. Chan, *Source Book in Chinese Philosophy*, 177.

6. Watts, *Way of Zen*, 132.

7. Lao Zi, *Tao De Jing*, Ch. 34.

8. Hall and Ames, "Correlative Thinking: Classical China and the Purification of Process," a paper presented to the Society for the Study of Process Philosophy, 1989.

Yin-Yang Thinking

Another important feature of Chinese Dao Thinking is *Yin-Yang* thinking, which permeates all aspects of Chinese thought and culture. The *Yin-Yang* symbol, or *Tai Chi* icon, a perfect circle divided into two equal, contrasting, interpenetrating parts, has been widely used by all major Chinese traditions including Confucianism, Taoism and Zen Buddhism. It indicates the dynamic coincidence of opposites and "affirms the harmonious holding together of contrasts in a balanced synthesis, the integrating of divergence into a rounded whole."[9] According to *Yi Jing* or *The Book of Changes*, "Heaven and earth correlate with the vast and the profound; four seasons correlate with change and continuity; *Yin* and *Yang* correlate with sun and moon; the highest excellence correlates the goodness of easy and simple."[10] The relationship between *Yin* and *Yang* is that of a partnership. The universe would be impossible without their interaction.

Yin and *Yang* are primary constitutive principles. All things arise out of a combination of these primal cosmic principles. They are two polar forces, the interaction of which brings the whole universe into being. All its constituents, such as heaven and earth, night and day, men and women, movement and rest, are expressions of the underlying *Yin* and *Yang* in eternal interplay. "There is nothing in which *yin* and *yang* do not participate"[11]

More important, *Yin-Yang* thinking emphasizes mutual nourishment, that is, Yin and Yang nurture and complete each other. From Yin/Yang thinking, "Neither Yin alone can be productive, nor Yang alone can be productive"[12] According to Zhang Jingyue (1563–1640), "The man who is good at nourishing Yang must seek Yang in Yin. With help from Yin, his vitality becomes unlimited. Likewise, the one who is good at nourishing Yin must turn to Yang, learning to find Yang in Yin. With help from Yang, his or her Yin becomes an endless resource for life."[13]

The mutual complementarity between *Yin* and *Yang* has been regarded by the Chinese as an important principle for harmonizing conflicting principles, and it can help harmonize people's minds when faced with what seem to be irreconcilable conflicts in their religious identity. For

---

9. Smith, *The Faith of Other Men*, 70.

10. I Jing (*The Book of Changes*, in the *Xici* [Great Appendix]).

11. Smith, *The Faith of Other Men*, 71.

12. Cheng Hao, *Er Cheng I Shu· Cheng Hao's Discourse*, 73.

13. Zhang Jiebin, *Jingyue Completed Works*, 974.

Chinese thought, the task of thinkers is to synthesize and harmonize the two seemingly opposite events based on the idea of interrelatedness and interdependence.

The visual image of the *Yin-Yang* symbol not only deconstructs the binary either/or thinking and advocates a non-binary both/and thinking, but also promotes a thinking of mutual complementarity, which makes room for co-existence and co-growth, mutual permeability, mutual learning and mutual enrichment of different religious traditions. Even as the Jew and Muslim might have their own identities, they can learn from one another. And so can the Christian and the Buddhist and the Confucian and the Taoist. In the world today, there are not two poles to Yin and Yang; there are as many poles as there are religions. Yin-Yang complementarity is like that of a rainbow with many colors, each of which adds to the whole. The need on the part of members of all religions is to say: "I see something of you in me and me in you, even as you are more than me and I am more than you. Deep down, we are all equal." Thus, in contrast to the thinking of Heim and even Hick, the concept of mutual complementarity between *Yin* and *Yang* provides a third way—a healthier way—of coping with the conflicts among different religions.

Harmonious Thinking

Harmonious thinking is another important constituent underlying Chinese Dao thinking. From Confucians to Taoism, although different Chinese philosophical traditions have their distinctive emphases, all of them recognize the primacy of harmony. To some extent, harmony can be regarded as a "deeper faith" in Whitehead's sense, which refers to "the trust that the ultimate natures of things lie together in a harmony which excludes mere arbitrariness."[14]

Confucianism especially emphasized harmony at the social level. The harmonious relationships among people and inside of a person were called Ren[15] by Confucius. In his book, *The Analects of Confucius*, Ren as a concept, occurs 107 times. He has defined "Ren" as "love others."

In addition, *Shuowen* has offered another explanation of "Ren": Ren is "忎." It has two parts: body (the upper part: 千) and heart (the lower

14. Whitehead, *Science and the Modern World*, 18. This quote is inspired by Dr. George Derfer who has been exploring the concept of deeper faith by Whitehead.

15. There are the several translations of Ren in English 人, like *authoritative conduct, benevolence, goodness, humanity*, etc.

part: 心) ("从身从心"). It says that the good relationship between body and heart is the starting point to love others. Harmony is regarded as "the biggest beauty in the heaven and earth."[16]

Like Confucianism, Taoism emphasizes Harmony. Unlike Confucianism, it pays a great deal of attention to the harmony of nature and the harmonious relationship between humankind and nature. "The ten thousand things carry the yin and embrace the yang, and through the blending of the material force (ch'i) they achieve harmony."[17] Chuang Tzu (bet. 399 and 295 B.C.) said "the harmony with mankind is called the music of mankind; the harmony with heaven is called the music of heaven."[18] "The ideal person is the one who was born with heaven and earth and who with others became the wholeness."[19]

In China, the sages are always open to harmonious engagement and thus exhibit this faith. For Confucius, "achieving harmony (*he*) is the most valuable function of observing ritual propriety (*li*)."[20] So "at the core of the classical Chinese worldview is the cultivation of harmony."[21] What is the meaning of harmony? We dealt with the concept briefly in the introduction to this chapter. Here we want to say more.

It must be stated again and again that harmony is different from sameness. Yan Ying, the prime minister of Qi in Warring Period, said:

> Harmony is like soup, there being water and heat, sour flavoring and pickles, salt and peaches, with a bright fire of wood, the cook harmonizing all the ingredients in the cooking of the fish and flesh. . . If water be used to help out water, who could eat it? If the harp and the lute were the same, who would delight in them? In this way sameness is of no practical use.[22]

Thus harmony is a creative process, amid which things are balanced with one another, but amid which something new also emerges. Harmony

---

16. Tung Chung-Shu (c.179–c.104 B.C.): *Ch'um-ch'iu fan-lu (Luxuriant Gems of the "Spring and Autumn Annals")*. 董仲舒. 春秋繁露[M]. 济南：山东友谊出版社，2001.第643页. 天地之美，莫大于和

17. Wing-Tsit Chan, *Source Book in Chinese Philosophy*, 160 (Lao Tzu: *Tao-te Ching*, chapter 42. "万物负阴而 抱阳，冲气以为和)

18. Chuang Tzu (c.399 and c.295 B.C.) 庄子. 天道："与人和者，谓之人乐；与天和者，谓之天乐。"

19. Chuang Tzu (c.399 and c.295 B.C.)《庄子•齐物论》："天地与我并生，而万物与我为一"

20. Ames and Rosemont, *Analects of Confucius*, Book 1.12, 74.

21. Ames, *Sun-tzu, the Art of Warfare*, 62.

22. Zuo Qiuming, *Zuo Zhuan*. http://www.artx.cn/artx/detail.asp?id=4834

is itself a building up, not a tearing down. The salt flavoring is the other to the bitter, and the bitter is the other to the salt. With these two "others" combining in due proportion, a new flavor emerges, and this is what is expressed in "Harmony" and what brings things into existence. Where water helps out water, the result is just the flavor of water, and that is what is expressed in "sameness supplementing sameness," and "sameness having no offspring."[23] In Shi Bo's words, "It is harmony which produces things. Sameness has no offspring."[24] Harmony is different from sameness. Sameness is destructive; harmony is constructive.

The founders of Chinese traditions saw this healing effect in harmony. For example, Confucius said that "a nobleman values harmony but not sameness, while a petty person values sameness but not harmony."[25] To Chinese thinkers, harmony is closely related to the openness described above. Whereas sameness is built on closing things off by pretending they are identical, Harmony (*he*) is built on cultivating difference or respecting otherness. In Neville's words, "Harmony is a mixture of components and patterns, requiring each and giving each equal importance."[26] The harmony that respects otherness or cultivates the maximum benefit from difference is the ideal state of all personal, social, and political interactions.

Harmony in the religious field does not mean different religions become one and the same. Harmony does not mean swallowing differences. Chinese harmony fully values difference. According to it, each religion is unique in itself. Willows are beautiful in their greenness and red flowers are beautiful as red flowers. It is the uniqueness that makes the religious world colorful. Harmony does not mean losing one religion's uniqueness, but recognizing the uniqueness of others and respecting it. The red flower has red light, the yellow flower has yellow light. All of these flowers are independently beautiful. Working together harmoniously, they make the whole garden beautiful without losing the beauty of each. No one is superior to the other.

Different religions include each other but still maintain their own basic stance and features. As Cobb points out, "The world is full of opposites, but these opposites are co-resident in all things or events. They

23. Yulan Fung, *Spirit of Chinese Philosophy*, 107–8.

24. Guoyu, in *Selected Works of Chinese Aesthetic History*, edited by Philosophy Department, Peking University (Peking: China Publishing House, 1980) 8.

25. Confucius, *Analects: Zilu*, 244.

26. Neville, *Behind the Masks of God*, 61.

require each other, inform each other, and even constitute each other."[27] The key point is to search for "an appropriate harmony."[28]

Following Two Courses at the Same Time

The fourth plank of Chinese Dao Thinking can be called "following two courses at the same time."[29] This doctrine indicates a typical Chinese way of thinking: "Always try to be comprehensive in viewpoint, by transcending one-sidedness."[30] Zhuang Zi offers an illustration by pointing out that the sage harmonizes the extremes and "rests in natural equalization." This means "following two courses at the same time" is not an artificial construct by a Chinese thinker. On the contrary, it is a natural state, an organic state, a harmonious state.

This way of thinking plays a vital role in the Chinese mentality. The value of Dao lies in its power to reconcile opposites on a higher level of consciousness. To use this power to reach a balanced way of living and a higher integration is the essence of Dao. Wang Yangming proposed the concept of "middle person" to strengthen this thinking. A middle person is a person who keeps the middle way rather than "going to the extreme." For Wang Yangming, only the middle person, who is open to the possibility of realizing harmony and integration, can gain access to the Tao."[31]

In the Chinese context, this notion of a mind seeking wider or more inclusive perspectives is not limited to Taoism. "The Mean" of Confucianism also represents the same train of thought. For Confucius, "The Mean is the supremest virtue."[32] According to Zhu Xi, "Achieving the Mean is the name for not erring to one side or the other, for being neither too much nor too little." This is the highest form of goodness, but it is also the hardest to achieve.[33] Zhuang Zi realizes that "petty biases" are the obstacles to Tao. That is why he strongly rejects man-made divisions.

27. Cobb, "Post-Conference Reflections on Yin and Yang," 421.

28. Ibid.

29. Zhuang Zi, chapter 2 in *Source Book in Chinese Philosophy*, 184.

30. Sun, "Chinese Metaphysics and Whitehead," 167.

31. Wang Yangming, *Chuanxilu*. In *Selected Works of Chinese Philosophy History* (Beijing: China Bookstore, 1982) vol. 2, 205.

32. Confucius, *Analects· Yongye*, 100.

33. Fung, *Spirit of Chinese Philosophy*, 106.

THE REJECTION OF THE TRADITION BY THE FIRST ENLIGHTENMENT

The First Enlightenment

By the First Enlightenment, we refer to two things. We refer to (1) the historical intellectual movement in Europe in the seventeenth and eighteen centuries that advocated reason and individual freedom. And we refer to (2) the May 4th movement in 1919 in China, which advocated democracy and science. In China we called them Master Democracy and Master Science. At that time people in China believed science could solve every problem and that it could even provide answers to the meaning of life. Although there is a gap in time between the Chinese version of the First Enlightenment and the European version, there is also an intrinsic connection between the two Enlightenments not only historically, but also spiritually. Both involve an unfettered devotion to—indeed a worship of—science and reason. For this reason we speak of both as the First Enlightenment.

There is little doubt that the First Enlightenment in both Europe and China played a revolutionary role in liberating people from *feudal tyranny* and ignorance. Some fruits of the Enlightenment included the notions of liberty, democratic participation, and the dignity of the individual. These fruits should still be highly valued and preserved. Given China's circumstance, in which a feudal ideology is still very influential, it is especially important to promote these values.

However, it would be irresponsible if we did not point out the limitations of the First Enlightenment after postmodern thinkers in the West already have pointed out the social and ecological costs. The Enlightenment played a central role in the justification for modernization. A worship of economic growth in modernization can be conceived as a manifestation of the First Enlightenment's emphasis on the individual who only seeks his own good and is "indifferent to the success or failure of other individuals."[34] Let us consider these limitations more closely.

The Limitations of the First Enlightenment

We find five shortcomings in the First Enlightenment, all of which are closely related.

34. Daly and Cobb, *For the Common Good*, 159.

An imperialistic attitude toward nature

The First Enlightenment carried with it a disrespectful attitude toward nature. Starting from an anthropocentric stance, this attitude treated nature as an object to be conquered, manipulated, dominated, and exploited by humankind. For Francis Bacon, one of the leading thinkers of the Enlightenment, Nature must be "hounded in her wanderings" and made a "slave".[35] In the words of Adorno and Horkheimer, the authors of *Dialectic of Enlightenment*, "What men want to learn from nature is how to use it in order wholly to dominate it and other men."[36] Nature was treated as a slave under the imperialistic attitude. The attitude is closely related to the disrespect for women because both nature and women are seen by the Enlightenment culture as "irrational, uncertain, hard to control, fuzzy."[37] Therefore, many people now realize that, in order to liberate women from oppression, people must also liberate nature, at least insofar as the two have been symbolically linked in the Western imagination.

A nihilistic attitude toward tradition and the past

The First Enlightenment also carried with it a nihilistic attitude toward tradition and the past, believing that in order to be fulfilled humans must sever their relations with tradition. In Europe, the past was treated as the "dark ages." In China, tradition was treated as trash that should be totally and completely abandoned. "Down with Confucianism" was the most famous slogan at that time. This radical rupture with tradition cut off the intrinsic link to our own tradition, leading us to abandon excellent spiritual resources in our tradition such as "respect for the heaven and awe of the Dao," "harmony with difference." We are now struggling to reclaim these traditions.

Moreover, it is the nihilistic attitude that causes the loss of faith and values in China today. Lacking any faith or sense of the divine, people come easily to treat something secular, such as science or money, as the object of worship. That explains why scientism and worship of money are now so widespread in China and in the West as well.

35. Merchant, *The Death of Nature*, 169..
36. Horkheimer and Adorno, *Dialectic of Enlightenment*, 4.
37. Dobson, *Green Political Thought*, 192.

The worship of science

Science was worshipped by almost all the First Enlightenment thinkers. It seemed to them to be the only correct and valid way to know the universe. Based on this assertion, all other ways of knowing the universe—such as religious, artistic, intuitional, emotional knowing—were viewed as unscientific. Therefore they were to be suppressed and demolished. In effect, advocates of the "science only" approach to life were scientific chauvinists. According to Li Yusheng, during the May 4th, Chinese Enlightenment, scientists in China deeply believed that truth was on their side and that the progress of China would totally rely on them. "I believe in science, therefore, I am superior to you both mentally and morally."[38] Most scientists held such an arrogant attitude toward their adversaries when they debated with them. Chen Duxiu, one of the leading Enlightenment thinkers in China claimed that only science and democracy could save China from "all dark sides including political, moral, academic, thought Levels."[39]

There is little doubt that science has made a great contribution to promote human civilization. However, it is very dangerous to treat science as an object of worship. It is the worship that makes people, both in China and in the West, neglect the limits of science. In fact, the Western science the enlightenment thinkers worshiped was based on Newtonian physics characterized by mechanism and reductionism, which succeeded in many respects but misled in others. In this science, the world was viewed as a machine, nature, "a dull affair, soundless, scentless, colorless."[40] In Max Weber's phrase, the world is disenchanted by modern science. According to Ulrich Beck, a well-known German sociologist, it is science that constituted "a potential cause of civilization-induced mass immiseration."[41]

The worship of reason

Closely related to the worship of science was the worship of reason. The first Enlightenment has been regarded as an "Age of Reason," because, in it, "Reason becomes the unifying and central point of the century, expressing all that it longs and strives for, and all that it achieves."[42]

---

38. Lin Yusheng, "The Rise of Scientism in China since May 4th."
39. Chen Duxiu, "Defense of New Youth."
40. Whitehead, *Science and the Modern World*, 54.
41. Beck, *Ecological Enlightenment*, 50.
42. Cassirer, *Philosophy of the Enlightenment*, 5.

Enlightenment thinkers believed that reason, especially "pure reason," which is "untainted by emotion, sensate knowledge, social constructions, and noncognitive awareness,"[43] was the drive of progress and could build a brand new civilization.

However, much historical evidence has now shown that the reason with pure pedigree not only failed to improve the human condition, but also failed to solve the problems of oppression of women and ethnic groups. Reason did not keep its promise to bring us a beautiful new world. One of the weaknesses of reason, in our opinion, when it operates in abstraction from the cultural and spiritual norms, is its lack of a moral dimension. It separates itself from value, and it then becomes only instrumental reason, which oppresses anything that is not rational in that limited sense. It is both player and judge. In this sense, it is a dictator.

Still another shortcoming of a "reason-only" approach to life is its tendency toward compartmentalization. Reason has various forms such as social reason, political reason, economic reason, technical reason, functional reason; each of them dominates one part of human life. The dominance of these types of reason can be viewed as "the defining feature of modern industrial society."[44]

Of course this is not all that reason is. In Greek thought, for example, reason included emotion and value, and was understood as a comprehensive way of understanding things. But in the First Enlightenment, reason was reduced to instrumental reason and lost its capacity for far-reaching vision.

Closely related to the above, the third shortcoming of modern reason is its individualism, which assumes that "rational self-interest" is the fundamental motive for human activities. According to this view, which has had an inordinate influence in Western neo-classical economic thinking, rational people only care about maximization of their interest and have no reason to take the consequence of their actions for others into account.

A one-dimensional understanding of freedom

"Freedom" was a ubiquitous slogan of the Enlightenment, which played a very positive role in encouraging people to fight against the oppression of feudal tyranny. However, the concept of freedom that Enlightenment thinkers promoted had its limits. Briefly, freedom was understood

43. Spretnak, *Resurgence of the Real*, 220.
44. Baber and Bartlett, *Deliberative Environmental Politics*, 19.

abstractly by Enlightenment thinkers primarily as a possession of the isolated individual, and not as a way of being connected to community, and it was limited to freedom of speech, freedom of thought, and (in John Locke's thought) freedom to own property.

The Negative Consequences of Modernization

The achievements of China's modernization are remarkable, especially its rapid GDP growth. Nevertheless, due to the limitations of the First Enlightenment, modernization based on it has caused serious problems. These include an ecological crisis, an increasing gap between the rich and the poor, and the loss of faith among Chinese people, the imbalance between people's physical lives and spiritual lives. While China is a developing country to a large extent, in some respects, it is "more modern" than the West. For example, 70 percent of rivers and lakes in China have been polluted. The drinking water in half of Chinese cities failed to meet the standard. China has become the number one polluted country in the world.

In addition, because of the lack of faith, consumerism has become many young people's religion. It is reported that China's consumption demand for luxury goods shows 20 percent annual growth. China emerged second as a global luxury market, after Japan, with young customers prepared to spend US $26.4 billion by 2016, compared to US $18 billion by their older counterparts. By 2015, China's consumption of luxury goods will increase by an estimated US $80 billion a year.[45] Don't misunderstand that only rich people in China buy these luxury goods. Deeply influenced by consumerism-driven lifestyle, many young people of modest means are also enthusiastic buyers of luxury goods. Faced with the question why she spent 12,000 yuan (US $1,446) on a famous-brand handbag when her average monthly salary was 3,000 yuan (US$361.45), Pan Zhimin, a new, 24-year-old employee of a consulting company, says the answer was simple. "It was a sign of the lifestyle I desire."[46]

45. "China Luxury Summit"; online: http://www.chinaluxurysummit.com/.

46. http://service.china.org.cn/link/wcm/Show_Text?info_id=128850&p_qry=SARS

A SECOND ENLIGHTENMENT BASED
ON PROCESS PHILOSOPHY

The limitations of the First Enlightenment led to destructive consequences, making it necessary to move beyond modernization towards postmodernization. The Second Enlightenment can be called postmodern since it includes but transcends the greatest achievements of the modern or First Enlightenment. What are the defining features of the Second Enlightenment?

From Anthropocentrism to Ecological Awareness.

Given the fact that anthropocentrism is responsible for the ecological crises faced today, the Second Enlightenment rejects it and its manifestation: an imperialistic attitude to nature. Unlike the First Enlightenment, which treated nature as an object of exploitation, the ecological awareness promoted in the Second Enlightenment regards nature as a 'subject.' It challenges people to realize that we are a part of an unfolding process, inherently linked with the stars, the winds, the rocks, the soil, the plants, and the animals. Ecological awareness emphasizes that it is nature that protects us. Nature not only provides our food and clothing and nurtures our body, but it also nurtures our mind. Therefore, we should not only protect her but also love her, respect her, and be in awe of her. Closely related to this new attitude toward nature, the Second Enlightenment calls us to respect peasants and the land. It challenges us to pay attention to the value of traditional farming and to the old idea of nurturing the land.

From Western-centeredness to Complementary Awareness

Modernization is often identified with the West. Some Chinese Enlightenment thinkers like Hu Shi and Chen Xujing, declared that only Western culture, especially Western science and democracy, could save China. They proposed that China should completely adopt Western ways, including its political, economic, and cultural systems. Few people in China today accept this theory fully, but it is still very influential, making it difficult to promote postmodernization. For example, *Crying for Yellow River*, a very popular TV program in China, praised Blue civilization (Western civilization) and denigrated Yellow civilization (Eastern Civilization).

From Homogenization to Diversity

By homogenization thinking I refer to modernity's preference for unity over plurality. This entails a negative attitude toward diversity. The destruction of indigenous cultures by globalization reflects homogenization thinking, which is an act of violence against the 'other.' The Second Enlightenment respects and appreciates diversity, including ethnic, racial, sexual, cultural, and religious difference. For Alfred North Whitehead, one of the founders of constructive postmodern philosophy, it is diversity and plurality that provide the condition for higher development.

From a One-dimensional to a Multi-dimensional Understanding of Freedom

The Second Enlightenment reveals freedom's complexity and richness, especially in its social dimension. Foucault's theory of power undermines the notion of absolute freedom because freedom itself is an effect of power. Power produces the possibilities of action, and the conditions for the exercise of freedom.

The First Enlightenment emphasizes freedom of thought, the press and religious opinion. For the Second Enlightenment, freedom of action and practical purpose are more important. It emphasizes the social dimension of freedom and reveals the intrinsic relation between freedom and responsibility. For Emmanuel Levinas, responsibility to others pre-exists freedom and there is no freedom that pre-exists the responsibility to others. Freedom is not to be free from others but to be dedicated to serve others. For the Second Enlightenment, individual and community values are interdependent. We liberate ourselves first, and then we can pay respect to others. At the same time, we realize our individual freedom only when we have respected others.

From Pure Reason to Aesthetic Wisdom

We need fresh wisdom in order to cope with the emerging issues of our time. The Second Enlightenment calls for aesthetic wisdom.

Postmodern aesthetic wisdom is organic, respectful of nature, respectful of diversity, free yet responsible, scientific yet spiritual, humane and ecological. This kind of wisdom is needed by China and the world today if we are to move beyond the shallowness of consumerism into a more meaningful way of living. The Second Enlightenment can build upon the First while moving beyond its more destructive aspects. A major shift is necessary to actualize the Second Enlightenment.

THE ACCEPTANCE AND IMPACT OF PROCESS THOUGHT IN CHINA

Finding Value in Chinese Traditions

The philosophical foundation of the Second Enlightenment is process philosophy. It is process thought that has encouraged the Chinese to re-value their traditions and attempt to recover those aspects that will build a China that is socially just, ecologically sustainable, and spiritually satisfying. This explains why process thought has been so well received in China in the past ten years.

Since the May 4th movement, which we call "China's First Enlightenment," our ancient tradition has been treated as something to be completely abandoned. "Down with Confucianism" was the most famous slogan of that time. The Chinese abandoned the spiritual resources of their tradition, such as: respect for heaven, awe of the Dao, and "harmony with difference." We are now struggling to reclaim these traditions. Lacking any faith or sense of the divine, people easily worship the secular. That explains why scientism and worship of money are so widespread today in China as well as in the West.

However, process thought and its representation, Constructive Post-modernism, help the Chinese find value and charm within their past because of its respectful attitude towards tradition. This partly explains why the Chinese people would like to embrace postmodernism in its constructive form rather than the deconstructive one, and why process thought is accepted so quickly in China. In a speech at Claremont, Kang Ouyang, a leading Chinese scholar and vice-president of Huazhong University of Science and Technology, said, "as a Chinese scholar, I especially noted that many constructive postmodernists are very friendly to Chinese people and Chinese culture. The Center of Process Studies has set a good example in this regard. Many postmodernists stress the importance of Chinese culture in overcoming modern problems and try to find enlightenment from traditional Chinese culture. This will certainly stimulate Chinese scholars to study their own traditional culture, to discover other possible resources, and to enlarge its influence in the further development of world culture."[47]

Realizing the Value of Religion

Inspired by process thought, today more and more people have realized the important role religion can play in promoting a harmonious society and an ecological civilization. In the words of Ye Xiaowen, chief of the State Administration for Religious Affairs of China, "Religion is a positive, valuable force in building a harmonious society."[48] For Pan Yue, "From the Taoist view of the Tao reflecting nature, to the Confucian idea of humans and nature becoming one, to the Buddhist belief that all living things are equal, Chinese religion has helped our culture to survive for thousands of years. Chinese religion can be a powerful weapon in preventing an environmental crisis and building a peaceful harmonious society."[49] Inspired by Constructive Postmodernism, Dedong Wei, a researcher of the Chinese Academy of Social Sciences, felt the convergence between Constructive Postmodernism and Buddhism. In his opinion, "Buddhism is postmodern in the real sense. It is very possible and realistic for Chinese to cherish, study, and highlight the excellent elements in Buddhist ecological outlook in order to avoid the detour of modernization."[50]

Provides a Philosophical Foundation for Environmentalism

As Griffin argues, Constructive Postmodernism based on process thought is ecological in the real sense because it "provides support for the ecology . . . "[51] Therefore; there is an intrinsic connection between process thought and the environmental movement in China. According to Yijie Tang, philosophy professor at Peking University, a top scholar in traditional Chinese philosophy and culture, "Process philosophy criticizes binary thinking and views nature and humans as an interrelated bio-community. This idea has important implications for the solution

47. Ouyang Kang, "Contemporary Marxism in China and Process Thought," a lecture delivered at Center for Process Studies, Claremont, August 21, 2001)

48. Ye Xiaowen, "Religion and Social Harmony."

49. Pan Yue, "Green China and Young China." http://www.cctv.com/docu/special/C19398/20071112/102775.shtml

50. Dedong Wei, "Buddhist Ecological Outlook."

51. Griffin, "Introduction to SUNY Series in Constructive Postmodern Thought."

of the ecological crisis facing us today."[52] This explains why Chinese environmentalists "prefer Constructive Postmodernism represented by process thinker David Griffin,"[53] said Fanren Zeng, former president of Shandong University, who is a founder of eco-aesthetics in China. Xiujie Wang, Chair of Liaoning Literature Association, is well known in China as an "ecological female author," and believes that "Constructive Postmodernism is the philosophical foundation of ecological literature." To Xiaohua Wang, "the fate of human beings and the whole ecosystem will be determined by whether the postmodern turn succeeds."[54] Among Chinese environmentalists, Sheri Liao has been most successful in putting Constructive Postmodernism into the practice of environmental protection. With a major in philosophy, Liao is China's best-known environmental activist and journalist. She founded the Global Village of Beijing in 1996, and has received commendations from the United Nations and the White House. The focus of her work has been on promoting a sense of individual responsibility and empowerment in relation to environmental issues in China.

Over the years, though, she became convinced that a genuine environmental movement in China must have a spiritual foundation that draws upon the intuitive wisdom from the Chinese past. She gradually found that constructive postmodern thinking or process thought can provide a philosophical grounding for that environmental movement. According to Sheri Liao's understanding, the constructive postmodern movement is a reflection on and a correction of modern fragmental and hegemonic thinking. Constructive postmodernism focuses instead on "wholeness, difference and uniqueness, while promoting ecological economy, organic agriculture, natural Life cultivation, co-architecture, spirituality, and simplicity of life—qualities that have sustained Chinese civilization for 5000 years."[55]

Illuminating the Sociopolitical Field.

This is the richest and fastest-growing field in the process movement in China. Realizing the value of process thinking, Chinese scholars are

52. Yijie Tang, "Reflective Western Scholars View Traditional Chinese Culture."

53. Fanren Zeng, "Ecological Aesthetics."

54. Xiaohua Wang, "China's Environment Movement and Constructive Postmodernism," a lecture at Center for Process Studies, Claremont.

55. "Liao Xiaoyi: A Thinker in Action," *Finance Times*, Oct. 28, 2007.

applying this approach or way of thinking to the sociopolitical field in order to solve the various pressing issues facing China. For example, Guihuan Huo, a senior researcher of the Chinese Academy of Social Science, has explored the significance of Constructive Postmodernism in resolving the conflict between science and the humanities.[56]

The following list of articles can provide readers with a clear impression of this literature:

1. "The Inspiration of Constructive Postmodernism for China's Higher Education" by Fei Li (*Education Today* 1 [2008]).

2. "The Inspiration of Constructive Postmodernism for Creating a Harmonious Society" by Desheng Bu, Yi Ma, and Xiaohui Liu (*Journal of Shanxi Party School* 2 [2008]).

3. "The Inspiration of Constructive Postmodernism for Moral Education of Graduate Students" by Wei Zhang (*Degree and Graduate Education* 3 [2005]).

4. "The Inspiration of Constructive Postmodernism for Chinese Medicine" by Yuanzhao Wang (*Journal of Liaoning Chinese Medicine* 5 [2006]).

5. "The Relationship between Science and Religion from a Constructive Postmodern Perspective" by Xiong Sun (*Journal of Zhejiang Party School* 6 [2003]).

6. "Analyzing Economic Man from the Perspective of Process Philosophy" by Yunqiu Gao (*Orient Forum* 5 [2005]).

7. "On Constructive Postmodern Reconstruction of Postmodern Education" by Jian Feng (*Journal of Hunan Normal University* 5 [2005]).

8. "Constructive Postmodernism and Chinese Party History Studies" by Chuanliang Shen (*Party History Studies* 1 [2006]).

9. "Promoting a Constructive Postmodern Culture of Birth" by Mingxing Zeng (*Population* 4 [2004]).

10. "Constructive Postmodernism and Chinese Jurisprudence" by Xuebin Liu and Yingjun Ma (*Journal of Shanxi Party School* 3 [2006]).

11. "Reflect on and Promote the Development of China's Modernization from a Constructive Postmodern Perspective" by Yougang Zhuang, (*Marxism and Reality* No.2 [2007]).

56. Huo, "Hegel, Marx and Whitehead."

Moving from Modernization to an Ecological Civilization

Process thinking has challenged the Chinese to rethink modernization by pointing out its negative consequences. Treating GDP growth as the main goal of a nation without considering social justice and morality is a typically mechanical understanding of development, which is a merely "Western notion."[57] Today more and more Chinese are realizing that Westernized modernization is not the only way for China to develop. Chinese leaders are now talking about a new form of healthy modernization and "Green GDP," which bypass the worst aspects of Western modernity. Healthy modernization is now understood to be "constructively postmodern" development. The concept of ecological civilization aiming at harmonious development of humanity and nature proposed by the Chinese government at the seventeenth National Congress of the Communist Party of China whose goal is to basically form "an energy- and resource-efficient and environment-friendly structure of industries, pattern of growth and mode of consumption,"[58] reflects an important shift in the Chinese government's understanding of development. Rather than stressing GDP growth as the core of development, as it did in the past, the government now recognizes that, to be sustainable, development requires a harmonious relationship between man and nature. Such a concept did not develop in a vacuum; Constructive Postmodernism has played a significant role. In the words of Pan Yue, head of the Environment Department of China, "Socialist ecological civilization is a critical absorption of environmentalism, eco-ethics, and postmodernism."[59]

In the words of Huibin Li, an official scholar of the Central Bureau of Compilation and Translation, a top think tank of the Chinese government, "If ecological civilization is a civilization after industrialization and postmodern means after modern, then, ecological civilization and postmodern civilization originally should be the same topic."[60]

From the process perspective, "ecological civilization" can be regarded as a postmodern civilization, considering its transcendence of modern industrial civilization. Proposing ecological civilization can be conceived as a significant contribution China makes to the postmodern movement in the world. There is little doubt that Chinese Dao thinking can play a

57. Xiang, "China's Reform should Get Rid of Westernize Dogmas."

58. Hu Jintao's report at 17th Party Congress; online: http://www.china.com.cn/17da/2007–10/24/content_9119449_4.htm.

59. Pan, "On Socialist Ecological Civilization."

60. Li, "Postscript to Ecological Civilization and Marxism," 227–28.

crucial part in creating such an ecological civilization due to its emphasis on process and harmony.

BIBLIOGRAPHY

Ames, Roger. *Sun-tzu: The Art of Warfare*. New York: Ballantine, 1993.

Ames, Roger T., and Henry Rosemont Jr. *The Analects of Confucius: A Philosophical Translation*. New York: Ballantine, 1998.

Baber, Walter F., and Robert V. Bartlett. *Deliberative Environmental Politics: Democracy and Ecological Rationality*. Cambridge: MIT Press, 2005.

Bacon, Francis. *Novum Organum*. Chicago: Encyclopedia Britannica, 1952.

Beck, Ulrich. *Ecological Enlightenment*. New Jersey: Humanities Press, 1995.

Cassirer, Ernst. *The Philosophy of the Enlightenment*. Translated by Fritz C. A. Koelin and James P. Pettegrove. Princeton: Princeton University Press, 1951.

Chan, Wing-Tsit. *A Source Book in Chinese Philosophy*. Princeton: Princeton University Press, 1969.

Chen, Duxiu. "Defense of New Youth." *New Youth* 1/1 (1919).

Cheng, Hao. *Er Cheng I Shu· Cheng Hao's Discourse*. In *Selected Works of Chinese Philosophy History*. Beijing: China Bookstore, 1982.

Daly, Herman E., and John B. Cobb Jr. *For the Common Good: Redirecting the Economy toward Community, the Environment, and a Sustainable Future*. Boston: Beacon, 1989.

Dobson, Andrew. *Green Political Thought*. London: Routledge, 1995.

Fung, Yulan. *The Spirit of Chinese Philosophy*. Translated by E. R. Hughes. London: Kegan Paul, Trench, Trubner, 1947.

Griffin, David. "Introduction to SUNY Series in Constructive Postmodern Thought." In *The Reenchantment of Science: Postmodern Proposals*, edited by David Griffin, ix–xii. SUNY Series in Constructive Postmodern Thought. Albany: SUNY Press, 1988.

Huo, Guihuan. "Hegel, Marx and Whitehead: Viewing the Conflicts between Sciences and Humanities from the Basic Transformation of Mode of Thinking in Western Philosophy Embodied by 'Process.'" *Journal of Jiangsu Administration College* 5 (2006) 18–23.

Hartshorne, Charles. "Process Themes in Chinese Thought." *Journal of Chinese Philosophy* 5 (1979) 323–36.

Horkheimer, Max, and Theodor W. Adorno. *Dialectic of Enlightenment*. Translated by John Cumming. New York: Herder & Herder, 1972.

Li, Huibin. "Postscript to Ecological Civilization and Marxism." In *Ecological Civilization and Marxism*, edited by Huibin Li, Xiaoyuan Xue, and Zhihe Wang, 227–28. Beijing: Central Compilation and Translation Press, 2008.

Lin, Yusheng. "The Rise of Scientism in China since May 4th." *Science Time*, June 7, 2006.

Merchant, Carolyn. *The Death of Nature: Women, Ecology, and the Scientific Revolution*. San Francsco: Harper & Row, 1980.

Neville, Robert Cummings. *Behind the Masks of God: An Essay toward Comparative Theology*. Albany: SUNY Press, 1991.

Pan, Yue. "On Socialist Ecological Civilization." *China Economy Times*, Sept. 26, 2006.

Smith, Wilfred Cantwell. *The Faith of Other Men.* New York: Harper Torchbooks, 1972.

Spretnak, Charlene. *The Resurgence of the Real: Body, Nature, and Place in a Hyper-modern World.* 1997. Reprinted. New York: Routledge, 1999.

Sun, George Chih-Hsin. "Chinese Metaphysics and Whitehead." PhD diss., Southern Illinois University, 1971.

Tang, Yijie. "Reflective Western Scholars View Traditional Chinese Culture." *The People's Daily*, Feb. 4, 2005.

Watts, Alan W. *The Way of Zen.* New York: Vintage, 1999.

Wei, Dedong. "Buddhist Ecological Outlook." *China Social Sciences* 5 (1999).

Whitehead, Alfred North. *Process and Reality: An Essay in Cosmology.* Corrected Edition. Edited by David Ray Griffin and Donald W. Sherburne. New York: Free Press, 1978.

———. *Science and the Modern World.* New York: Free Press, 1967.

Xiang, Lanxian. "China's Reform Should Get Rid of Westernized Dogmas." *Global Times*, Feb. 4, 2008.

Ye, Xiaowen. "Religion and Social Harmony." *The People's Daily*, Nov. 28, 2006.

Zeng, Fanren. "Ecological Aesthetics: A Brand New Ecological Aesthetics in the Postmodern Context." *Journal of Shanxi Normal University* 3 (2002).

Zhang, Jiebin, editor. *Jingyue Completed Works.* Shanghai: Shanghai Science and Technology Press, 1959.

8

A Taste for Multiplicity
The Skillfull Means of Religious Pluralism

—Roland Faber and Catherine Keller

EDITOR'S INTRODUCTION

This book as a whole consists of chapters written from—or in the Chinese case, about—traditional perspectives that have endured and developed through the centuries. These perspectives have well-established strengths but also recognizable problems and limitations. In response to these problems and limitations they have changed and developed in each new historical epoch. These chapters offer proposals as to how in our time of rapid change everywhere, the thought of Whitehead may be useful to them. This final chapter in this series argues that the thought of Whitehead can be useful to Whiteheadians as well, as they also find themselves in a rapidly changing context.

Even though the Whiteheadian community is quite small, it is itself divided into several philosophical groupings. The major ones are sometimes labeled: radical empiricism, historicism, rationalism, and speculative philosophy. Thinkers in these diverse traditions have found help in Whitehead in advancing their work and some have become members of the Whiteheadian family.

Another label that has been applied to Whitehead's thought as early as the 1960s is "post-modern." In Science and the Modern World*" he clearly indicated that the basic style and categories of modern science and modern philosophy were no longer adequate. He spoke of William James as inaugurating a new era in philosophy in his essay, "Does Consciousness Exist?" Clearly for him what was emerging was "post-modern," but the term played a negligible role in the wider discussion until its use by French philosophers made it philosophically and culturally important.*

Many of the specific criticisms of modernity by Whiteheadians and by the great postmodern philosophers in France are similar. But there was a major difference. Whiteheadians were articulating systematic alternatives to modern thought. Their focus was the construction of a comprehensive new vision. The French saw in all such efforts a kind of intellectual imperialism that was not separate from cultural and economic colonialism. The sensibility of a generation of cultural and scholarly leaders has been deeply informed by this form of postmodernism. To them, earlier distinctions between empiricists, rationalists, historicists, and speculative thinkers seem insignificant and passé.

Yet some in this new community also have found help in Whitehead's thought. They see that Whitehead himself transcended the categories by which his followers defined themselves. His followers have not been wrong to affirm the constructive element in his work, but their tendency to fix and systematize it has been alien to his spirit. Freed from the narrowing and rigidifying work of his interpreters, Whitehead can be a vital participant in today's postmodern conversation. That conversation focuses on diversity and plurality. In a book written from diverse perspectives, this chapter is a call for celebration.

In a small wooden box concealed behind a sliding pane in his sleeping quarters Lord Hauksbank of That Ilk kept a collection of beloved "objects of virtue," beautiful little pieces without which a man who traveled constantly might lose his bearings, for too much travel, as Lord Hauksbank well knew, too much strangeness and novelty, could loosen the moorings of the soul . . . the silk handkerchief of a pagan goddess of ancient Soghdia, given to a forgotten hero as a token of her love; a piece of exquisite scrimshaw work on whalebone depicting the hunting of a stag; a locket containing a portrait of Her Majesty the Queen; a leather-bound hexagonal book from the Holy Land, upon whose tiny pages, in miniature writing embellished with extraordinary illuminations, was the entire text of the Qur'an; a broken-nosed stone head from Macedonia, reputed to be a portrait of Alexander the Great; one of the cryptic 'seals' of the Indus Valley civilization, found in Egypt, bearing the image of a bull and a series of hieroglyphs that had never been decoded, an object whose purposes no man knew; a flat, polished Chinese stone bearing a scarlet I Ching hexagram and dark natural markings resembling a mountain range at dusk; a painted porcelain egg; a shrunken head made by the denizens of the Amazon rain forest; and a dictionary of the lost language of the Panamanian isthmus whose speakers were all extinct except for one old woman who could no longer pronounce the words properly on account of the loss of her teeth

—Salman Rushdie, *The Enchantress of Florence*[1]

SACRED COMPLEXITY

In Salman Rushdie's satiric narrative of early modern global encounters, Lord Hauksbank of That Ilk is a free-floating cosmopolitan, a pirate admiral occasionally commissioned by Her Majesty. His "objects of virtue" seem to mirror and mock a postmodern desire for difference, our delight in multiplicity, our escape from simple locality. For those of us who treasure religious diversity often delight in the gifts of other wisdoms. Though our initial motives may be ethical or democratic, something more comes into play than a mere ecumenical ethics or strategy for interreligious peace. We grow an appetite for their difference. Our pluralism deepens.[2] And it multiplies: our pluralism is not one! This volume demonstrates the plural resonances of several religious traditions with Whitehead's cosmology and with process theology. Indeed, it displays how specifically Whiteheadian approaches to pluralism develop a *taste for religious multiplicity itself*. So we focus in this essay not on the relations of process thought to particular religions, but on a Whiteheadian understanding of the *inherent multiplicity of religion—and of the religious character of multiplicity.*

But how, then, might we distinguish between an apparently growing attraction to religious multiplicity and the pirate admiral's collection of multicultural treasures? How might we value, as process thinkers, at once the beauty of spiritual bricolage and the justice of intercultural encounters, the wisdom of eclectic explorations and the integrity of particular

1. Rushdie, *Enchantress of Florence*, 16.
2. Griffin, *Deep Religious Pluralism*.

traditions? Can we, with Whitehead's support, examine the multiplicity of traditions transforming the single tradition, indeed perforating the boundaries of its singularity? One might love for instance the neighborhood yoga class spliced with Zen teachings and led alternately by a young Muslim from Istanbul, and an aging Jewish feminist. Rhythms of interfaith marriage, ecumenical Qur'anic study, Pentecostal Sunday mornings supplemented with a Wednesday evening Ashanti women's ritual, churches sharing building and soup-kitchen with synagogues, theistic respect for certain rigorous atheisms, ecological alliances with a Native American inflection—such routine hybrids ripple fluently through the expanse of a cosmopolitan life. It takes a sweeping hypocrisy to dismiss such a spectrum as "new age" or "syncretistic." But, then, what dividing line remains between the complex resonances collected in this book and Lord Hauksbank's cabinet of treasures? If the present endeavor implies a pluralism that many would call postmodern, does that make us pirates?[3] Is our taste for multiplicity perhaps still more symptomatic of the voracious Euroamerican consumption of "too much strangeness and novelty"—whatever remains exotic after centuries of appropriation—than of ecumenical respect?

We could of course take the route of much responsible interreligious work. We could lodge ourselves within the clear boundaries of a religious identity and a cultural context, from which we reach out carefully to representatives of other religions. We might practice a *separative pluralism* in order to avoid the risk, or at least the charge, of appropriation of the religious other. Yet the very notion of "religion" is being contested by some scholars of religion, as indicative of a pristine sense of simple identity, externally related.[4] It represses not only the obvious syncretism of much current practice, but also the internal complexity of the so-called great religions—not to mention the multiple sources of their orthodoxies. John Cobb, who had blazed the trail "beyond dialogue" of such complexities as "Buddhist Christianity," is now calling the traditions *Wisdoms* rather than

---

3. Unfortunately, such an understanding of postmodernity has also befallen theological reflection. See Ward, *The Postmodern God*.

4. As John Thatamanil puts it in "Comparative Theology after 'Religion,'" the term "religion" has a provincial Western origin but has come to be employed by traditions that do not resemble its presuppositions. For example, "the notion of a singular religious identity, in circular fashion, is generated by and in turn generates the idea that religions are neatly separated by clearly demarcated and impermeable borders." Moore and Rivera, *Planetary Loves*, 243. Also see Boyarin on the Christian creation of "religion," in *Border Lines*.

"religions."[5] The way of process theology to enliven participation in specific spiritual communities and their deep institutional and textual traditions (as demonstrated in this book) could never confine itself tidily to any bounded identity. It proceeds on the presumption that a mutual participation, and indeed, transformation issues from the contact between the Wisdoms; and that when process thought is involved, it is, intentionally activating their internal complexities. It is the endeavor of this chapter to emphasize these connective preconditions. In other words, the constructive proposals for the diversification of process theology within different Wisdoms form a matrix of 'sacred interactivity' under, within, beyond, and between the traditional boundaries of religions. The process approach does not, then, settle for the pluralism—so prone to piracy—of many separate ones, but opts for a *relational pluralism*. If these traditions live, in fact, only in process and in interaction, then only such relationalism can actually disclose the concrete, contextual life of Wisdom traditions.

If the identities of these traditions are not fixed but fluent one towards the others, then neither can we presume that there will be any single identity of process theology, ready to impose its new paradigm upon all Wisdom traditions. Instead, we find that in their complex exchanges, process approaches and Wisdom traditions connect and disconnect within multi-dimensional flows of resonance. They may, we hope, release "sacred complexities," forming amidst their meandering infiltrations and mutual contaminations unexpected and unsettling alliances. Energized by its relational pluralism, why would we attempt to formalize process theology into some new, orthodox, pluralism, ready-made for any tradition it engages? Instead, we find that a process sense of the plurality of expressions of the divine or the sacred within, between, across, and beyond religious traditions resists the deceptive unity of an already tamed plurality, of what Whitehead calls "a neat little system of thought, which thereby over-simplifies its expression of the world" (RM 50).

Process pluralism goes all the way down. Instead of a tidy system that will handle the plurality of traditions from *the* process point of view we find that process theology, from the start composed of a variety of theological and philosophical influences, was itself always a multiplicity. Evolving from Whitehead's complication of physical cosmology with divinity, process theology assembled a dramatic diversity of modes of thinking.[6] And as with Whitehead, this assemblage has always been ex-

5. Cobb, *Spiritual Bankruptcy*.
6. See Faber, *God as Poet of the World*, part 1.

perimentally interlinked with the labyrinthine multiplicity of the world's Wisdoms. Although some of its routes were conceptualized within the context of Christianity, process theology never intended to become either the expression of *one* religion, or the articulation of wisdom *as* One.

On the contrary, remaining true to Whitehead's cosmological vision means attending to the world as a polyphony of experiential and interpretive processes. Its pluralism reflects the vastness of an irreducible multiplicity of becomings. It thus heightens sensibilities towards the adventurous in human—and also in nonhuman—nature. As this pluralism discovers connective differences, it activates an experiential space of uncharted intensities and forms uneasy harmonies of "togetherness" (PR 22). Amidst our varied religions, process pluralism has always valued the movement of the improbably wandering wisdoms. It has understood multiple influences as important instances of "concrescence" ('growing together') in, between, and across these traditions. Following Whitehead's intuition that process thought "seems to approximate more to some strains of Indian, or Chinese, thought, than to western Asiatic, or European, thought" as it makes "process ultimate" (PR 7), process theologies appeal to an eros of relational differentiation that reveals the divine, or the sacred, in *and* beyond religions, in *and* beyond all inherited identities.

Hence, when a process theology exceeds the orthodoxies of a massively Euro-Christian tradition, its intent is not to *supersede* any of these orthodoxies (and so merely mirror their competitive oppositions) but to highlight—in light of a connective sacredness—their own fluency. Cobb's game-changing *Christ in a Pluralistic Age,* for instance, deconstructed— with the help of Buddhism—the unifying substance metaphysics of classical Christianity, yet did so as a way of receiving key features of the Nicene and Chalcedonian logos-Christology.[7] Whitehead himself discerned, in the classically unassimilable logic of the trinity, the break-through of a "doctrine of mutual immanence" in a "multiplicity" (AI 168). Such a gesture need not deploy the promising multiplicity of the trinity in competition with a stereotype of Jewish and Muslim monotheism. Rather, this relational pluralism of process theologies might let the divine reveal itself, for example, as a variant of the "plurisingularity" of the name *Elohim.*[8] Similarly, rather than trapping Asian thought within a mere One or a mere Nothing, we discover among the living options of Buddhism the example

---

7. Cobb, *Christ in a Pluralistic Age.*

8. See Keller, *Face of the Deep.*

of the beautiful play of multiplicity in the *Lotus Sutra*.[9] This many-folded matrix thus may be disclosed as theistic divine *and* a nontheistic sacred. Indeed 'S/He/It' has been acquiring a singular multiplicity of names!

By embracing many elements of many orthodoxies—along with many of the others they exclude—such a polyphony certainly eludes any essentialist unity. But it also means to avoid the piracy of an appropriative pluralism. Not content to espouse an oppositional heterodoxy or a defiant heresy, this differential process understanding of a sacred interactivity offers, instead, what we may call a *polydoxy*—an inherently multiple teaching of the multiple.[10] It does not take the place of our various traditions of "right teachings" and "right practices," but rather tracks the differences that connect them. Hence, a process pluralism is a *sapiential* polydoxy from the start: it does not assemble a mere many, nor yet a pirate admiral's exhibition of stolen treasures. On the contrary, as the various chapters of this book demonstrate, it displays the folds of a wisdom that we find enfolded only in multi*pli*city: the *pli,* which makes the difference connective and opens the connections into difference.[11] A polydoxical multiplicity connects the folds one to another in the very act of valuing the otherness of the engaged Wisdoms. It honors that which interlinks, pleats, or braids the flows of their difference together; it encourages living the intensities that its differentiations release.

Pirates do not just disappear, however. Some become emperors; others attack the empire's integrity. We seem to find ourselves in a historical period of renewed interreligious conflict and theocratic wills to power—largely variants on the sibling rivals of Abraham, vying with each other and with state secularism for dominance. Therefore we consider the cultivation of this *taste* for 'connective differentiation' and 'differential connectivity' not only joyful and nourishing, but *necessary* for the planetary weal. Without it, the energy for a decolonizing ecumenism and for a pluralist ethic quickly dissipates. Of course the postcolonial worry must remain: we may love those exotic others to death and appropriate their treasures. Hence, engaging sacred interactivity may only avoid separation or piracy by recognizing the *risk*, within the neoliberal globalism, of transgressive entanglements. In other words, a polydox multiplicity recognizes its harmonics not only as joyfully complex, but also as uneasily com*pli*cit.[12] If

9. See Reeves, "Divinity in Process Thought and the Lotus Sutra," 257–369.

10. See Keller and Schneider, *Polydoxy.*

11. See Deleuze, *The Fold.*

12. Cf. Spivak, *Critique of Postcolonial Reason.*

a certain "postcolonial ambivalence"(Homi Bhabha) has complicated the discourse of liberation, it does not pretend it could return to an original purity of the native or the ethnic. Postcolonial theologies do not imagine either a founding or a final purity of a separated, socially just religious community.[13] Difference does not separate. It does not protect authenticity from piracy by restoring over-simplification and mutual exclusion. Once I begin to *feel*—to "prehend"—the other (how am I separate from him/her/it?)—have I not taken some of that difference into self, effecting an "other in self"?

Attention to complicity—the *tricky* ways we are "folded together"—does not suppress our taste for multiplicity. It holds it *responsible*. It releases the flows of resonance that make response possible. Yet, as the multiple engagement of process understandings of different Wisdoms collected in this volume demonstrate, their multiple entanglement does not hinder, but in their "togetherness" encourages complex commitments across and among traditions. *This* taste for the multiple is what process thinking cultivates as the very manifestation of the "Divine Eros" (AI 277). If we, living with these Wisdoms, become mindful of the sacred multiplicity that always already constitutes their own process, we may experience a love that instigates a relational pluralism and then nourishes it. We call this love—*polyphilia*.[14] In what follows we explore a process theory of multiplicities as "skillful means,"[15] in the irreducible uncertainty and the loving possibility of its becoming.

BECOMING MULTIPLICITIES

Polyphilia is not omniphilia, polydoxy not omnidoxy. When we consider relational pluralism as a complex landscape of sacred foldings, its activating transformations take the most concrete, contextual, and conflictual forms. In the past half century, an unruly crowd of theories and practices has complicated religious and theological study, and therefore also comparative studies in religion and theology. These studies have enmeshed the problems of the ancient Wisdoms in a plurality of competing issues (race/gender/sex/class/ecology) multiplied by cultures (traditions/ nations/ethnicities/ diasporas), all intensified by historic urgency.

13. Cf. *Postcolonial Theologies*, edited by Keller, Nausner, and Rivera.
14. See Faber, *Poet*, Postscript.
15. See Faber, The *Divine Manifold* (forthcoming).

One might almost sympathize with various conservative recoils from this "multiplication" of indignantly politicized identities within and between the Wisdom traditions. Even more, one might (almost) understand why all these issues—race, gender, sex, class, and ecology multiplied by cultures, traditions, nations, ethnicities, and diasporas as addressing life or death for a critical mass of earthlings—have been kept at bay in the institutionalized forms of interreligious dialogue. The complications seem to multiply into a chaos of irreconcilable demands, accusations, and impossibilities. Nonetheless, the Wisdom discourses—the theologies—show signs (amidst this entanglement) of a mysterious metamorphosis: polyvocal and promiscuous, haunting and queer, grounding and ungrounded, situated and planetary. A theological polydoxy answering to the manifold of Wisdoms does seem to be emerging. And for all the indubitable confusions, a certain 'coherence' does seem to be evolving. We are all—in such a volume—learning to embrace its sources both within and beyond the history of relevant orthodoxies. But how will such an identity-engulfing polyphony hold together?

Its logic would not resemble that of an abstract order of pyramidal meaning. Polydoxy, unlike the orthodox self-understandings it intersects, clings together by a connective, a *sticky logic*: "to cohere" means first of all "to stick together." Inconclusive and becoming, this stickiness, this mutual entanglement, seems to reflect something about all our relations. It is that which is, by definition, hard to unify in thought—something luring us to seek new ways to understand 'togetherness.' William James first dubbed this 'something' the "pluralistic universe," indeed, presciently, the "multiverse." "Pluralism lets things really exist in the each-form," he wrote, emphasizing the concrete particularities of the world. Everything concrete exists "at all times in many possible connexions which are not necessarily actualized at the moment." James thus originates at the same moment pluralistic reflection on religious experience and on the cosmos. "If the each-form be the eternal form of reality no less than it is the form of temporal appearance, we still have a coherent world, and not an incarnate incoherence, as is charged by so many absolutists. Our 'multiverse' still makes a 'universe' . . . through the fact that each part hangs together with its very next neighbors in inextricable interfusion."[16]

Ernesto Cardenal, the great Salvadoran theo-poet, sets this cosmos in *verse*: "Why say universe, as if it were only one / and not pluriverse?"[17] The

16. James, *A Pluralistic Universe*, 130–31.

17. Cardenal, *Pluriverse*, 212.

inextricable interfusion keeps crossing disciplinary boundaries. William Connolly, a Jamesian and Deleuzian (he calls himself a 'Jamesleuzian'), intercepts the multiverse for the purposes of a political theory centered in the problem of religious and irreligious pluralism. The philosophy of a pluralistic universe, he writes, "suggests that human civilization is an event that might not have happened, and that it is most apt to survive if we attend to the fecundity, volatility, and complexity of interconnections in which it is set."[18] Such interconnections—political, physical, spiritual— may be evoking the pluralist coherence we seek.

Another metaphor for this 'cohesiveness' would be the polyphony of an orchestra in concert—its logic is that of *sounding together* in the plurisingularity of a matrix of experienced meaning. The polyphony is enacted as *sym-phony*—without a singular, sovereign conductor and without the imposition of a unified form and program. Indeed, the emblem of Whitehead's plural "togetherness" is this "symphonic form" in which we obtain a "sense of multiplicity" of "the experience of unity, of multitude, of transition" (MT 84). This 'concrescence' is thus a 'living together.'[19] In its metaphysical form—as stated by Whitehead's Category of the Ultimate (PR 21–22)—this conviviality appears as the creative togetherness of the process of the multiplicity of becoming. Of all of Whitehead's "tentative formulations of . . . ultimate generalities" (PR 8), this one offers a plu- ralistic coherence amidst imperialist attempts of (philosophical, religious, or political) totalization and indifferent relativism alike. Its generation of the rhythms and harmonies of coherence explores mutually relative multi- plicities in process—unification of multiplicities, multiplication of unities, and their resonance in a creative advance into the unprecedented. In such a sympathetic multiverse, perhaps in itself, *nothing* is ultimate—*except* the very concrescent cohesiveness of the polyphonic convergences and diver- gences.[20] We sound or live together as mutual surprises in a symphonic complexity.

Gilles Deleuze,[21] perhaps the most eminent philosopher to be deeply appreciative of Whitehead's symphonic pluralism, echoes Whitehead's infinitely variable connectivity in a "Harmony of Harmonies" (AI 296) with a "polyphony of polyphonies." Transforming "harmonic closure to

18. Connolly, *Pluralism*, 92.

19. See Faber, "Theopoetic Justice: Towards an Ecology of Living Together," Inau- gural Lecture for the Kilsby Family/John B. Cobb, Jr. Chair in Process Studies, April 22, 2010, Claremont School of Theology.

20. See Faber, review of *Die Wahrnehmungen der Organismen*, 124–28.

21. See Faber and Stephenson, *Secrets of Becoming*.

an opening onto a polytonality,"[22] its multiplicity avoids the total One and the disjunctive Multiple, but also the pirate-captain's collection of many ones. He draws on Whitehead's "play that diverges" and honorifically dubs his symphonic pluriverse—in allusion to James Joyce—the "Chaosmos."[23] In its nets and webs of bifurcating and moving, cohering and criss-crossing foldings, what 'lives together' discloses itself as event of heterogeneous connections. Its imperative is: "Be neither a One nor a Many, but multiplicities!"

As a multiplicity "doesn't begin and doesn't end, but is always in the middle, between things, interbeing, *intermezzo*,"[24] we are asked to become *from the middle*, always *in between*, in the rhythms, alliances, and resonances of our living together. In this "motley world,"[25] 'unity' always appears as a *finite* fold of multiple relations. Nothing is fixed; nothing is perfect; nothing is forever; but everything is vibrating, living, and resisting false unifications that defy multiplicity and life. This polyphonic pluralism employs an ethos of undoing oppressive hierarchies (sanctified ultimates and eternal orders) by creating folds of difference. Conversely, the imperial desire for the One is the desire for death; it is guided by a conservativism that for Whitehead "is fighting against the essence of the universe" (AI 274).

Does this resistance to the colonizing Oneness, this ethics of relational multiplicity, not also demand that pluralism exceeds relativism? Wouldn't the latter, if it harbors an ethos, not foster the ethics of global piracy, or perhaps worse, of mutually indifferent locations? Especially against the mutual isolation of closed contexts, interrupted by acts of aggression, we emphasize the excess of the polyphonic harmonics and symphonic rhythms of 'living together.' This excess of connective cohesiveness is produced not by the quantity of its relata but by the folds of the connection *between* them. Because these connections are folds of difference, not boundaries of separation, they also always exceed any bounded context. A separative pluralism is always tempted to simply identify with its own local context and leave others to do the same. Such localism belies the tangled interdependencies of the multiverse. An effectual pluralism of differential foldings, however, will instead require us to transgress closed contexts as false expressions of relationless units.

22. Deleuze, *Fold*, 82.
23. Ibid., 81.
24. Deleuze and Guattari, *Thousand Plateaus*, 25.
25. Deleuze, *Fold*, 81.

Our differential pluralism will understand multiplicity in its *transcontextual* valences, transgressive of the sealed boundaries of any single context, religious or cultural.[26] For its ethical claims must transgress the sealed boundaries of any single context, religious or cultural (your religious practice may justify a ritual sacrifice of animals repugnant to me, but less violent than my carnivore people's industrial practices; at the same time, it may not justify irresponsible mass production of CO_2 or of populations even among poor nations). Without this *connective* appeal, no pluralism can develop right teachings and right action—from an eightfold or a manifold path—whereby we persist in the transmutation of our quantitative pluralities into a qualitative planetary multiplicity.

Relational pluralism thus distinguishes itself from relativism in the cultivation of what we could call 'strange attractions': towards the others, the neighbors, the strangers, the stranger neighbors, with whom we find ourselves in relation—personally or planetarily—even before we can "identify" ourselves in difference from them. But in so doing, we open, and are opened by, the *fold between self and other*, the margin of stickiness or *jeong*,[27] overlap, hybridity, miscegenation, contamination, vibratory interference. Here, we join the tricksters[28] and ancestral lures,[29] the intermediary spirits and between-figures, charting the sacred interactivity of those older wisdoms that were superseded by the so called 'great world religions' (if this is not, in itself, already an imperialist simplification).

We are suggesting that it is only in the discovery of such constitutive or *prehensive relationality* that pluralism escapes from the banal plural of a mere many, or a series of separate ones. This enfoldment however is never reducible to one; in each fold the other is enfolded—partially, contiguously, stickily, symphonically. Each fold is a universe of others, each likewise "holographically" enfolding universes and "cryptographically" instigating new universes. While this com*plic*ating condition gets necessarily simplified by orders of abstraction, preference, and justice, notice that even sim*plic*ity—contrary to its classical connotation of pure unity—involves secretly a folding. The singular is already plural: "Being does not preexist its singular plural."[30]

26. See Faber, *Poet*, §36.

27. Jeong, a Korean word for attachment, is developed as theological trope in Anne Wonhee Joh, *Heart of the Cross*.

28. For the trickster figure as a device for postcolonial hermeneutics, see Grau, *Of Divine Economy*.

29. Coleman, *Making a Way out of No Way*.

30. Nancy, *Being Singular Plural*, 29.

The taste for multiplicity gives rise to a trust that changes the meaning of faith and the sacred. It can, perhaps, be most deeply cultivated *from within the mysteries* of the respective pluralisms possible to specific traditions—even to those traditions that, in the rise of the West, fused with the forms of theology and science least historically amenable to pluralism. To the extent that any of us are rooted in a historic religion, we work *with* its resources *of* and *for* complexity. To the extent that our Wisdoms remain entangled with the separating simplifications of their orthodoxies, we work "prehensively" *towards* their symphonic and sticky connectedness. Christian pluralisms cannot therefore operate long without Muslim, Hindu, Buddhist, or Hopi pluralisms. If these are embraced in a polydox alliance, they spread the recognition that multiple teachings are always already constitutive of any specifically chosen tradition. As the various Wisdoms also need enough coherence, however, they will inevitably create, anew, simplifications of abstraction, preference, and justice in order to both exceed the indifference and constrain the piracies of a hostile plurality.

The spiritual impulse to *become* multiplicities, then, arises from a transformation of oneness-*into*-manyness. Its conviviality becomes possible when we let go of any presupposed static and world-capturing sacred totality and its corresponding isolating contextualism of a oneness-*without*-manyness. In this transformation, we activate the enfolded multiverse that always surpasses itself, that unfolds differences in becoming and asks us to always enfold its community anew. Within and between Wisdom traditions, we risk the adventure of seeking the sacred interactivity in, between, across, and beyond those very traditions. But in invoking process folds of the divine, or of the sacred *in* multiplicity, we do not envision yet another—a "better"—religion. In light of the war-ridden exclusivities of simple identities that create sibling rivalries the self-designated "great world religions" and the primordial ways not even recognized as religions, the appeal to become multiplicities within diversity and entanglement takes on an incarnate urgency.

As we envision this embodiment of relational and differential multiplicity, we affirm also that the sacred or divine *in* multiplicity can never be reduced to only *one kind of* experience and understanding. This is not just a matter of ecumenical generosity. Rather we may understand the sacred or divine in the Wisdom traditions to reveal itself *in* an irreducible polydoxy. Because it *is* the very sacred or divine activity of enfolding, this multiplicity will allow us to discern it not only *in* multiplicity, but also *as* sacred or divine multiplicity. With Whitehead, we suggest that "the actuality of God must also be understood as a multiplicity of components in the process of creation" (PR 350).[31] And with Deleuze, as he muses on Whitehead, we affirm that the sacred interactivity is not that of "being a Being," but that which "becomes Process."[32] Desiring this divine *in* multiplicity inherently directs our pluralistic gaze towards a trust no longer driven by fear of becoming, difference, and flux, but filled with anticipation of the *mutual embodiment,* of the *inter-carnation,* of encounters, conjunctions, and interferences of Wisdoms. Whether we evoke the plurisingularity of *Elohim,* or the manyness-in-oneness of the Christian trinity, or the sacred intertwining of *samsara* and *nirvana* in the Buddhist 'co-origination' (*pratîtya-samutpâda*), or the complexity of the trickster of native religions, we 'prehend' the *sacred folds* of multiplicity. S/He/It, we might say, not only *insists on* multiplicity but *becomes as* its very interactivity—not as the one, not as the many, but as *the sacred or divine (in) multiplicity.*[33]

We (like all the authors of this volume) who speak from within specific and various spiritual traditions, in their development and in their dotage, find ourselves invariably 'between'—enfolding ourselves in an enfolded pluralism. As with the pirate admiral, the moorings of the soul get loose. So much the better: polyphilia! We may be learning to move with a more fluent grace, with less need and greed, amidst strangeness and novelty. We may at moments enfold a postcolonial ethics along with precolonial hints of wonder, evolutionary sciences of emergence along with religious narratives of creation, bodhisattvas along with Christ, the Bible along with the *Lotus Sutra.* In unfolding the mystery of this *enfolded divine (in) multiplicity,* our polydoxy may become *upaya*—"skillful means"—of the greater healing.

SKILLFUL MEANS

Might the multiple, here collected process approaches to Wisdom-folds offer a *pluralism of skillful means?* Maybe we should approach their multiplicity like the opening of the Chakras—healing through flow of potentialities folded down into ourselves. The folds we have blocked (our relations, our cultures) and their interrelations may not be allowed to express a reality of rigidly bound Ones—wounded and wounding in their enforced

31. Faber, "God in the Making," 179–200.

32. Deleuze, *Fold,* 81.

33. See Faber, "Bodies of the Void," 200–23.

separations. For our bodies no less than our traditions, may the violence of the "engendered monsters" (of the enclosed totality of appropriation, or the multiple totalitarianisms of separation) be broken when we realize that the "states of things are not unities or totalities but multiplicities"? May the realization that the "many states of things (where each state would be a whole)" where "each state of things is multiple (which would only be an indication of its resistance to unification)" are but the illusion of the united or divided One. May we instead open, or unfold, the "points of unification, centers of totalization, points of subjectivation" so that "multiplicity grows from the middle like grass"?[34] Healing begins where elements become less important than what is the 'between' of the elements—the many folds of relationships, inseparable from one another.

This is the *Lotus Sutra's* doctrine of *upaya*. Indeed, what rises off the pages of the *Lotus Sutra*, what billows and balloons and fills the reading gaze, is its multiplicity of multiplicities. These multiples multiply mountainously, vertiginously. These lists start with the great audience of Buddha on Holy Eagle Peak, an audience of millions: of so many *categories* of worthies, starting, strategically with individual *arhats* representing the very ideal about to be superseded. Women are named from the start, two famous nuns and their thousands of followers. Then the eighty thousand *bodhisattvas*; and the tens of thousands of various kings and deities—*Indra* alone is accompanied by "twenty thousand children of heaven"—and such marvelous collectives as the dragon kings and the centaur kings and the wheel-rolling kings and each of their tens of thousands of followers. As all these collectives collect themselves along with the narrator, this healing truth about multiplicity is disclosed: that every Buddha has been closely associated with hundreds of thousands of billions of buddhas in the past, fully practicing the way of the immeasurable *dharma* that is demonstrated by a polydox polyphony and held together through the infinite folds of the Buddha insofar as his *"innumerable skillful means* save living beings."[35]

The multiplicity of means is seen to be skillful by the infinitely *many* sentient beings and leads to the recognition of the *one* truth of salvation. The *Sutra of Innumerable Meanings*, which classically accompanies the *Lotus Sutra*, names this truth of the relational multiplicity of becoming, *pratitya samutpada*: "all things are originally empty and calm, ceaselessly changing, arising and perishing in an instant."[36] We can we read their

34. Deleuze, *Desert Islands; Two Regimes of Madness*, 309–10.
35. Reeves, *Lotus Sutra*, 95, our emphasis.
36. Ibid., 37.

"oneness"—sought in T'ien–t'ai's teaching of the "three thousand worlds in one thought-instant,"[37]—as code not for a simplifying, homogenizing unity, an annihilation of difference that assures the eventual collapse of the multiple, but instead as the *dynamic interdependence* of oneness-and-manyness: "The buddhas, the most honored of people, know that *nothing exists independently*, and that *buddha-seeds arise interdependently*. This is why they teach the one vehicle."[38] In the Hua-yen tradition, again, this one-multiplicity appears as the "interpenetration of part and part" (*shih-shih wu-ai*) and of the "interpenetration of part and whole" (*li-shih wu-ai*) in which recognition we release the healing process of the many-in-one of every single event as one-among-many amidst infinitely many events.[39]

Multiplicity as *mutual interdependence*, again, as articulated in the *upaya*, resonates with Whitehead's conviction that any conceptualization of 'ultimate realities' demands *a creative process of healing* by which it "converts the opposition into a contrast" (PR 348). Multiplicity as *mutual interdependence of part and whole* is clearly reflected in Whitehead's profound contention that every happening (as it gathers itself from its relations) "repeats in microcosm what the universe is in macrocosm" (PR 215) such that it, at the same time, "pervades the whole world" (PR 28). Multiplicity as *mutual interdependence of part and whole* reflects Whitehead's contention that, since there is no absolute context, there are no absolutely separated contexts either. Hence, the very environment of a polydox articulation of the sacred or divine (in) multiplicity must be polyphonic in nature, in order to be healing from occupations and separations. The world as a "whole," as Whitehead says, "is a multiplicity" (PR 348). It is, in other words, a "community of actual things" in "an incompletion in process of production," this 'process of incompletion' is healing because in it "no two actualities can be torn apart: each is all in all" (PR 214–15). Such a relational complex meets the heart of the healing process of multiplicity: *polydoxy demands polyphilia and polyphilia releases polydoxy.*

In *Religion in the Making*, Whitehead indicated such skillful means by evoking a threefold characterization of healing interdependence of the mutual enfolded plurality of Wisdoms *across* religious traditions. There is the complexity of religious experiences that in its specific expressions in multiple modes of living (values) and thinking (dogmas) as well as their mutual interpretation (metaphysics) necessitates a *mutual resonance*

37. See Odin, "Peace and Compassion," 371–84.

38. Reeves, *Lotus Sutra*, 95, our emphasis.

39. See Odin, *Process Metaphysics and Hua-Yen Buddhism.*

between them that cannot be reduced to only *one* true experience, religious teaching, or cosmological understanding (cf. RM 47ff). In order to allow for each fold to remain valuable, their togetherness must remain open to ever-new modes of interference. In Whitehead's typology of religious interpretations of the interrelations of the sacred or divine interactivity within the world, again, he demonstrates their *mutual incompleteness*. The "Eastern Asiatic concept" of "immanence," the "Semitic concept" of "transcendence," and the "Pantheistic concept" in which "the actual world is a phase of the complete fact" that is the divine are complexly intertwined (RM 68–70). And in an unprecedented "contextualization" of the sacred or divine *within* a multiplicity of ultimate aspects of reality—the multiplicities of worlds, values, and creativity (cf. RM 90)—Whitehead points at the *mutual immanence* of every folding of the sacred or divine and, hence, at the intercontextual nature of a multiverse in becoming. As in James, it never yields an absolute standpoint. Rather, its healing capacity lies in its profoundly processual relationality by which all of our abstractions, simplifications, and justifications must always be refolded again and again so as not to block their enfolded multiplicity.

As these threefold means of interdependence—of resonance, incompleteness, and immanence—arise in Whitehead's subtleties of thinking, what every process *upaya* of multiplicity will recognize at one point or another is this: what connects *and* differentiates all processes is their profound *mutuality*. With Plato, Whitehead calls this the *khora*—"the medium of intercommunication" (AI 134).[40] As the multiplicity of *dharmas* in the *Lotus Sutra*, Whitehead's *khora* unfolds into the irreducible dimensions of a healing multiplicity in which polydox complexities never stabilize, but always generate new dimensions, contingent one to the other and without any unified framework of deduction.

As this healing mutuality releases the sacred or divine *into* the finite processes of becoming, the *upaya* of the infinitely many buddhas reveal only *one* truth: their infinite multiplicity can only become healing when they skillfully direct us towards a polyphonic harmonics of the mutual embodiment of the sacred or divine *with* and *within* multiplicity. And enfolding the multiplicity of Wisdom traditions in their respective mystery, we may be surprised by the "one" truth of the *Lotus Sutra*—the healing character of the manifold. Its polyphonic interdependence is not indifferently all-inclusive, however, but rather dislodges any assumption that the sacred or divine controls the world or that only *one* religion can be true or

40. See Faber, "Immanence and Incompleteness."

that in *all* religions it would be only *one* expression of the sacred or that all the religions are indifferently true. Against these obstructions, Whitehead, like the *Lotus Sutra,* awakens a taste for sacred multiplicity with its healing character in terms of images of concern, care, tenderness, patience, love, intimacy, and peace.

Whitehead's divine (in) multiplicity fosters a comparable multiplicity of folds—releasing their healing capacity only in their mutual resonance, incompleteness, and immanence among themselves (*shih-shih wu-ai*) and with the universe (li-shih wu-ai): from the "principle of concretion" in *Science and the Modern World* with its multiplicity of names (SMW 179) to the "divine event" in *Religion in the Making,* vibrating between impersonal and personal modes (as pertaining to Buddhist and Christian orthodoxies alike); from the multiplicity of ultimate realities to the complex nature of 'God' in *Process and Reality,* with a multiplicity of poles and oscillations; from the multiple names of the sacred in *Adventures of Ideas* (initial Eros, final Fact, tragic Beauty, Supreme Adventure, Harmony of Harmonies, Love, Peace) to the Deity of *Modes of Thought* that mediates our experience of the corporality of the multiplicity of the universe, Whitehead intensifies in a multiplicity of means skillfully arousing, always anew and differently, the healing multiplicity in us, in our religious traditions, and in the unfathomable universe.[41]

Although process theologies have, in general, concentrated only on a few of these complex images of the sacred, they have developed a variety of openings for, and beyond, these images. While some process theologies limited their inquiries to the explicit use of 'God' in Whitehead, others dwelled in the multiplicity of ultimate realities as sacred. While some sensed the need to engage with the Abrahamic orthodoxies, others found it more useful to resonate with the characteristic of creativity and beauty of Eastern Wisdoms. In its "speculative imaginations" (PR 5) process pushed toward an astonishing and transgressive multiplicity: from a divine 'event' to a divine 'society'; from a sacred 'creativity' to a 'divine matrix.' Always, however, we should think that it would be fatal to the *healing* process of multiplicity that the *Lotus Sutra* suggests if we would become tempted to understand these images as closed systematization of that which Whitehead only approximated in terms of "tentative formulations of ultimate generalities" (PR 8).

Multiplicities of skillful means as offered by Whitehead and process theologies will have to *risk* these and other polyphilic *uncertainties—healing*

41. See Faber, "'The Infinite Movement of Evanescence,'" 171–99.

uncertainties, as it were—in the midst of the closures of orthodoxies. As long as we sense in them the humble love for the poetics of the open universe in its infinitely many finite connections (cf. PR 346), we will excite their healing capacities against monopolies of truth, separatism, or piracy. When we use these uncertainties *as upaya* and the *upaya as* healing uncertainties—as the many different approaches of process theology to the diverse Wisdoms in this volume demonstrate—we *can* resist embalming our religious lives in intra-contextual blindness. When we approach the sacred in, and in love of, the very multiplicity of unique perspectives, these *skillful uncertainties* will excite the very *concrescence* of our 'living together.' By interrupting our captivity to our most beloved abstractions, they will release us back into the ethical and spiritual demands of a sustainable conviviality.

UNCERTAINTY AND COMPLEXITY

Whitehead's connective pluralism of the sacred (in) multiplicity, unfolding the Buddhist *upaya* of a healing multiplicity, will also *enfold* itself so as to arrive on the path of meditative silence at the mystery of its "one" truth. At a certain point, where differences of belief and orthodoxy become obstructive to our 'living together,' what we may call the 'interreligious uncertainty principle' kicks in. Uncertainty, as we have suggested, is implicated in multiplicity, as multiplicity will unfold into uncertainty—both as humility and as excess.

Since there "is no 'control' that doctrine can place on divinity, especially in the theory-resistant multiplicity of divine immanence,"[42] we suggest that the uncertainty of multiplicity names that excess. But it utters it *apophatically*, that is, it speaks its unspeakability. The apophatic tradition is deeply rooted in the "world religions," and in profound ways in Christian orthodoxy, as negative theology. So, the *upaya* of uncertainty does not silence but overflows the orthodoxies, religious discourses, and theologies as a silence that honors the apophatic plenitude of the sacred (in) multiplicity.

As polyphilic planetarity calls for unprecedented attention to polydoxic uncertainty, it is not that suddenly one sells short one's own conceptual or doctrinal commitments to Wisdom traditions. It is not a sudden swerve into relativism. Nor is it a merely strategic pause, a polite silence until one can reassert one's own position more cunningly. Rather, the complexity of positionality here practiced—including the entire multiplicity of

42. Schneider, *Beyond Monotheism*.

teachings—is, we suggest, itself rooted in a profound *nonknowingness* or exercised as the very *process of unknowing.*

It is here that the verbose process tradition, confidently unfolded from Whitehead's affirmative metaphysics, may better practice the gesture of negative theology.[43] Process thought has quite kataphatically emphasized the complex mutuality of God and the world, underscoring their coherence—and, hence, the creative production of multiplicities at the relational heart of reality. Just as for Whitehead "no entity can be conceived in complete abstraction from the system of the universe," all key notions, or metaphors, in a system of thought, "presuppose each other." Yet Whitehead's very concept of "coherence" is, as we noted above, set forth in a quasi-apophatic gesture. For the resistance provided by concrete interrelations against mere separation of abstract terms does not mean that the signifiers "are definable in terms of each other. It means that what is indefinable in one such notion cannot be abstracted from its relevance to the other notions" (PR 3). The unknown is not excused from relation.

Khoric intercommunication, in Whitehead, is the relational process of the *unprecedented*—the opening of, and to, the uncertainty as the unknowing of "identification." Like tentacles feeling out the unknown, Whitehead's polydoxic theopoetics leaves us on the shaking grounds of an apophatic uncertainty on which the sacred (in) multiplicity cannot be "identified" with either God or ultimate reality. For the latter also indicate multiple sites of our unknowingness. Whitehead's 'coherence of the unprecedented' appeals to an uncertain *manifold* of complex differentiations, overflowing into unexpected creative relations.

Emitted from its special resonances with Whitehead's mutual immanence of the world and the divine, we have for some time been riveted to the *docta ignorantia*—the 'learned unknowing'—of the Nicolas of Cusa. This version of the mystical tradition, with its apophatic forcefield of uncertainty and its auto-deconstructive unknowing of "identities," does not leave us with a valueless equality of orthodoxies, but with a polydoxy that values an enfolded pluralism of the unprecedented ways of Wisdom as folds unfolded into the overflow of a positive cosmology of boundless mutual complication.

Enfolded in Whitehead's "contrasted opposites" (PR 348) of the multiplicities of the world and the divine in their movement towards mutual enfolding and unfolding is an anticipation of Cusa's *complicatio/explicatio* rhythm. This vision of mutuality marks, for us, a historical beginning for

43. See Faber, "'Gottesmeer,'" 64–95.

the theopoetics of relational uncertainty. *Complicatio* names this mystery as the *apophatic* infinity of the finite in which all relations are enfolded such that it is the enfolded potentiality (*posse ipsum*) of all folds. Cusa already realized that it is its very *unknowability*—its 'coherence' as infinite complexity—that prevents us from knowing that the religious other is wrong. Resonant with Whitehead's "mysticism" as the "insight into depths as yet unspoken" (MT 174)—as enfolding the *unprecedented*—Cusa extends this unknowingness of the *docta ignorantia* with unexpected 'coherence' to all enfolded creatures. And yet, such is the manifold enclosed in the divine—as enfolded multiplicity—that it begins, with Cusa, to break up and out into the world. What is 'complicated' in the infinite enfolds the finite and *unfolds* in the finite. It is not a one that is opposed to the many; it is folded out—as the divine *explicatio* itself—*in* and *as* multiplicity in all creatures.

In Cusa's cosmology of an acentric or omnicentric manifold, early modern science is germinating. He comes close to intuiting the connection of uncertainty to nonlocal entanglement that is at the cutting edge of quantum physics. Whitehead was already dimly aware of the uncertainty principle and energized by the quantum principle in his imagination of connective multiplicity (cf. SMW, ch. VIII). In its reverberating relevance, it will instigate an epistemic humility that should, by rights, grow in proportion to the amount of information. There are parallels between the interactions of science with religion to that of one religion with another that we cannot pursue here, but they root inextricably in the founding impulses of process thought.

In a wider polydox teaching, with its polyphilic eros, this unfolding into the multiplicity is enriched in beauty and restrained in appropriation by an ethic of finite multiple embodiments. Each relation comes unfolded out of an excess of relation. It therefore enfolds all its relations, even the most overexposed, in unknowingness. The fold of relation itself is shadowed—which is not to say overshadowed—by unknowing. As in Judith Butler's later parlance: "Perhaps most importantly, we must recognize that ethics requires us to risk ourselves precisely at moments of unknowingness, when what forms us diverges from what lies before us, when our willingness to become undone in relation to others constitutes our chance of becoming human."[44]

It is by way of an ethos of learned unknowing that we may stimulate the healing capacity of Whitehead's 'skillful means.' In its enfolding

44. Butler, *Giving an Account of Oneself,* 136.

and unfolding of the divine (in) multiplicity, its uncertainty leaves us with a profound 'apophatic plenitude' in any meaningful approach to the Wisdoms. The contrast between 'personal' and 'impersonal' aspects of the sacred ('God' and 'creativity' in Whitehead's parlance) becomes *theopoetic adventure*.[45] The contrast as it pertains, for instance, to the Abrahamic ('God,' Yahweh, Allah) and Indian/Chinese religions (*narguna brahman, tao, sunyata*), is familiar to Whiteheadian interreligious considerations—as is the sacredness of the 'world' for indigenous religions or the inclusive relationality (*pratîtya-samutpâda*) as 'personal' complication in Eastern traditions (Amida Buddha) and the 'impersonal' complication of 'God' in Western mysticism (Eckhart's 'Godhead,' Schelling's *Ungrund*).[46] The mystery of 'the sacred or divine interactivity' will only unfold as long as we don't create orthodox animosities, but a healing uncertainty, a complexity of *upaya,* a complexifying opening of blockings of the flow of sacred multiplicity.

And, instead of colonizing them into a stable super-metaphysic that identifies and coordinates Wisdoms, we understand these sacred adventures as *processes of unknowing* in which their 'contrasts' theopoetically, for the greater healing, gather the enfolded complexity of 'ultimate reality' differently in relation to the polydoxic heart of different Wisdom traditions. They constitute a 'community of unfolding' the enfolded mystery of the divine multiplicity. Therefore, it will be the very medium of intercommunication in which, irreducible one to another, their relational differences form *healing constellations* with one another. The ecumenical consequences of this unknowing—within, across, and beyond Wisdom traditions—become revolutionary, indicating the path *not* taken in the West for interreligious dialogue.

When the cardinal Cusa deploys the *docta ignorantia* against a Christian ignorance of their own ignorance, he produces an unprecedented knowledge. Cusa had taken part in a great ecumenical expedition to Byzantium. Then, in 1453, Mehmet took down Constantinople, migrants flood Europe with tales of horror, and the Ottomans push on. The pope calls for a new crusade. The cardinal opposed it. Within weeks of hearing the news, personally devastating, he writes *De pace fides*—a vision of religious peace. It invents an argument for interreligious dialogue. In nuce, because we finite beings cannot "know" the truth, which is infinite,

45. See Faber, *Poet*, §32.
46. See Bracken, *Divine Matrix*.

neither can we exclude the truth of other religions.[47] We have no excuse to force conversion or to war over belief. Connolly offers a postmodern analogue: "when you encounter unfathomable mystery in your faith in the right spirit, you may become inspired to appreciate corollary elements of paradox, mystery, or uncertainty at different points in other faiths . . . "[48]

This is the 'one' polyphilic truth of the mystery as it unfolds its healing capacity in its infinitely many *upaya:* that the infinitely enfolded mystery of sacred or divine multiplicity cannot be expected to be 'the same' or a countable plurality of manifestations. Wisdom, we say, is not about the "repetition" of existing modes of knowing, but about *creative unknowing* within the multiplicity of a polydoxic plenitude of the ever anew arrival of the sacred or divine. Whitehead encourages us to plunge into this irreducibly creative process of creative unknowing by noting that the creative constitution of new foldings (contrasts), when they form ever-more complex syntheses, can never be reduced to simpler contrasts of opposites. As its complexity is *emergent* und thus uncertain, such a process of contrasting Wisdoms produces an *infinity of categories*; complexity produces always new constellations of ways to connect. Engaging Wisdom traditions, for process theopoetics, must be a process of *incompletion*—the *processual* rhythm of diffusion (*implicatio*) and differentiation (*explicatio*).[49] The infinite potential of constellations of the complicated aspects of ultimacy can and will produce—and, in fact, has always produced—ever-new events with a *unique character of their togetherness*. Then its 'sacred discourse' does not reflect a mere archaeology of Wisdom traditions—as if we know already their identity and number. Rather it must become sensible to the incredible capacity of the unprecedented *event* of the sacred in a creative

47. Therefore if the Jew and the Muslim will recognize that they need not take our trinity as a personalist tritheism but as the "identity, equality and connection" of the infinite to itself; if the Hindu polytheist will admit that in each of the gods and goddesses "divinity itself" is being worshipped—then we have "one religion with many rites." Not religious pluralism, but the opening of the door to a dialogue of difference, an agonistic respect, that would make a heartier pluralism eventually possible. But as Simone Weil points out, Cusa represents the lost possibility for an alternative modernity for Europe, which would have obviated the endless religious war. The negative theological background for an affirmative corporeality of nonseparable differences in Cusa unfolds in a new apophatic ecumenism. It cannot go all the way to the polydox pluralism that we need—and that Christianity also needs and is in its academies at least rehearsing.

48. Connolly, *Capitalism and Christianity*, 128.

49. See Faber, *Poet*, §40.

multiplicity of Wisdom traditions. And these events are always events of stickiness, of the 'concrescence' of 'living together.'

In a sense, this gesture beyond "dialogue"—much appreciated when performed out of the certainties of the "identifications" with one's own tradition and the "otherness" of the other traditions—is always an apophatic leap of faith. Or is it the event of enlightenment? Whether or not it is said or unsaid to be such, this "third space" in which mutual transformation might occur can be symbolized with Whitehead's *khoric* 'medium of intercommunication' or Cusa's "Spirit," the 'connection itself.' It implicates every relation in the "negative infinity" of divine *complicatio,* a sacred *plenitude of enfolded multiplicity.* As in Whitehead, this infinite cannot close off the multiplicity as an 'infinity without finitude' or close down the multiplicity into a monistic whole. Au contraire, as Levinas pits 'infinity' against 'totality' and Whitehead proposes 'infinity' only '*in* finitude,' their mutual *perichoresis* is the unfinished, the indefinite, the indefinable *in the process* of enfolding and unfolding.[50] *Un dieu defini serai un dieu fini.*[51]

The ethical and spiritual call of the unprecedented sacred polyphony immerses our miseries of hate and fear in the light of our healing capacities to be called forth from the unknowingness of the mystery into the unknown fragilities of 'living together' in religious peace.

POLYPHILIC PLURALISM

The process pluralism we suggest here is an enfolding and unfolding pluralism, a relational and differential pluralism in a process of ever-new constellations of complication and uncertainty—an uncertainty that is complex because it names a mystery that cannot convey the sacred without an inherent love for the manifold in which it is enfolded. If this process pluralism is not to devolve into the piracy of a mere raid on whatever exotic differences globalization has not yet exhausted, then the emerging complexity remains, always, a work of self-critique—always a suspension of our presumptions that serves as a constraint upon a pluralism that intends to be a healing event. Only in this manner does the value of multiplicity activate an ethics and spirituality of radical interdependence.

But the apophatic moment of this mystical suspension, as we have argued, is just the backside of the *more*: the excess of meaning, life, difference, embodied in all our relations and the relations embodied in our

50. See Faber, "De-Ontologizing God," 209–34.

51. Scholem, *Major Trends in Jewish Mysticism,* 25.

differences. A mutual embodiment invoked in all our ultimates. No single incarnation contains it. And so, what *limits* our pluralism to an ethics of nonviolent encounter, intolerant of intolerance, exclusive of exclusion, disrespectful of disrespect, would be the very criterion of mutuality we have set forth. The sacred interactivity of Whitehead's cosmic Eros drives an alternative concept of power—if it should yet be named "power" at all—in process theology. Persuasion replaces coercion at the level of supreme purposefulness, but without any purpose of subjection. Love comes into play, as well. The pluralism we seek is not only discourse in the form of polydoxy, but life in the character of *polyphilia—the imitation of the sacred love of multiplicity.*[52]

Of course, the supremacy of 'love' is dangerously deformed by the history of Christian dominance. Moreover, it can never pretend to the role of common denominator for the dialogue (nor can *any* references to metaphysical ultimates). Process pluralists, however, do not wait for a common denominator, but engage in common projects in which conversations yield shared aims of mutual resonance, immanence, and incompleteness. The lure would be neither ground nor goal, but means—skillful means (of healing) or medium (of intercommunication)—the affirmative expression of the *upaya* in its productive suspension of certainty. The uncertainty principle of interreligious discourse—from which unfold the dynamisms of the infinite emergent complexity—requires the motive force of *polyphilia*, the love of this polyphony of multiplicities. The process pluralism we propose will not always worship polyphilic love as God; but it will always worship God as polyphilic love. For we suspect that whenever a God *is* worshipped, the primacy of the love-attribute will be the best check against the rapacity to which his/her/its followers are tempted. This is the point: the negation, the constraint of polyphilic pluralism, is the backside of the affirmation.

This affirmation, experienced in the loveable achievements of novel harmonies and intense contrasts, motivates not only religious but political pluralism. The sacred or divine in the image of such polyphilic love reveals itself as a love that *activates* us toward the respect of the fragility of the differences within the political and spiritual world. The affirmation of its complex values in their differentiation will draw attention to ever-new experiences as profound religious impulse in the changing landscape of Wisdom traditions. The *love* of the appearances of a multifarious world will arouse a practice of caring fragility of our living together in its ecological

52. See Faber, "Ecotheology, Ecoprocess, and *Ecotheosis*," 75–115.

complexity. Hence, we are seeing the surprising emergence of a "politics of love," as a mimicking of the language of biblical love, or of "agonistic respect," a subliminal paraphrase of love of the enemy. Seemingly, nontheistic approaches to multiplicity, such as Deleuze's, in their own work yield another motivation *for* Wisdom: the mystery of multiplicity, a new spirituality of value and virtuality, reverberating from Cusa's *complicatio*. Its *ethical, political, and spiritual impulse* always to reverse the coercive simplifications issues a divine Eros of suspension of simplifications in seeking ever-new and ever-more-beautiful contrasts of complexity. Whitehead's 'God' is an image of the insistence of such a love of the manifold. In such a manifold, it is for us to recognize polyphilia as the manifestation of the sacred or as divine revelation; for us to live its tenderness as if it is our lives through which it may never be lost.

In the radical practices of *bodhisattva,* compassion has already long entered into subtle contrasts with Christian love, offering a nonclinging wisdom to our calamitous western passions, while drawing into Asia a prophetic politics. The Whiteheadian divine lure—seeking ever-skillful means—is the arousal of non-violent modes of acting and thinking in a universe that in its vastness tends towards unprecedented intensities and ever-new harmonies with the tenderness of a compassionate valuation of the least of its folds. Yet the language of 'God' would, from the perspective of such a God, itself be subject to both western mystical negation and Asian impersonal sublation. For the *upaya* will never stop demanding of us fresh uncertainties and surprising connections. They cannot be stored in a treasure chest. Yet they will be released not in the name of any divine or sacred or ultimate, but *in the name of the living* in the fragility of their lives. The figure we offer at this moment, hoping no pirate will use it, is that of a *polyphilic pluralism.*

BIBLIOGRAPHY

Boyarin, Daniel. *Border Lines: The Partition of Judaeo-Christianity.* Philadelphia: University of Pennsylvania Press, 2004.

Bracken, Joseph. *The Divine Matrix: Creativity as Link between East and West.* Maryknoll, NY: Orbis, 1995.

Butler, Judith. *Giving an Account of Oneself.* New York: Fordham University Press, 2005.

Cardenal, Ernesto. *Pluriverse: New and Selected Poems.* Edited by Jonathan Cohen. New York: New Directions Books, 2009.

Cobb, John B. Jr. *Christ in a Pluralistic Age.* 1975. Reprinted. Eugene, OR: Wipf & Stock, 1998.

———. *Spiritual Bankruptcy: A Prophetic Call to Action.* Nashville: Abingdon, 2010.

Coleman, Monica A. *Making a Way out of No Way: A Womanist Theology.* Minneapolis: Fortress, 2008.

Connolly, William E. *Capitalism and Christianity, American Style.* Durham, NC: Duke University Press, 2008.

———. *Pluralism.* Durham, NC: Duke University Press, 2005.

Deleuze, Gilles. *Desert Islands and Other Texts, 1953–1974.* Los Angeles: Semiotext(e), 2004.

———. *The Fold: Leibniz and the Baroque.* Translated by Tom Conley. Minneapolis: University of Minnesota Press, 1993.

———. *Two Regimes of Madness: Texts and Interviews, 1975–1995.* Edited by David Lapoujade. Translated by Ames Hodges and Mike Taormina. Semiotext(e) Foreign Agents Series. Los Angeles: Semiotext(e), 2007.

Deleuze, Gilles and Felix Guattari. *A Thousand Plateaus: Capitalism and Schizophrenia.* Minneapolis: University of Minnesota Press, 1987.

Faber, Roland. "Bodies of the Void: Polyphilia and Theoplicity." In *Apophatic Bodies: Negative Theology, Incarnation, and Relationship,* edited by Chris Boesel and Catherine Keller, 200–23. Transdisciplinary Theological Colloquia. New York: Fordham University Press, 2010.

———."De-Ontologizing God: Levinas, Deleuze and Whitehead." In *Process and Difference: Between Cosmological and Poststructuralist Postmodernisms,* edited by Catherine Keller and Anne Daniell, 209–34. SUNY Series in Constructive Postmodern Thought. Albany: SUNY Press, 2002.

———. "Ecotheology, Ecoprocess, and *Ecotheosis*: A Theopoetical Intervention." *Salzburger Zeitschrift für Theologie* 12 (2008) 75–115.

———. *God as Poet of the World: Exploring Process Theologies.* Louisville: Westminster John Knox, 2008.

———. "God in the Making: Religious Experience and Cosmology in Whitehead's *Religion in the Making* in Theological Perspective." In *L'experience de Dieu: Lectures de Religion in the Making d'Alfred N. Whitehead,* edited by Michel Weber and Samuel Rouvillois, 179–200. Janvier: Ecole Saint-Jean, 2005.

———. "'Gottesmeer'—Versuch über die Ununterschiedenheit Gottes." In *"Leben in Fülle": Skizzen zur christlichen Spiritualität,* edited by Thomas Dienberg and Michael Plattig, 64–95. Münster: LIT Verlag, 2001.

———. "Immanence and Incompleteness: Whitehead's Late Metaphysics." In *Beyond Metaphysics? Explorations in Alfred N. Whitehead's Late Thought,* edited by Roland Faber, Brian Henning, and Clinton Combs, 91–107. Amsterdam: Rodopi, 2010.

———. "'The Infinite Movement of Evanescence'—The Pythagorean Puzzle in Plato, Deleuze, and Whitehead." *American Journal of Theology and Philosophy* 2/1 (2000) 171–99.

———. Review of *Die Wahrnehmungen der Organismen. Über die Voraussetzungen einer naturalistischen Theorie der Erfahrung in der Metaphysik Whiteheads,* by Michael Hampe. *Process Studies* 25 (1996) 124–28.

Faber, Roland, and Andrea Stephenson, editors. *Secrets of Becoming: Negotiating Whitehead, Deleuze and Butler.* New York: Fordham University Press, 2010.

Grau, Marion. *Of Divine Economy: Refinancing Redemption.* London: T. & T. Clark International/Continuum, 2004.

Griffin, David Ray, editor. *Deep Religious Pluralism.* Louisville: Westminster John Knox, 2005.

Joh, Anne Wonhee. *The Heart of the Cross: A Postcolonial Christology*. Louisville: Westminster John Knox, 2009.

Keller, Catherine. *The Face of the Deep: A Theology of Becoming*. London: Routledge, 2003.

Keller, Catherine, and Laurel Schneider, editors. *Polydoxy: Relation and Multiplicity in Theology*. London: Routledge, 2011.

Keller, Catherine, Michael Nausner, and Mayra Rivera. *Postcolonial Theologies*. St. Louis: Chalice, 2004.

Moore, Stephen D., and Mayra Rivera. *Planetary Loves: Spivak, Postcoloniality, and Theology*. New York: Fordham University Press, 2010.

Nancy, Jean-Luc. *Being Singular Plural*. Stanford: Stanford University Press, 2000.

Odin, Steve. "Peace and Compassion in the Microcosmic-Macrocosmic Paradigm of Whitehead and the Lotus Sutra." *Journal of Chinese Philosophy* 28 (2001) 371–84.

———. *Process Metaphysics and Hua-Yen Buddhism: A Critical Study of Cumulative Penetration vs. Interpenetration*. SUNY Series in Systematic Philosophy. Albany: State University of New York Press, 1981.

Reeves, Gene. "Divinity in Process Thought and the Lotus Sutra." *Journal of Chinese Philosphy* 28 (2001) 257–369.

———. *The Lotus Sutra: A Contemporary Translation of a Buddhist Classic*. Boston: Wisdom Publications, 2008.

Rushdie, Salman. *The Enchantress of Florence*. New York: Random House, 2009.

Schneider, Laurel C. *Beyond Monotheism: A Theology of Multiplicity*. New York: Routledge, 2007.

Scholem, Gershom. *Major Trends in Jewish Mysticism*. New York: Schocken, 1921.

Spivak, Gayatri. *Critique of Postcolonial Reason: Toward a History of the Vanishing Present*. Cambridge: Harvard University Press, 1999.

Thatamanil, John. "Comparative Theology after 'Religion.'" In *Planetary Loves: Spivak, Postcoloniality, and Theology*, edited by Stephen D. Moore and Mayra Rivera, 238–57. New York: Fordham University Press, 2011.

Ward, Graham, editor. *The Postmodern God: A Theological Reader*. Oxford: Blackwell, 1998.

Whitehead, Alfred North. *Process and Reality: An Essay in Cosmology*. Corrected Edition. Edited by David Ray Griffin and Donald W. Sherburne. New York: Free Press, 1978.

9

A Retrospective
What It All Means

—Sandra Lubarsky

T HE ESSAYS IN THIS volume are an overture to the rich and extended conversations that can arise from mutual receptivity. Together they constitute an intellectually demanding exploration of the usefulness of process thought for those who are committed to a variety of wisdom traditions as well as an appraisal of process theology by the measure of these traditions. To read the essays individually is to observe a process that is much more than the usual exercise in critical thought; it is to see a creative exchange undertaken with a "penetrating sincerity," what Whitehead deemed the most important of religious virtues. To read the essays as a whole is to become alive to the dynamism of multiple Wisdoms meeting one another in a companionship of inquiry.

In his introduction, John Cobb talks about how putting on "Whiteheadian glasses" helps people to "see the world in fresh and valuable ways." He remembers how in his own life, the glasses issued by the University of Chicago's humanities division magnified the strains in the fabric of Methodism. At the same time, those prescription lenses curved the light sideways so that any of religion's counterclaims to modernity were obscured. Of course, "seeing" always comes harnessed to a metaphysics; no corrective lens can overcome this state of affairs. And we know that on a neurological level, visual patterns shape and sustain our worldviews. To see the world differently, then, is a daunting task. It requires attention to evidence that exceeds the narrow band of our current visible order. Against limited "schemes of thought" that arbitrarily illuminate only a small range of life, Whitehead said, "There is greatness in the lives of those who build up religious systems . . . [and] in the rebels who destroy such systems" (PR, 337–38).

Nonetheless, it is no easy thing to make a perceptual shift, either as a trailblazer or a rebel. Cobb speaks of the pain that was involved in shifting worldviews. "One has to ask oneself again and again whether it's wise to go one's own way in spite of the social, scholarly, and intellectual pressures to go other ways." When much is at stake, as it was for Cobb and as it is for many of those who have written for this volume, the decision to open oneself to a new way of seeing—and thus also to new vulnerabilities and responsibilities—is not uncomplicated. To embrace a process metaphysics is to separate, on the one hand, from many of the assumptions of the dominant metaphysics of the modern world (Cartesian-Newtonian materialism), and on the other, especially for those who identify with monotheistic traditions, from many of the long-embraced theological assumptions that shaped their traditions prior to modernity.

In an essay on painting, novelist and art critic, John Berger writes, "the painter knows that far from being able to control the painting from the outside, he has to inhabit it and find shelter in it."[1] Such is also true for the kind of work that is being done in this volume. These are not essays that are written at a distance. Each is written from personal commitment to a particular Way. Each is a positive prehensive effort to incorporate a philosophical system and a wisdom path. It is an enactment, writ large, of Whitehead's central metaphysical principle: the inclusion of one event into another. Which aspects and how they are incorporated is the occasion for much creativity. Above all, each writer is motivated by the desire to strengthen and sustain the vitality of the Way that informs his or her life. The challenge is to satisfy the enthusiasm for relevance and coherence with the larger scheme of things without undoing the very wisdom that provides reason for reaching beyond itself. What is required is "order entering upon novelty" and "novelty . . . reflected upon a background of system."[2] Whitehead urges caution in this process, care that new energies do not sweep away the "the delicacies of contrast between system and

---

1. Berger, *Shape of a Pocket*, 31.
2. Whitehead, *Process and Reality*, 339.

freshness." He counsels that those involved in the effort to renew traditions "deal tenderly"[3] in the conjoining of affections, and this is, in fact, the approach taken in each of the essays in this book. We see the building up of traditions and the securing of more habitable shelters, refuges not *from* the world, but *within* it.

This book is framed as an opportunity for representatives of diverse communities to consider the value of process thought for their work. It is not assumed, as Catherine Keller and Roland Faber state so well in their essay, that there is a "single identity of process theology, ready to inscribe its new paradigm upon all Wisdom traditions." Rather, the assumption is that the many valuable Wisdoms will find their own patterns of relation, some of which will be particular to a singular Way, others of which may recur within several traditions. Where there are repetitions, they come with variations on the theme; such is the case with the theme of divine influence, taken up in the essays on Judaism, Islam, Christianity, and Hinduism, each time given fresh resonance. This approach to dialogue aligns with the model that Cobb has pioneered throughout a lifetime of cultivating openness as a theological practice. There is no hint of apologetic, no justifying, defending, or bending one's tradition in order to gain respectability or legitimacy from what has been predetermined to be a superior philosophical system. Nor is it a desultory dialogue without real commitment or purpose, with participants trying to find common ground by smoothing over differences. The starting premise is that each tradition has its own cognitive strategies and social location, its own systemic wholeness, and that an internal dialogue between the tradition and process thought may be mutually enhancing. It is dialogue without compulsion or threat. And thus, this public thinking-aloud, done forthrightly and without polemics, allows readers to see the creative process unfold, sometimes tentatively and sometimes boldly, within distinctly different ways. The manner in which this unfolds is of interest and value not only to those who stand within the traditions, but for those standing outside as well. For me, as a Jew, it is helpful to learn how a Muslim thinker struggles with the question of divine power. Partly this is because of the inescapable principle of internal relations, partly it is because of the close kinship between the two traditions, and partly it is because of the contrasts between the two traditions. I look to this and other exchanges between process thought and the various Ways also for the unexpected insights that may arise from the asking of new questions and from what Keller and

3. Ibid.

Faber call the "processes of unknowing" that constitute part of the "sacred adventure." They seem wise themselves when they write that "wisdom is not about the 'repetition' of existing modes of knowing, but about *creative unknowing* into the multiplicity of polydoxic plentitude of the ever anew arrival of the sacred or divine."

And so the dialogue within traditions becomes in this volume also a dialogue between traditions, and the reflection on the usefulness of process thought becomes also a reflection on the pluralism of wisdom traditions. The progression is natural and related when the beginning assumption is not only that all traditions have value both for themselves and for others, but that there are several different approaches to the ultimate character of the universe. Cobb credits Whitehead with helping him to understand Buddhism, but it is Cobb's contribution to have correlated Whitehead's concept of "creativity" with the Buddhist notion of "dependent origination" and his further articulation and clarification of the idea of multiple ultimates that has changed the landscape of religious dialogue.[4] Whereas superficial pluralism maintains that when all is said and done, the many varieties of traditions—Eastern, Western, indigenous, Humanistic—are all speaking about the same ultimate reality, "deep pluralism" affirms Cobb's insight that the many traditions are directed toward different ultimates: creativity/emptiness; God; the world. We do not thereby have three competing supreme values but rather three complimentary "features of reality" (Cobb's language), each fundamental and each reliant on the other. We can acknowledge that there is real difference between the various Wisdom ways at the same time that we can recognize that what is being said is important to all of us. Though we may continue to orient ourselves around one particular ultimate, we can do so without denying the legitimacy of traditions that shape themselves in relation to a different ultimate. More than this—much more—is the fact that deep pluralism carries us on a great current toward deep, uncharted waters upon which we now hover, poised before new chapters in our wisdom histories. These are the chapters to be written as we negotiate and celebrate the new relations that become possible when the intimacies between ultimates are disclosed. What might be the shape of a Judaism—or any monotheistic tradition—that seriously entertains dependent origination and sets impermanence side by side with everlastingness? What God-centered doctrines and liturgies will be reformed to correlate with Earth-centered wisdoms? Where will the centers and the borders be in these new forms of "togetherness" that arise

4. Griffin, "John Cobb's Whiteheadian Complementary Pluralism," 39–66.

from the "dynamisms of the infinite emergent complexity" made possible by deep pluralism? The adventure is great. It will undoubtedly be accompanied by such dangers as bootlegging and piracy, condemned by Keller and Faber at the beginning of their essay. But it holds out the promise that we may learn "the requirement of love . . . the love of this polyphony of multiplicities" as well.[5]

Whitehead and Cobb speak in aesthetic terms about what dialogue can yield—richness, contrast, intensity; it is language that shifts away from judgments of either-or and from exclusion. It assumes a vibrant palette of possibilities. These possibilities arise in the process of receptivity, of dialogue, of opening to the extraordinary and the ordinary. "The impulse to paint," writes Berger, "comes neither from observation nor from the soul (which is probably blind) but from an encounter: the encounter between painter and model—even if the model is a mountain or a shelf of empty medicine bottles." It begins with receptivity and on this point Berger quotes the Chinese artist, Shitao (1642–1707):

> Painting is the result of the receptivity of ink: the ink is open to the brush: the brush is open to the hand: the hand is open to the heart: all this in the same way as the sky engenders what the earth produces: everything is the result of receptivity.

Receptivity arouses collaboration and participation. "Paintings," Berger says, "are not first and foremost about a young woman, a rough sea or a mouse with a vegetable; they are about . . . participation." When is a painting alive? "When the painted image is not a copy but the result of a dialogue."[6] And so it is also with the creative process in general, including the theological and metaphysical arts.

Rabbi Bradley Artson's essay is remarkable in its depth of dialogue with process theology, its breadth of application, and its correlations between Jewish tradition and process theology. Artson surveys many of the central concepts of process thought and shows how they are not only compatible with but "faithful" to the Jewish tradition. Indeed, he argues that it is process philosophy, not Greek metaphysics that supports the basic covenantal structure of Judaism. "Reality as relational . . . should sound familiar to any Jew because our word for that dynamic relating is *brit*, covenant . . . Covenant is always interactive, always connecting, and always relational." In a succession of examples, Artson makes the case that "[p]

---

5. Quotations are from Keller and Faber's essay in this volume.

6. All quotes are from Berger, *Shape of a Pocket*, 18–21.

rocess thinking offers a way to recover a more biblically and rabbinically dynamic articulation of God, world, and covenant."

Divine omnipotence, omniscience, and impassibility are shown to be incompatible with covenantal theology and unsupported by either Hebrew Bible or Talmud. Divine-human partnership requires human freedom and responsibility, neither of which can be reconciled with divine omnipotence or omniscience. Moreover, divine omnipotence can only lead to the inference of divine accountability for evil. On either count, the logic of covenant is undermined. Instead, Artson affirms an image of God who acts persuasively in the world, "meet[ing] you in the next choice, with the next possibility," without violating either human freedom or natural law.

Citing Torah, Talmud, and Zohar, Artson finds much in Jewish thought that is aligned with and provides support for the insights of process theology. He rejects the idea of creation *ex nihilo* for textual reasons and because it implies divine omnipotence. He affirms both creation and revelation as ongoing, continuous processes that attest to renewed creativity, divine presence in the world, and God's "steady relational love." Every moment can be a departure from the wilderness and a coming into the "pulsing relationship of love" that is given through Torah. Importantly, Artson links this dynamic with the covenantal expectations of ethical action. "Such covenantal love also, of course, elevates the place of ethics, and it means that morality becomes the capstone of religious Jewish life."

Artson's contribution stands out as one of the first, systematic examinations of process theology and Conservative Judaism. "Walking with God" is the goal of Jewish tradition. To "be on the way"—*ba-derek*—is to align a dynamic, processive Judaism with process thought.

Mustafa Ruzgar, writing from the perspective of Islam, also finds process philosophy to be a more compatible philosophical system than Greek philosophy. As Artson found for Judaism, Ruzgar finds for Islam: that process philosophy supports "more authentic perspectives that resonate with the main outlines of the Qur'anic worldview and human experience." He arrives at this conclusion by engaging in the kind of lively intellectual conversation between philosophy and religion that, until recently, had long been a hallmark of Islamic thought. And he urges a return to this tradition of dialogue, both in order to insure internal authenticity and in order to maintain the vitality of Islam in the modern world.

Ruzgar takes up the problem of evil as his "case study" in the usefulness of process thought for Islamic theology. It is a pivotal problem, of course, bearing on many of the central issues related to the God-world relationship. His starting point is twofold: the Qur'an's affirmation of the empirical fact of genuine suffering in the world and the Qur'an's insistence on God's genuine concern for humanity. That there is real suffering in the world rules out the arguments that evil is either a privation of goodness (and hence not anything real) or a necessary contrast to the good (and hence not really evil), both of which Ruzgar attributes to Greek philosophical reasoning. That God is genuinely concerned with human life means that God's goodness, mercy, and compassion cannot be treated separately from God's agency in the world.

Ruzgar explains that, as Fazlur Rahman has put it, God's power and mercy are "fully interpenetrating and fully identical." Thus, Ruzgar argues, it is both more philosophically coherent and more accurate to Qur'anic sensibilities to conceive of divine power as persuasive, creative power rather than coercive power. Persuasive-creative power is power expressive of God's care for the world. At the same time that it gives distinct expression to the Islamic notion of "fully interpenetrating" power-mercy, it makes room for human freedom–and thus affirms the Qur'an's dual focus on divine agency and human freedom. There is real evil in the world caused not by God, but by free human beings who "are conceived of as more than passive respondents to God." God acts mercifully and compassionately in this world, promoting (in Rahman's words) "orderly creativity, sustenance, guidance, justice, and mercy fully . . . as an organic unity."

Ruzgar's conclusion, reached after a careful analysis of the theological and philosophical traditions of Islam, is that the process understanding of God's power is more Qur'anically appropriate than other philosophical solutions that have been proposed in the history of Islamic philosophy. His is an important analysis, based as it is on the desire to be faithful to the Qur'an and to the Qur'anic worldview as well as to do honor to the tradition of Islamic theology and its quest for philosophical coherence.

In a breathtaking spin, Marjorie Suchocki turns the conversation on divine power inside out, making omnipotence a background element to divine omnipresence. Building on the process understanding of power as persuasive, Suchoki's essay can serve as a meditation on Keller's and Faber's suggestion that power, absent the corrosions of oppressive hierarchies, should perhaps not "yet be named 'power' at all." Ruzgar's call for the conception of power-mercy, drives in this direction as well. From within the Protestant tradition, with particular reference to Wesleyan theology, Suchoki offers the word "grace" as a fuller, more faithful way to name God's influence in the world.

To emphasize omnipresence is to raise high the process notion of divine relativity. Suchocki describes omnipresence as "an ultimate power of 'withness,' which is essentially an enabling power." She makes it clear that from a process perspective, divine omnipresence is a necessity. God is "with" in several ways: *within* the world, in each actual occasion as an element of its becoming; *with us* in the sense of being on our side, actively encouraging and adding to our capacities; *working with* all actual occasions in a co-creative way. From a process perspective, there is nothing passive about the divine pervasive presence.

Grace, then, is not a matter of whether God is present and with an individual, offering gifts. It cannot be otherwise. Indeed, grace is at work even apart from human receptivity, precisely because God is omnipresent. "A God of Presence is a God of Grace," writes Suchocki. And yet, God's grace, omnipresent though it is, does not reduce freewill; it awaits response, freely given. "The enabling, gracious power of God works with the responsive, free power of the becoming present."

With process thought as her weft and Protestant theology as her warp, Suchocki weaves an intricate, new pattern—one in which grace is God's energy in the world, enabling each individual to reach beyond themselves to work with God in ways that exceed their own self-interest.

Father Joseph Bracken writes with great appreciation for Bernard Lee's processive account of the Roman Catholic tradition, giving an elegant summary of his theological interpretation. But Bracken is troubled by what he believes is an overemphasis in process thought and in Lee's theology on "the Many"—on the individual actual occasions (on the micro-level) and on the individual parishioner (on the macro level)—at the expense of "the One," the unity of the church as an institution. He applauds Lee's event-oriented approach for its ability to enliven religious experience in such a way that the Jesus-event has a vivid immediacy for individual believers. Precisely because he believes that "Whitehead's philosophy can have a significant impact on Roman Catholic belief and practice"—and a positive one—he offers both a critique and a modification of process theology that is intended to strengthen its relevance for Roman Catholics.

It is the particular social and institutional location of Catholicism that drives Bracken's revision of the Whiteheadian notion of "societies." Bracken is sensitive to the importance of institutional structure for the integrity and stability of a religious system and he is equally sensitive to the diversity of traditions within Christianity. Is there a way, he asks, to leaven the process emphasis on individual experience and novelty with greater attention to the influence of enduring social structures on individual lives and the "unity of the Body of Christ?" Bracken's answer is affirmative and he proposes that "Whiteheadian societies should be understood as enduring structured fields of activity for their constituent actual entities." In this model, every actual entity arises within a field which provides a "governing structure" as the individual takes shape; each individual then contributes its own "self-constitution" to the field. The structured field of activity reconciles what Bracken believes to be a greater emphasis on "top-down causality"—the weight and stability of structures of authority—with the processive nature of reality. Reinterpreting the process notion of society in this way, Bracken hopes, will help process thought to be of greater relevance for the Roman Catholic tradition.

For Hinduism and other non-Western Ways, "the challenges are different from those posed by the Abrahamic traditions," writes Jeffery Long. His essay is a fascinating overview and exploration of the mutually enhancing relationship between process thought and various forms of Hinduism. Because the affinities run deep, Long believes that a "third, new 'hybrid' system can arise, a Hindu process theology, which sheds new light on both Hinduism and process thought." His essay begins to lay out the factors involved in shaping such a hybrid.

Among those factors is the way that process thought can help in the recovery of an important aspect of the Tantric concept of *maya*. One consequence of simplifying the extraordinarily rich tradition of Hinduism under a singular identifying label—the tendency of much Western, academic scholarship—has been to understand *maya* in only one of its meanings, as "illusion." Long proposes that the encounter with process philosophy can lead to a renewed emphasis on the Tantric tradition's interpretation of maya as "creative transformation." This notion of *maya* is related to experiencing reality as "essentially relational, organically unified, and creatively transformative." Such a view of reality can lead, according to Long, to the very important revaluing of the natural world and so, to efforts to sustain it. In a time of great ecological crisis, such a revaluation is no small thing.

Long also lifts up several ways in which Hindu traditions can be of benefit to process thought. In light of the essays by Artson and Ruzgar, his emphasis on the Hindu notion of a non-omnipotent deity is particularly germane. Long reflects on the difficulty that members of Western traditions have had in overcoming the notion of divine omnipotence, fearing that a non-omnipotent God could not be worthy of worship. Within Hindu traditions, deities are not assumed to be omnipotent—reality consists of a multitude of free beings—or to have the capacity to create ex nihilo. And yet, Hindus have not felt incapacitated in their worship. Long suggests that the example of Hindu reverence for a non-omnipotent god can serve as evidence that the attribute of omnipotence is superfluous to intense theistic devotion.

"The basic Vedantic model of reality," writes Long, "is, in its essentials identical to the idea of process thought that reality is a manifestation of a principle of creativity." Long's essay is an energetic introduction to the very rich correlations between Hindu traditions and process thought.

As Long notes in his essay, one of the strengths of process thought is the philosophical foundation it provides for valuing all of life. In the essay by Christopher Ives, we are treated to a dialogue that plays like a fugue, the "voices" of Buddhism and process philosophy introducing and answering, announcing and transposing themes in the composition of a Buddhist environmental ethic.

While there is much within Buddhism on which to build an environmental ethic, Ives recognizes that there are limitations as well. An environmental ethic that is faithful to the philosophy of Buddhism, he argues, will require a careful and demanding rethinking of several of the central principles of Buddhism.

Ives begins with the theme of intrinsic value, so important to conferring standing to non-human life. Does Buddhism provide a basis for intrinsic value? Can it be anchored in the notion of "buddha-nature"? Can it be fastened to the idea of "having feeling" so that it is attributed to all sentient beings? Is there a hierarchy of intrinsically valuable beings? Can an ecosystem have intrinsic value apart from the value of individual occasions of experience? Ives turns to Buddhist tradition, Buddhist scholarship and process philosophy, listening appreciatively to each articulation. He finds the process idea that "experience is the locus of value" to be useful in locating value in every living event even as the processive nature of reality is affirmed. He draws on David Griffin's distinction between intrinsic and ecological value for help in clarifying the value of more and less complex individuals. And he turns to John Cobb for an understanding of the role an ecosystem plays in increasing or decreasing the intrinsic value of individual occasions of experience.

Ives also considers the question of teleology in a tradition where "interrelational arising (*pratîtya-samutpâda*) holds for all facets of reality, including damaged ecosystems" and which seems not to favor any particular social or natural outcome. After determining that Buddhism clearly seeks the alleviation of suffering, Ives suggests that this goal can be augmented by the process aim at increasing value. And he suggests that Whitehead's teleology of beauty can provide Buddhists a way to "delineate their own ecological teloi." With its affinities to both Buddhism and ecology, Ives finds process philosophy to be exceedingly helpful in clarifying and extending Buddhism's ability to address ecological concerns in ways that are authentic to the tradition.

Meijun Fan and Zhihe Wang also write with great attention to the current context of environmental decline. With 70 percent of Chinese rivers and lakes polluted and half of all Chinese cities supplied with contaminated drinking water, they propose a revaluation of classical Chinese thought as part of a "second enlightenment based on process philosophy." When the "harmonious thinking" of Chinese Dao is coupled with process thought, they believe the result will be "healthy modernization" as manifested in an "ecological civilization."

Fan and Wang give a lucid summary of the guiding principles of Chinese Dao; in each case, the correspondences between Daoism and process philosophy are striking. The Dao is "a dynamic process, the creative advance of the world;" the Yin-Yang dynamic is that of harmonious opposites and "mutual nourishment;" the cultivation of harmony serves as the ground for novelty; and the reconciliation of opposites is possible by means of greater inclusion and wider perspective. Sadly, with the First Enlightenment in China, these traditional ideas were supplanted by scientific materialism and its attendant convictions regarding instrumental reason and value-free knowledge.

In a country as large and complex as China, the failures of the First Enlightenment are conspicuous. Fan and Wang contend that what is needed is "fresh wisdom to cope with the emerging issues of our time." They look to the "aesthetic wisdom" of Chinese Dao and process thought as the primary sources for rethinking modernization and moving into a Second Enlightenment. Process philosophy is seen as being especially congruent with the goals of the Second Enlightenment, providing both an appreciative assessment of Chinese philosophy and of the role of religion in society as well as the philosophical ground for an eco-aesthetic value system. The marriage of process philosophy with Chinese thought can usher in a new enlightenment and lead to the building of "a China that is socially just, ecologically sustainable, and spiritually satisfying." For this reason, Fan and Wang declare that "the philosophical foundation of the Second Enlightenment is process philosophy."

From Keller and Faber we are given a portending of possibilities, both cautionary and celebratory. Simply to take interest in Ways that differ from our own does not insure "a sacred interactivity" in which new forms of togetherness arise. Indeed, given our inexperience with the pluralistic endeavor and burdened in so many ways by tendencies and practices that defeat relational pluralism, we can hardly be confident that we will not indulge in "the piracy of an appropriative pluralism." Keller and Faber are quick to acknowledge this likelihood and they urge an awareness of "the tricky ways we are 'folded together,'" a confession of our complicity in partaking of that which has not been ours, and responsibility for the relationships that ensue.

But they also clearly rejoice in the possibilities released by the coming and becoming multiplicities. The Whiteheadian rhythm—the Many becoming One becoming Many becoming One—beats strongly and steadily, even as unexpected connections form. Keller and Faber echo Whitehead's insistence that even "the actuality of God must also be understood as a multiplicity of components in the process of creation;" they offer even stronger language: "sacred or divine multiplicity . . . not only *insists on* multiplicity but *becomes as* its very interactivity—not as the one, not as the many, but as *the sacred or divine (in) multiplicity.*" The Many becoming One is to be understood as "the *dynamic interdependence* of oneness-*and*-manyness."

Such interdependence is a "skillful means," a source of healing. But its power can be subverted if it is not accompanied by a "healing uncertainty," the knowledge that both the process of creativity and its outcomes cannot be either fully known or fully completed at any point. This unknowing is a sort of profound knowledge; knowledge of our ignorance can keep us open to new possibilities and relationships; knowledge of the unfinished nature of the process of folding and enfolding can curb our addictions to fixity and certitude. It is the "sacred love of multiplicity," with its infinite complexities and unforeseeable outcomes that holds out the gift of deepened wisdom and joy.

This book began as an invitation and continues as one. It is more prologue than epilogue. Indeed, there is no concluding this discussion for those who embrace a process model of reality, who have put on Whiteheadian glasses. If the process judgment about the nature of reality is correct in its most fundamental principle—that creativity is the unending process which characterizes reality—then what we have been given in this book are folds of connections that, if we are lucky, will multiply our relations with one another.

BIBLIOGRAPHY

Berger, John. *The Shape of a Pocket*. New York: Vintage International, 2001.

Griffin, David Ray. "John Cobb's Whiteheadian Complementary Pluralism." In *Deep Religious Pluralism*, edited by David Ray Griffin, 39–66. Louisville: Westminster John Knox, 2005.

Whitehead, Alfred North. *Process and Reality: An Essay in Cosmology*, Corrected Edition. Edited by David Ray Griffin and Donald W. Sherburne. New York: Free Press, 1978.

Index

Index

Sachedina, Abdulaziz, 76–77, 79–81, 97

sacrament, 43, 45, 49, 59

sacraments, 35, 37, 42, 44–45, 47, 49–52, 54

sacred, 35, 38, 44, 46, 52, 122, 132, 184–87, 191–93, 195–99, 201–5, 211, 219

Śākta, 118, 120–121

Śakti, 120–121

salvation, 28, 54, 58–62, 67, 70, 125, 194

śāstras, 104

science, 2, 21, 38, 53, 107, 110, 158, 166–68, 171, 173, 176, 179, 181, 192, 200

sentience, 139–43, 145–46, 148

Singer, Peter, 139, 141, 153, 156

societies, 24, 38–39, 42, 49–52, 124, 136, 150, 215–16

substance, 39, 47, 50–51, 100, 102, 109, 136, 159, 185

substantialism, 102, 115

Suchocki, Marjorie Hewitt, 54–55, 214–15

suffering, 4, 6, 14, 21–24, 56–57, 66, 74–78, 82, 97, 108, 137, 139–43, 145–48, 151–53, 214, 218

śūnyatā, 126

Sutra, 186, 193–97, 207

sûtra, 149

Sūtras, 108, 111

sūtras, 104

sva bhava, 136

Talmud, 3–4, 6, 11, 14, 18, 24, 26–27, 29–30, 213

Tao, 160, 163

tao, 159–60, 165, 174, 201

Taoism, 160–163, 165

telos, 149–53

text, 16, 18, 27, 38, 94, 107, 170, 181

texts, 68, 94, 106–8, 110, 116, 130, 140, 151–52

theodicy, 56, 74, 79–81, 84, 87–88

theology, 1–4, 6–7, 9, 23, 27, 30, 34–35, 38, 45, 54–55, 57–59, 72, 75, 80, 84, 87, 95, 101, 104–5, 118, 121, 131, 152, 182, 184–85, 187, 192, 198–99, 204, 208, 210, 212–16

theopoetic, 201

theopoetics, 199–200, 202

Theravâda, 140, 151, 153

Thomism, 35–36

Torah, 3–4, 6, 11, 24–28, 33, 213

tradition, 1, 6, 25–26, 44, 58–59, 67, 69, 71, 92, 98, 100–104, 106–8, 110, 113–14, 117–18, 120–121, 123, 127, 129, 131–32, 136, 138–40, 157–59, 166–67, 173, 183–85, 192, 195, 198–99, 203, 210–218

traditions, 1–2, 6, 29–30, 72, 98–100, 102–4, 106–7, 110, 115–16, 121–23, 125–27, 132–33, 137, 154, 157–58, 161–62, 164, 167, 173, 180, 182–88, 192–98, 201–4, 208–11, 214–17

transformation, 159, 178, 184, 192, 203

Transformation (creative), 101, 118, 120–122, 132, 216

truth, 4, 29, 37, 101, 105, 110, 134, 168, 194, 196, 198, 201–2

truths, 104, 107, 137

ujô, 139

unity, 47–48, 53, 70, 85, 91, 101–2, 106, 109–10, 113, 118, 123, 129–30, 133, 172, 184, 186, 189–91, 195, 214–16

unknowingness, 199–200, 203

upaya, 193–96, 198, 201–2, 204–5

Vatican, 34, 37, 48

Veda, 107

Vedanta, 134–35

Vedānta, 102–4, 107–20, 123–26, 128, 130, 132, 134

Vedāntic, 101, 105, 107–11, 114–17, 122, 125–26, 128–29, 131

Vedas, 107

vidyāmāyā, 121

Vivekānanda, Swami, 103, 107, 124, 134

Wang, Zhihe, 157, 218

Made in United States
North Haven, CT
19 June 2022

20407172R00150